Doctor Kate
Angel on Snowshoes

THE STORY OF
KATE PELHAM NEWCOMB, M.D.

by Adele Comandini

Ri
NE

Grateful acknowledgment is made to Leo Feist, Inc., Music Publishers, for permission to reprint two lines of the lyrics of "K-K-K-Katy" by Geoffrey O'Hara, Copyright 1918. Copyright renewal 1945 by Leo Feist, Inc.

PUBLISHED SIMULTANEOUSLY IN CANADA BY

CLARKE, IRWIN & COMPANY, LTD., TORONTO

To Dr. Kate's family, to her many old (and young) friends in Woodruff and its neighboring towns and forests, and to the countless thousands of new friends who have sent her their blessings in the form of pennies, nickels, dimes, quarters, bills and checks, with wonderful letters that brought a glow to her heart, this book is gratefully and affectionately dedicated.

Contents

Contents

Doctor Kate
Angel on Snowshoes

Katie's First Grief

KATE PELHAM sat on the top step of the porch, her stubby brown button shoes planted firmly on the step below. Her solemn gaze scanned the country road beyond the gate, and her round chin was set with determination. She was waiting for Mama to come home.

It had been three whole days since Mama had gone away in the big carriage. Katie had last seen her sleeping in a long shiny bed, all pretty with silk and flowers. Then she had gone.

Before that Katie had tiptoed into the bedroom and had seen Mama in her own bed, looking very pale.

"Are you sick, Mama?"

Mama had kissed her and smiled, saying, "I'll soon be well again, darlin'."

There was a lilt of brogue in Mama's speech, for she was a daughter of the Callahans who spoke only Gaelic, and so the music of Erin's tongue was part of Kate Pelham's heritage.

Katie had been promised a baby brother or sister, but there was no baby in the new crib, and Mama was gone. Papa had stayed away for a long time, too. Then Uncle

John had brought him home, looking so different, with his head bowed and his eyes red and swollen, and he didn't speak to Katie but shut himself in the bedroom. Nevertheless Katie was sure Mama would come home soon.

She heard Papa's step on the porch floor behind her.

"Katie," he said in a deep, rough voice she hardly recognized. He sat down beside her. He had a blue bowl in his hands and the aroma of warm soup drifted to Katie's nose as he stirred it with the spoon. It was the kind of soup she liked, but she wasn't hungry. He asked her if she would have some, but she looked at him gravely and said, "When Mama comes."

She had eaten nothing for two days.

"Katie——" Her father's voice broke and he set the bowl on the steps and put his arm around her. "Katie, darling. Mama isn't coming. Don't wait, Katie; please don't wait—any more." He dropped his face into his hands and she saw the tears trickle through his fingers. Katie could not take in the strangeness of seeing Papa bent over, his body quivering, his face in his hands. Papa was always so straight and strong and quiet.

Katie put her hand on his knee. "Mama will come soon, Papa," she said.

Nothing could shake her belief that the warm, loving arms would soon be around her again, and the light laughing voice would say, "Has my Katie been a good girl, now?" Her body ached for the softness of her mother's breast, the fresh fragrance of Mama's dress against her cheek. Papa was wrong to think Mama would not come back to give Katie her supper and tell her stories and hear her prayers and put her to bed. It had always been so, and she would surely come.

4

Papa got up and stumbled into the house, and Katie heard the bedroom door close.

She waited and waited. The sun began to go down.

Katie awoke in her own crib. It was morning. She must have fallen asleep and missed her mother's arrival.

"Mama," she called. "Mama." It was grandmother who came in answer to her call.

"Did you have a good sleep, darling?" Grandmother asked, kissing her and smoothing back her tousled hair. Grandmother sounded the way Katie did when she had a cold. Her pretty doll-like face was pale under the fringe of brown curls, and the lids of her usually bright brown eyes were swollen, like Papa's.

"Did Mama come home?" Katie asked eagerly, climbing out of her crib and starting toward the door to see for herself. Grandmother caught her and held her.

"Katie," she said slowly, as if it were important to make her understand, "Mama has gone to heaven. She can't come back. You mustn't wait for her."

"Why?" demanded Katie. "Why did she go there?"

Grandmother held Katie close.

"She was very sick, dear, and God took her away from her pain."

Katie searched her grandmother's face with anguished unbelief. What was she saying?

"Where's the baby?" Katie asked. She had been promised a baby, and now they said Mama wasn't coming home and there was no baby. How could this be?

"She took the baby with her," said Grandmother, her handkerchief to her streaming eyes.

"But why?" said Katie desperately.

5

"I don't know, Katie. I don't know," Grandmother wept. "Maybe God needed her to take care of the little angels who had no mother of their own."

Katie thought this over, but it did not comfort her. Why should God take her mother to heaven to care for strange angels, and not let her come home to care for Katie?

"I want Mama!" Katie demanded, her round face darkening with rebellion. "Tell God to send her back!"

The days passed, and Katie continued to importune God in her prayers. But He did not send her mother back. She would stand at her father's side and ask her unanswerable questions: Couldn't they go where Mama was and bring her back? Wouldn't God let her come home if they asked Him? Had she gone away because Katie had been naughty?

"No, child, no," he would answer in that strange choked voice. Grandmother would take Katie into the garden and tell her stories, trying to make her forget to ask questions about Mama. But everything Katie saw brought Mama back into the conversation: Mama's flowers. Mama's chair. Mama's gloves. Mama's sunbonnet hanging on the nail.

Katie's grandparents soon decided to give up their Brighton, Illinois, house and come to Leoti to look after their son and his little girl. They took Katie to Brighton with them when they went back to pack up, hoping the change might distract her. It would relieve Tom of the anguish of seeing her run to the gate and look hopefully down the road. The child's stubborn hope kept his own wound bleeding.

When Katie arrived at Grandmother's, she went from room to room, opening doors and looking in to see if Mama might not be in one of them. They had often played hide and seek together, and perhaps she was just waiting for Katie to find her. But she was never there. Time and again Katie searched, while her grandparents watched her with brimming eyes.

There were new things to see at Grandmother's: pigeons in the yard, a cat with kittens, and aunts and uncles who came to see Katie and made much of her. And there were cousins for her to play with. The ache began to diminish, but at night, when she was alone in her bed, she missed her mother again. She felt a deep, dark resentment against God in her heart. How could she believe God loved her when He took her Mama away? No, she decided in her busy and rebellious little mind, God didn't love her. In the bitterness of her uncomprehending grief, she told God in no uncertain terms that she didn't love Him, either. It was bad of Him to take a little girl's mother away. Why had He done it? Why? Why? This question was to become the motivation of Kate Pelham's life.

"The Sweetest and Best"

GRANDMOTHER PELHAM did her utmost to fill the void in Katie's life and the little girl clung to her for the affection she sadly missed. She continued to speak of her mother, but now she thought of her as an invisible presence, hovering close. Often Grandmother Pelham came upon her in the arbor, or sitting in her little rocker on the porch beside the larger one where her mother had sat, repeating the rhymes and stories Mama had taught her, pretending that Mama was in the empty chair, listening and answering.

Katie's nimble imagination and determined character frequently involved her in mischief which, while it was logical to herself, baffled her elders.

For instance, on a hot Fourth of July morning four-year-old Katie, dressed in starched white with a huge pink butterfly sash and hair ribbon, sat in the parlor waiting for Uncle Ed Callahan to call for her. She was to march beside him at the head of the G.A.R. parade. "Judge" Ed Callahan was the chairman of the local chapter and one of Leoti's most distinguished citizens. Katie had been duly impressed with the honor of being chosen to lead the parade with him, but as she waited, a corroding doubt began to cloud her elation. She recalled the rhyme Mama had taught her:

> But whether in pink or whether in blue
> They found her the sweetest and best,
> They tried and they tried
> For a year to decide,
> But as yet they had never quite guessed.

Should she, perhaps, have worn the blue sash and hair ribbon to be considered "the sweetest and best"? She knew Grandmother would not change her sash at this late hour, unless, of course. . . .

It was never explained to Grandmother Pelham or to Uncle Ed or to the G.A.R. Fourth of July Parade Committee just why small Katie had gone out to the yard and backed her pink butterfly sash into the horse trough. She wore the blue sash and hair ribbon instead of the pink, but the necessity for changing her clothes from the skin out took the better part of an hour, and the parade was held up in the broiling sun until Uncle Ed arrived with blue-sashed Katie in tow.

In the late summer of 1890 a devastating cyclone struck Leoti and the surrounding prairies. Grandfather and Grandmother hustled small Kate to the cellar where they sat listening to the terrible roar and percussion of the demonic wind, with the house shaking above them and the sound of screaming fowl and animals piercing the pandemonium with notes of terror. Grandfather shook his head and remarked that it was blowing "like the wrath of God." Katie lifted her face from his shoulder and asked, "What's 'wrath of God,' Grandpa?" Grandfather said it meant anger. Katie wanted to know why God was angry. Grandmother said it was because people didn't love Him as they should. This was all Katie needed to convince her that she, and she alone, had been the cause of the twister because she had told God, in her anguish, that she hated Him for having taken her mother to heaven. It took all of Grandmother's persuasion to dispel Katie's conviction that God had sent the "spiral" to punish her.

The cyclone of 1890 leveled Leoti and took many lives, though the twin houses of Tom Pelham and John Hardesty, built at the same time by the two friends, remained intact. For weeks after the blow, Katie was in a state of near-hysteria. The fallen houses, the homeless families, the dead animals—the unforgettable nightmare haunted her dreams for years afterward.

To distract her, the little girl's father sometimes took her to the bank with him. She was an entertaining chatterbox, and her visits were always welcomed by the office staff. They were amused at hearing Katie read the newspaper, which she did proficiently, having learned to read before she was quite three by memorizing verses and hymns and then identifying the words on the printed pages. One day she read that funds were needed to rebuild the shattered homes of Leoti. On her next visit, while the bank staff was checking the cash for the state examiners who were to arrive the next day, Katie nonchalantly helped herself to four bundles of bills and carried them away in her lambskin muff.

Hours elapsed before Grandmother discovered Katie's treasure under the hall rug. The bills totaled thirty thousand dollars and by the time they were returned to the bank several gray hairs had appeared in Tom Pelham's brown thatch. Katie blandly explained that Papa had a lot more money in the bank and she had taken just a little to help the people rebuild their houses. Needless to say, her visits to the bank came to a sudden halt.

On one of his trips to the East on business for the bank, Tom Pelham set in motion an event which was to make a profound change in Katie's life. He had received a letter of condolence from his late wife's friend, Nona Fenton, who taught school in Mayville, a small town in Chautauqua County, New York. She had been a family friend of the Callahans since they first settled in Mayville upon their arrival from Ireland, and she and Kate Callahan had formed a close friendship. Nona had once been engaged to Kate's brother, James David—a young Harvard professor—who had died an untimely death some years before.

Nona Fenton had never married. When Katie was born, in Wellington, Kansas, where Tom and his bride had moved from Brighton, Illinois, Nona had come to visit her friend Kate Pelham during her summer vacation, and it was then that she became baby Kate's godmother.

Now, deeply touched by Nona's letter of condolence, Tom Pelham came to Mayville to call on his lost Kate's dearest friend.

The two wept together, and Nona relived her girlhood years with the brilliant and vivacious Kate, seeming to conjure up her presence as she described her quick wit, her delicious Irish expressions, and her trick of rattling off Gaelic to confound her importuning admirers. Nona still had letters in which Kate described her romance with the young schoolteacher she had met in Brighton where they were both teaching school.

Was it any wonder that the young widower, then only twenty-six years old, felt strongly attracted to this plain but appealing young woman who seemed to embody the spirit of his lost wife and could evoke her living presence?

Returning to Leoti, Tom felt a nostalgic longing for Nona's companionship. He seriously considered the idea of marrying her and discussed the matter with his mother. Emily Pelham knew that her son was not a man who could remain forever alone, companioned only by a grief-stricken memory. Besides, she felt that little Kate needed a mother's care, and who was better fitted to assume that responsibility than the child's own godmother, her mother's dearest friend?

When spring came, Tom returned to Mayville and asked Nona to marry him. She accepted and they were promptly married. After a brief wedding trip they returned to Leoti, and Katie was told that she now had a "new Mama" whom she must love and obey as if she were her own.

Katie's affectionate heart was only too ready to accept Nona as her "new Mama," but a temperamental difference between them soon made itself felt. Nona was volatile and her temper short. She had not been poured into the tender maternal mold that had made Kate Callahan a mother Katie was never to forget. Soon young Katie began to withdraw into herself to avoid the conflicts that arose.

At first, Grandmother and Grandfather Pelham remained at their son's home to ease for Nona the burden of keeping house and caring for Katie. But Nona's quick temper and possessive demands on Tom soon convinced them that they would be better away from their son's household. They went to live with one of their married daughters, though not too far away, for they knew Katie would depend on them for the love she hungered for.

A baby was soon on the way, and the rift between Katie and her stepmother widened. Nona was deeply absorbed in her own approaching motherhood, and Katie was left to look after herself. She would wander over the prairie to Grandmother's, or sit in the shade of the house, out of Nona's sight, watching the antics of the bright-eyed prairie dogs whose burrows dotted the flat meadows. She came to know them and their habits and loved them for the way they cherished their little ones.

Tom Pelham was deeply involved in his business at the bank and had also taken up the study of law. While he was aware that Katie was no longer the sunny chatterbox she once had been, he was too preoccupied to give much thought to the problem of the child's unhappiness. A business opportunity opened for him in Abilene, Kansas, and he decided to move his family there. Katie pleaded to be allowed to remain in Leoti with her grandparents, but Tom insisted that she must go with him and Nona. She would have a bigger, nicer house and also the baby sister or brother she had always wanted.

The move meant leaving the house in which Katie could believe her own mother still watched over her with angelic understanding. She could not visualize her mother in the strange surroundings of the new house and she suffered from the loss of familiar rooms almost as much as she had from the actual loss of her mother.

In Abilene, Katie was sent to school, and because she could already read, she was put in the second grade. School gave her a few hours of escape from Nona's irritable supervision. She hurried off eagerly each morning and returned reluctantly in the afternoon, wishing that school would last until bedtime.

The arrival of the new baby brother, who was named Thomas Walter Pelham, Jr. after his father, brought Katie a pang of remembrance. It was Mama who was to have given Katie a new baby brother. But now Papa was crooning and cuddling Nona's baby, while she, his Katie, appeared to be ignored or forgotten. Already, though she was only six, Katie had begun to taste the sadness of life.

After the birth of the baby, Tom Pelham moved his family to Buffalo. He had passed his bar examinations and was now a licensed corporation lawyer ready to start a practice.

Their Buffalo home was even larger and more elegantly furnished than the one in Abilene. But Katie's heart still remained in the old Leoti homestead where her mother's memory was enshrined. She carried every detail of that house in her mind to comfort her loneliness.

Four more children blessed the marriage of Tom and Nona Pelham, and Nona's irascibility seemed to increase as her family grew. Although they could well afford servants to care for the house and the children, Nona's temperamental outbursts sent even the most forbearing cooks packing, so that the burden of helping with the household tasks and caring for the smaller children fell largely upon Katie's young shoulders.

Robert

IN June, 1900 Katie graduated from Public School
19 in Buffalo and entered high school with the intention of following in her mother's footsteps and becoming a schoolteacher. Teaching did not especially appeal
to her, but she wanted a career and in those days there
were few professional opportunities open to women. She
really wanted to study medicine but her father had firmly
scotched the idea, declaring that medicine was "no profession for a lady." Kate had to content herself with his verdict since he was bearing the expense of her education.

It was during her freshman year in high school that
Katie experienced her first romantic attachment. Despite
her shyness and her cynical opinion of her own attractive-
ness, she became the object of devoted attentions from a
handsome and congenial fellow student who took to walking home from school with her and gave every indication
that he preferred her company to that of her more alluring
schoolmates. Katie was at first mistrustful, then grateful,
and finally, after a year of perseverance on the part of her
young admirer, deeply responsive to his attentions.

To her, Robert seemed a blond and radiant being from

another world. Whether they had long talks on their school subjects, or walked in companionable silence through snow, rain or fair weather on their way home, or sat in the school grounds eating lunch from their lunch boxes, or merely passed each other in the halls on their way to and from classes, the joy of belonging together was an endless miracle to the love-starved Katie. Her loneliness vanished in a new reason for living.

This "romantic friendship," which was innocent of any demonstration except an occasional holding of hands, took a serious turn in the spring of their junior years. One day, on their way home from school, Robert bluntly and blushingly told Katie that she was the only girl he would ever want to marry. Katie, then sixteen, could scarcely believe that she, with her drab straight hair, her tiny, thin, undeveloped figure, and her plain, bespectacled face, could have inspired such a profound emotion in the boy whose attentions were the envy of her classmates. It was some time before she could bring herself to say that she would not consider marrying anyone but him, although, of course, that would have to be in the indefinite future.

Katie's life now had direction. The "engagement" was kept a secret and, while Nona knew that a certain boy walked Katie home from school, she could not fathom the new glow that had come into her eyes and the serenity which she now displayed in all situations.

It was the winter of Kate's senior year. For several days she had walked home alone. Robert had come down with a heavy cold and had stayed away from school. He sent her a scribbled note through one of his classmates, telling her not to worry. It was nothing but a cold and he would soon be back at school. He missed her, and he signed the note: "Love, Yours, Robert." It was Katie's first love letter, and she kept it in the pocket of her dress.

For two weeks Katie continued to walk home alone. She missed Robert more each day. Then, one morning, as the class gathered for roll call, the teacher sadly announced that one of their fellow students had died of pneumonia— and she named Robert. The school was taking up a collection to send flowers, and the funeral would take place on such a day at such a place.

If the faces of some of her classmates were turned to look at her, Katie did not know it. She was struck dumb, blind and deaf. Her neighbor in the next seat was a new girl. She did not know about Katie and Robert. She did not even notice that Katie had turned deathly white. She thought the Pelham girl had a horrid complexion anyway.

In one day, Kate changed from a happy, blossoming young woman to a moody, embittered girl. She became perverse, hostile and rude. Robert's love had made her appear desirable, attractive. But with Robert gone, she became the same silent, withdrawn introvert she had been before. She spoke to no one, and would deliberately cross the street to avoid meeting people. The one consuming question in her mind was—*why?* Why did Robert have to die before he had even begun to live? Why couldn't he have been cured? Why did Mama have to die? Why hadn't they saved her and the baby? Why? It was then that her desire to study medicine became an obsession. Again she pleaded with her father to let her become a doctor. But he would not hear of it.

The Reluctant Debutante

BROODING constantly over Robert's death, Kate finished high school and after completing the required year of teacher's training, secured an appointment to teach the sixth and seventh grades at Public School 54. From the first, Kate felt ill at ease before her classes. She loved children, but she did not enjoy disciplining them. During all the years she taught school, she never overcame the feeling that she was playing an uncomfortable role.

Tom Pelham's career progressed rapidly and he became corporation counsel to the Gillette Razor Company. This meant moving his family to Boston, where the company had its offices. Katie remained in Buffalo and moved in with her friend and fellow teacher, Mabel Walters, and her mother. Though she missed her younger brothers and sisters, the freedom of being away from home was a novelty which more than made up for the separation.

Kate joined Mabel's church, the Parkside Baptist, and also became a member of the Women's Christian Temperance Union. She entered into their activities and found this vigorous movement a satisfying outlet for her pent-up emotions. She sang at their rallies, and her voice was laughingly described as being in the "key of H," but her enthusiasm left nothing to be desired.

Gradually the shy and introspective Kate began making friends. There were several doctors in the Parkside Baptist congregation, among them a woman physician, Dr. E——, to whom Kate had gone for treatment when she was run-down from overstudy and indifference to nourishment. Learning of Kate Pelham's frustrated desire to become a doctor, the kindly Dr. E—— drew her into a circle of doctors who sympathized with the young teacher's passion for a medical career and encouraged her not to abandon hope of achieving her dream.

Kate also had a group of friends her own age whom she had met through the Sunday School classes at Parkside Baptist and at the school where she taught. This was Kate's "crowd," and for the first time in her life she experienced the carefree happiness of youthful companionship, unburdened by the care of younger children and filled with the gaiety and laughter she had missed during her childhood. These young people spent their vacations together at Gull Lake, in Muskoka, and in the Adirondacks where several of the families had summer homes. During the school year they went riding, boating or hiking "over the river and through the woods" on picnics and to the shore for oyster stews and lobster dinners. Several of "the crowd" were musical and Katie became a member of what they called "The Middy Quartet," so called because the girls wore the then popular "middy blouse" and skirt.

The friendships formed in that congenial group have lasted through the years and a holiday ritual which originated in that Buffalo circle has also endured and spread throughout the country. On Christmas Eve these young companions gathered at the home of one of them for a reverent ceremony to celebrate the birth of the Christ child. They sang carols, had a simple supper and performed the ritual of lighting the Christmas candle from which they lighted smaller individual candles. These were melted down to make the next year's Christmas candle, and so the sense of the ceremony was perpetuated from year to year.

As usual when life began to assume a harmonious aspect, there was a threat in the offing. For some time, Katie's father had been trying to persuade her to abandon teaching and join the family in Boston. He had to do considerable entertaining in connection with his business and Nona was not well enough to assume the many social duties involved in her husband's position (he was now president of the Gillette Company). Katie resisted all attempts to lure her to Boston, not only because she was reluctant to leave her friends, but because the role of society hostess appealed to her even less than did schoolteaching.

Nona's sudden death made Katie's presence in Boston mandatory. After the funeral, which Kate took leave from school to attend, her father implored her to stay and preside over his household. Kate tried to beg off, but Tom Pelham was accustomed to winning decisions, and she finally agreed to give up her teaching post and move to Boston. Actually, the pleading of her brothers and sisters influenced her decision. They missed her and longed to have her near them.

Kate completed the school term in Buffalo, resigned from her position, took reluctant leave of her friends and headed back to Boston. The train that carried her away from Buffalo seemed to be taking her away from everything that had meant happiness: the companionship of her "crowd," the hours of fascinating medical discourse, and the freedom from family interference which she had thoroughly enjoyed. How could she have let herself be talked into a life of social activity in Boston when she writhed at the ordeal of meeting even one stranger?

The Pelham home on fashionable Ivy Street was furnished as befitted a man of importance and staffed with trained servants who made Kate feel awkward and ill at ease. To her, the house was a huge, elegantly appointed trap designed to prevent her from fulfilling her own inclinations. Only the jubilation of her brothers and sisters at having her in Boston made up for her feeling of captivity.

Now began the onerous process of equipping "Miss Kathleen," as she was now decorously called, for her place in society. Kate knew nothing about clothes and cared less. Mr. Pelham's highly efficient woman secretary was assigned to see that Kate had a proper wardrobe for the many events which were scheduled on Papa's calendar. No captive princess being prepared for an unwanted wedding could have seethed with more rebellion against the endless fittings and shopping expeditions Kate had to endure under the patient if sometimes glazed eye of Papa's long-suffering secretary.

If a hat was found that seemed becoming, Kate was sure to put it on at the wrong angle. If a dress seemed to do something for her figure, she would decide it was too tight, or too low-cut or too frivolous. If a color relieved her sallow complexion, it was sure to be a color she detested.

Needless to say the experiment was not a success. "Miss Kathleen," seated at the foot of the table opposite her urbane and gracious father, frowned every time she saw wine poured, and deliberately inverted her glass to prevent one drop of the detestable stuff from being set before her place. This produced an outraged post-mortem in Papa's study. If she didn't want to drink the wine, she should simply leave it in her glass and not behave as though some terrible crime were being committed by those who did enjoy it. Katie listened patiently and then announced to her father that, in taking the temperance pledge, she had promised not only to eschew alcohol herself, but also never to allow it to be served in her home or at her table.

"This," snapped her father, "happens to be *my* home, and I'll thank you not to tell me what I can and cannot serve at my table."

Of course he was right, but then Kate had not asked to be served there either. It had been Papa's idea and she said so, braving his anger in the hope that he might decide that she was not cut out for the role of society hostess and let her return to Buffalo. Even teaching school seemed agreeable compared with what she was undergoing here.

But Papa was not a man to give up easily. He persisted in trying to mold Katie to the part he wanted her to play, believing too that it was necessary training for her future. He expected her to marry a young man suitable for the daughter of a prominent business executive like Thomas Walter Pelham. Though he was forced to admit Katie was not especially attractive, he intended to see to it that she married well and took her proper place in Boston society.

"Patience," he told himself. "Patience." He was already beginning to see some improvement. A big reception and ball was being arranged at the country club to honor visiting British nobility and the experience would be a valuable one for Kate's education as a hostess. Kate's own account of that impressive function needs no elaboration:

"The guests of honor that night were Lord and Lady Something-or-other and the crème de la crème of Boston and New York had been invited to honor them. My corsets were laced miserably tight—so my tight-fitting dress would hang looser—and my high-heeled slippers pinched my feet unbearably. I had smiled and shaken hands with what seemed like thousands of people. Papa was furious with me because I had refused to take dancing lessons. On our way to the club he had said something cutting about 'trying to act like a human being for a change.' I was tired and nervous and by the time all the guests had arrived I was ready to walk out right then and there and take the next train back to Buffalo.

"The only thing that prevented me from doing exactly that was the wink and smile I got across the room from Mr. Ulrich, a friend of Papa's whom I liked better than anyone I had met in Boston so far. He came to my side and whispered, 'Courage, Camille. You're doing fine. Don't abandon ship. It can't last forever, you know.'

"Mr. Ulrich and I were good friends. One day while he was waiting in our parlor for Papa to return from his office, Mr. Ulrich and I had had a long conversation. I had poured out to him, in a moment of overflowing discouragement, my aversion for the life I was leading in Boston, my distaste for social formality and my deep and hopeless desire to study medicine.

" 'And why haven't you studied it then, my child?' Mr. Ulrich had asked, putting his glasses on his nose to peer at me over them.

" 'Because Papa says it isn't ladylike,' I replied, 'and he would have to foot the bill.'

"Mr. Ulrich stood up and began to walk up and down the parlor, scratching his chin and turning to peer at me now and again, as if he were sizing me up against the observations he had undoubtedly made of my talents as a hostess.

" 'My dear girl,' he said at last, 'with all due respect to your father, who is a very fine man, I think he is making a mistake. If you really *want* to study medicine, and *he* won't pay for it, by Jove, *I'll* pay for it!'

"I jumped to my feet and ran to him. Clutching his arm—a gesture which I would never have permitted myself in a saner moment—I asked, 'Mr. Ulrich, do you really mean it? Would you do that—I mean, pay for my medical training?'

" 'Of course I would!' exclaimed Mr. Ulrich. 'The country needs doctors, and plenty of women are beginning to enter the profession. I have no children of my own, and it would be a privilege to pay for the medical education of a girl who wants one as much as you do.'

"I felt like hugging him, but of course I didn't. Instead, I began to cry and he loaned me his handkerchief and patted my shoulder. Papa's arrival sent me scurrying to my room. But now I saw a gleam of light. There was some hope that I might be able to escape from my 'gilded cage' after all. Of course, there was the matter of persuading Papa. But even if he refused, I could walk out and count on Mr. Ulrich to see me through medical school. What I needed now was the courage to defy Papa. . . . Well, here we were at the ball and Mr. Ulrich was telling me not to 'abandon ship,' and now the Grand March was beginning.

"Papa led the march with the wife of the guest of honor. I followed with her husband, the distinguished Lord Something-or-other, and when the orchestra struck up a waltz and the others began to dance, Papa glared at me and I suffered the humiliation of having to confess that I didn't know how to dance. Again, my friend Mr. Ulrich came to my rescue with a charming lady on his arm. Placing her in the arms of my disconcerted partner, he led me away on some pretext that I was needed in the banquet room. I have often remembered Mr. Ulrich in my prayers. By now, he has gone to his reward. I hope he has the finest wings and the brightest halo in heaven. He deserves them.

"Supper was a sumptuous affair that night. Silver and crystal and fine linen under the candlelight from great multiple candelabras made a glitter that was almost blinding. The tables were decorated with garlands of smilax and banked with roses. I sat at the foot of the table of honor, with Papa at the head, flanked by Lord So-and-so and his very elegant and bejeweled lady. The guests surrounding me and Mr. Ulrich, whom I had placed at my right for moral support, were all out of the blue book, and not picked at random either.

"The menu had given me several headaches until I'd had the good sense to turn over the entire matter to Papa's butler and the maître d'hôtel of the club and forget about it.

"Iced melon in a variety of colors opened the supper. Then a clear soup which contained pieces of something I couldn't swallow. Mr. Ulrich told me it was turtle, and that very nearly undid me. Then came a fish entree with a sharp sauce with things called capers in it. Then came the main course, which was squab served with tiny green peas and wild rice—probably from Wisconsin—scalloped potatoes and a salad.

"The squab was my undoing, and at the same time, the open sesame to my medical career. I had never been served squab before, and I was unfamiliar with its consistency and its habits. I moved in on it with my fork in a heavy flank attack, and without a chirp of warning that miserable bird skimmed off my plate and landed in the lap of a dowager from one of the best families in Boston.

"My father, who always kept a vigilant eye on me, was, of course, looking my way at that very moment. To say I was embarrassed would be a rank understatement. I felt the red flush creep to the roots of my hair and wished the floor would open up and swallow me.

"Chairs were pushed back and the migrant squab was rescued from the parquet where it had finally landed. A waiter hurriedly took it in custody and it was snatched away to the kitchen. My father's face was a study in incipient apoplexy. Mr. Ulrich was coughing into his serviette, nearly choking with laughter. But no one else laughed. If only they had! But they were much too polite. My father picked up the thread of interrupted conversation and decorum was restored. Another squab was brought to my place, but I refused to touch it. Nor have I cared for squab since.

"The following morning, before church, as it was Sunday, I was summoned before the bar of justice. My father was pacing his study looking as formidable as I expected he would. As I entered, he looked up without saying a word, thus giving me an opening for the set speech I had prepared in my feverish tossing the night before. It wasn't much of a speech. I said:

" 'Papa, I'm sorry about what happened last night, but it couldn't be helped. This is the end. I can't stand this life any longer. I'm going back to Buffalo and I'm going to study medicine. If you won't pay for my training, Mr. Ulrich will. He said so.'

"That was all. It was my declaration of independence. It was my emancipation proclamation. It was my farewell address.

"To my surprise, Papa said, 'That won't be necessary, Kate. I'll pay for your training myself. Perhaps I've been wrong in trying to force you into a pattern which is against your nature. I'm giving up.'

"We went to church that morning with our hearts filled with gratitude. I for being allowed at last to study for the profession I wanted. Papa, I'm sure, for ridding himself of a thoroughly incompetent and hopeless lady of the house."

Off to Buffalo

KATE had a long session with her father about expenses for her medical training. She had a budget at her finger tips, having gone over the figures many times while the possibility of achieving her ambition was still only a despairing hope.

Her father's surrender to her medical career transformed Katie's diffidence to radiant gratitude and enthusiasm. Tom Pelham sensed that there was an inner Katie he had all but forgotten. The vivacious little companion of his Leoti years emerged once more from the protective shell she had built around her vulnerable sensibilities, and her plainness was transfigured by a glow that made her seem almost beautiful. The brooding solemnity of her brown eyes was replaced by a sparkle of excitement. Her full lips lost their drooping curve and her even teeth flashed in the winning smile that even now disarms and captures her patients.

When the hour of her departure arrived, Mr. Ulrich insisted on escorting her to the station. As she was leaving the house, her father said something which has remained fresh in her memory through the years. He took her two hands and said:

"Katie, I hope, when you become a doctor, you will be able to save other mothers from dying as your mother died."

His eyes filled, and Katie realized that her father had never completely overcome his grief at her mother's death. She promised that this would be her unswerving determination.

Katie had written to Dr. E—— announcing her triumphal return to enter medical training. Upon arriving in Buffalo she was welcomed joyfully by the friends who had encouraged her to hope. Dr. E—— gave an informal reception at her home to celebrate the prodigal's return, and Kate related the saga of her Boston adventures, culminating in the ball at the country club and the mishap with the squab which turned a disaster into a victory.

It was then early spring and Kate could scarcely wait until September to begin her pre-medical studies. Meanwhile, Dr. Louise Hurrell and Dr. E—— gave her books to read which would prepare her, and she absorbed them so diligently that she was able to quote verbatim from their pages.

Those months of anticipation and preparation were a bright spot in Katie's life, although the summer brought a misadventure which nearly terminated her medical career before she had even begun training for it.

During the summer vacation, Mabel Walters and Kate joined Dr. E—— in a trip to the Catskills, where Dr. Hurrell had a summer cottage. While driving along a mountain road, Dr. E——'s car skidded, plunged down an embankment and overturned. Only its collision with a tree prevented its continued plunge down the mountainside into the current that swept toward the waters of Croton Dam. The three occupants of the car were stunned and bruised.

Kate was the first to recover her senses. Having made sure that none of her bones were broken, she proceeded to kick the window out of the car and climb out. She roused Dr. E——, who had succumbed more to fright than to injury, and pulled her out of the wreck. They both helped to get Mabel out of the precariously balanced car which threatened at any moment to slide away from the supporting tree.

Mabel groaned and refused to be budged.

"I'm dead!" she protested hysterically. "How can I get out when I'm dead?" They finally convinced her that she was still among the living and hauled her through the window to the comparatively safe steep incline. All three had been painfully cut and bruised, but they managed to scramble up the embankment by clinging to shrubs, roots and rocks, and they limped a mile to the nearest cabin where they telephoned for help. While they waited for it to arrive, they washed the dirt from their injuries and thanked their lucky stars that the catastrophe had not sent them all to Kingdom Come.

Dr. Hurrell, white with apprehension, arrived in a neighbor's car. When she saw that they were all comparatively safe, she dressed their bruises, excoriating the treachery of the "gasoline buggy" that menaced the lives of occupants and pedestrians alike.

Dr. Louise Hurrell, a "trail blazer" in the field of medical practice for women, is still, at this writing, one of Dr. Kate's dearest friends. This brave woman had overcome the handicap of polio, which had left her lame, and had worked to put herself through medical training. She laughingly described her wardrobe during her student years as "clo," her facetious term for the single dress she had to wear throughout her college years.

Now in her late eighties, Dr. Hurrell retired from active practice only six years ago. Her retirement was marked by a banquet given in her honor by the New York Medical Association. She sent Kate a clipping from a Buffalo paper describing the event and it crossed in the mail the first biographical article written about Dr. Kate by Lewis C. French and published in the *Milwaukee Journal* of October 17, 1948, which Kate sent to her old friend.

Dr. Hurrell is a gifted healer and a great humanitarian who believes that medicine is as sacred a calling as the ministry, and that the healing of the body goes hand in hand with the redemption of the human spirit from the corruption of evil. No economic considerations ever influenced Louise Hurrell's service to her patients, and Dr. Kate gives Dr. Hurrell credit for the philosophy of dedicated service to humanity which the senior physician instilled in her as a student.

In September, 1913, Kate Pelham entered the University of Buffalo and began her medical studies. Her first day at school was one of exultation. She returned to her room at the Walters' apartment feeling like a fledgling that has just taken its first successful flight. She was going to become a doctor, and a good one, so help her God!

"We Will Our Youth Lead on to Higher Planes. . . ."

WILLIAM SHAKESPEARE, *Henry IV*

O F her instructors at the University of Buffalo, Kate speaks with veneration. Dr. DeLancey Rochester, professor of internal medicine, whom the students affectionately called "Roxy," was one of her favorite teachers. His high ideals and deep spiritual philosophy made a lasting impression on his students. Describing him, Kate says:

"Roxy had no glamour. He was unimpressive except to those who studied under him. He lived only to teach medicine and to heal his patients. He had a strong spiritual feeling about healing, which he imparted to his students. He believed that healing was more than a science. To him, as to Dr. Hurrell, it was a sacrament. His words in this connection are well worth repeating. Roxy said to us—and I will never forget his face as he said it—'This do—whenever you enter a sickroom, enter with a prayer on your lips.'

"I have never failed to follow his advice, and I believe all those who studied under him have done the same."

On the first day of his course in internal medicine, this

unusual teacher said to his class, "Up to this time you have
been learning mechanics. Now you are entering your profession. If there are any here who feel that they do not like
the work and are unwilling to proceed with it, I myself, out
of my own pocket will refund the tuition of those who
so decide." These were his exact words, quoted verbatim
by Dr. Kate after forty years!

"He had no takers," Kate added reflectively.

Another unforgettable teacher was Dr. Bush, who conducted a first-year class which experimented on sick animals. The students were required to rig up their own
apparatus. The animals—cats, dogs, rabbits, guinea pigs,
even mice—were treated exactly as though they were ailing children. The class was instructed to make a diagnosis.
This was then checked with the laboratory report, and
Dr. Bush suggested the treatment which the students were
to carry out. He was a stickler for technique and no detail of the handling of "patients" was too insignificant to
be performed with accuracy.

One member of Kate's group, in giving an intravenous transfusion to a "patient," missed the vein with the
hypodermic needle. Dr. Bush seemed to have eyes in every
corner of the room. He came to their section and remarked,
"Things don't seem to be going well here, do they?"

The student who had fumbled the injection was deeply
concerned over his mistake. Dr. Bush knew who the fum-
bler was, but did not single him out or rebuke him. He
simply said to the students gathered around, "Did you stop
to think that it might have been a baby?" The student
never missed a vein again. Nor did the rest of the class.

It was Dr. Bush who also gave them a rule for diagnosis that is still a gem of common sense in medical practice. He made it very clear to his students that diagnosis,

33

while it must be painstaking, need not exceed the bounds of clinical practicality.

He said, "Let your diagnosis be sufficiently accurate for all clinical purposes." He meant that if a doctor was reasonably certain that the symptoms he had observed required certain treatment, and that treatment would not endanger the patient, he should proceed on the basis of that "sufficiently accurate" diagnosis, rather than risk delaying treatment to a point of endangering the patient.

Dr. Williams, who taught gynecology and obstetrics, was also a dynamic influence in shaping Kate's future. His crusading spirit in the cause of zero mortality in childbirth struck a responsive chord in Kate, since this had been the urge behind her early desire to study medicine. Dr. Williams' lectures, which Kate absorbed avidly, laid a solid foundation for her outstanding success as an obstetrician.

Dr. Thomas H. McKee, then Dean of Medicine at the University, was also highly regarded by Kate and her fellow students. He was a thoroughly conscientious specialist in contagious diseases, and the slow progress of science in their prevention and cure was "an iron in his soul." He taught the advanced grades, and serious cases were often brought before his classes for discussion.

Once a case involving meningitis was being discussed. At that time the disease was almost invariably fatal. The only treatment then known was the lumbar puncture, and that was inadequate. Dr. McKee knew there was no cure for the patient under his care, and this fact made him feel frustrated and helpless. For a long time he paced the room, his hands clasped behind his back, struggling with the unsolvable problem. Then he looked up at his class and said, "Well, I suppose the lumbar puncture will make the family feel better."

Dr. McKee took the loss of a patient very much to heart. For days afterward, his classes felt a pall of tragedy hanging over his otherwise lively and often humorous lectures.

Such was the caliber of the men who led Kate Pelham along the path to her medical degree, and the hallmark of their high standards was stamped indelibly upon her professional career.

"K-K-K-Katy, Beautiful Katy . . ."

KATE studied hard. She was slow and thorough and painstaking, but not a "brilliant" student. She drank in the lectures with trancelike concentration, her eyes fixed earnestly on the instructor as if to photograph his every word, his every idea irradicably in her mind.

One day Dr. Williams paused in his recapitulation of the subject he was expounding—abnormal deliveries with particular reference to the use of forceps. He looked at Kate in exasperation and said, "Miss Pelham, will you please get that blank expression off your face? I have explained this principle three times. If you don't understand it, I will explain it once more, if you will only get that look off your face!"

The class roared. Kate, whose tendency to blush had been used as a demonstration of that phenomenon before classes in dermatology, turned scarlet. She had been in one of her trancelike states and had failed to refocus her staring eyes and close her mouth. She understood the subject perfectly well, she stammered. Her classmates teased her afterward, but she didn't mind. Their joshing had no sting in it; it was all part of the fellowship of learning that made her feel at one with them.

Kate's college years were by no means all work and no play. Once or twice a week a group of about fifteen compatible students met at their various homes to discuss the subjects they were studying and to enjoy each other's companionship.

Kate's constant escort at these gatherings was a classmate whom his fellow students called Pat. He sat next to Kate in class as his name came after hers on the roll. He was an outstanding student, personable and quiet, with the same tendency to be meticulous and painstaking about his studies as Kate herself. They were both perfectionists, exploring every topic tenaciously until they were sure they had mastered it. The similarity of their scholastic temperaments drew them together. They had long discussions of their class work and drifted into a comfortable companionship which extended into their social activities as well.

Whether they went to the hospitals to observe cases firsthand, which was part of their curriculum, or spent evenings with their friends, Pat always accompanied Kate to her door. She enjoyed Pat's stimulating company and, before she realized it, their association began to assume a sentimental complexion.

One evening, returning from the inspection of an ice-cream factory to observe the sanitary measures employed under civil regulations, they stood at Kate's door for a long time, realizing that saying good night had become the most difficult thing they had to do.

Pat drew her to him, and for the first time Kate was thoroughly and unresistingly kissed. When he released her, Pat said quietly, "This is it, Kate. . . ." Nothing more. She knew what he meant and she agreed. It did not require a lot of poetic words or phrases to tell her that they were in love. She had known it for a long time.

Their romance was not without problems. Pat lived with his widowed mother and an ailing aunt who had made sacrifices to enable him to study medicine. He was financially dependent upon what little he could earn by teaching night school once a week during the school term, and he earned as much as he could during vacation to help defray his own expenses and assist his family.

Kate's allowance from her father was no more than enough to keep her fed, clothed and housed. There was little left, after she paid for her board, her books and her laundry, from which to put anything aside for her future with Pat. This economic stringency made their marital prospects necessarily vague, and as Pat tried to earn more money, their time together was reduced to seeing each other in class and on occasional Sundays. This added fuel to their ardor, and gave their romance the spur of desperation.

Their inseparable attachment during school hours was too obvious to be missed by their companions. They were teased, of course, but they only smiled at each other and endured the ragging without affirming or denying that they were engaged. A popular song came out at the time which their friends would whistle or sing whenever Kate and Pat passed:

"K-K-K-Katy, beautiful Katy,
You're the only g-g-g-girl that I adore."

Katie never failed to blush, but then, she blushed at everything. Pat grinned and joined the chorus.

Though she denies it vehemently, Kate seems to have been one of those unobtrusive charmers who have been known to change history and to leave a trail of broken hearts behind them, much to the amazement of those who purport to know much, but actually know very little, of the mysterious effluvium of feminine appeal.

All one can get out of Kate on this subject is, "I was shy and plain, wore glasses and never had much to say. In fact, I guess I was what the youngsters nowadays would call a 'square' or a 'drip.' I was a prude, and even the slightest hint of impropriety shocked and offended me. How I managed to go through my medical training without becoming hardened to the facts of life, I still don't know. Right up to my senior year, my face would turn scarlet whenever suggestive subjects were discussed. Here's a good one on me, though I should be ashamed to tell it:

"In our senior year we worked in groups and were assigned individual cases to analyze. We examined the patient and then retired to an anteroom in the clinic to discuss the diagnosis.

"My case, on this particular day, was a young woman with a growth in her abdomen which had been increasing in size for about four or five months. I went through a long dissertation about the symptoms, and the instructor interrupted me impatiently to say, 'Very well, Miss Pelham, but what is the diagnosis?'

" 'I think pregnancy seems the most probable,' I said, 'but, of course, that's impossible.'

" 'And why is it impossible?' asked the instructor.

" 'Well,' I replied, 'because her husband has been dead for two years.'

"You could have heard a pin drop for a split second. Then the class whooped. I stood there, the color of a

39

skinned beet, looking as dumb as I felt. It broke up the session.

"As we left the clinic building, Pat kept looking at me bug-eyed. Finally he suggested that I have a heart-to-heart talk with a woman friend and get straightened out on the facts of life. I didn't need to. It had dawned on me, if slowly, that the stork sometimes forgot to look for a marriage certificate."

Twinkling humor transfigures Kate's round, solemn face with something that, if it is not beauty, is certainly the stuff beauty is made of.

Whatever it is, it wove a spell around Pat's heart. Plagued by objections from his family at one end, and at the other, from Dr. E——, who claimed medicine and romance didn't mix, Pat and Kate suddenly decided there was only one thing for them to do—put an end to the arguments by getting married right then and there. It was three o'clock in the afternoon of a spring day. The city hall closed at four. There was no waiting period in those days; they could be married immediately after getting their license. They were both well over twenty-one and all that was necessary was to arrive at the city hall before closing time.

They ran to catch a streetcar and rode downtown in complete silence. Their main problem was over. Those that would follow would be solved in due course. They were getting married and thus putting an end to the harangues they'd been forced to endure.

As they reached the door of the license bureau, Pat turned to Kate and said, "Kate, you'll have to lend me a dollar. All I have in my pocket is twenty cents."

Kate looked at him, her eyes blank behind the ubiquitous glasses. "I haven't got a dollar," she said. "All I have is a quarter."

There was no escaping it. The license cost a dollar and they had forty-five cents between them.

"I guess it's fate," Kate said. And they walked slowly down the city hall steps.

Kate's Double-Header

AFTER school hours, Dr. E—— and Dr. Hurrell often took Kate with them on their rounds in order to give her a firsthand briefing in professional practice.

Their patients were largely among the working class, good respectable people of moderate means who had found the competent care, and the moderate fees, of these fine women doctors to their liking. They handled many confinement cases, and one day, while Kate was in Dr. E——'s office consulting with her on some of the difficult subjects of her senior year, the doctor was summoned by an excited relative to attend an imminent delivery.

"Come along, Kate," she said. "There's a baby coming, and since you're specializing in obstetrics, here's your chance to assist me and learn something."

Kate was only too glad to have some practical experience in the field that interested her most, and together they drove in Dr. E——'s new car to the modest neighborhood where her patient lived.

They climbed the narrow stairs to the cold-water flat on the third floor where they were admitted by the patient's mother. Everything seemed to be progressing normally.

Kate stood by while the doctor examined the patient, and as they waited for the next phase of labor pains to begin, Katie saw to it that everything was in readiness for the delivery and chatted with the young mother who was, in fact, considerably younger than herself. At twenty-one she had already had two children, and Kate talked about her own grandmother who, at nineteen, had already had four. The story of Emily and Ben Pelham's elopement and the Mississippi river boat marriage entertained the patient and made her forget to be nervous about the coming ordeal.

Suddenly there was a sharp knock at the door, and the patient's mother went to answer it. A man stood outside, gasping for breath, and asking for the doctor. Dr. E—— was summoned and she saw at once that the man was suffering from an acute attack of intractable asthma. He lived in the building and had learned that the doctor was in the Wagner apartment attending Mrs. Wagner, so he rushed there for help when the seizure came on.

Seeing the seriousness of the man's condition, Dr. E—— realized that there was no time to lose. She quickly put on her hat and jacket and told Kate to take charge of the delivery. Kate tried to protest, but Dr. E—— firmly told her that she was perfectly capable of handling a simple delivery. She herself would be back as soon as possible, perhaps even before the child arrived. But this man would surely die if she did not attend to him at once. She left abruptly with her gasping asthma patient, and Katie was alone with her first solo obstetrics case.

As she returned to the bedroom, fighting panic, she recalled Dr. "Roxy's" admonition, and prayed that she would be able to meet the responsibility that had been placed upon her without warning. The prayer calmed her, and as the natural course of events took place, she deliv-

43

ered a fine boy, slapped him smartly on the bottom, cut the cord, and handed him to his excited grandmother. Then she prepared to receive the afterbirth. But nothing happened. And what was even more alarming, the mother was still apparently in labor. What had gone wrong? Kate began to be frightened. Then, to her amazement, and that of the mother and grandmother as well, a second baby made its appearance. This time it was a girl. The astounded Kate repeated the former process, the afterbirth followed without difficulty, and she took care of the mother, who had begun to laugh hysterically when she realized she had produced a pair of twins. The grandmother immediately called the news down the shaft of the areaway, and the cries of joyous laughter that resounded through that cold-water flat were music to Kate's ears. Her first delivery had been a double-header, and everything had gone off perfectly. Perhaps this was a good omen for her future.

Dr. E——, arriving shortly afterward, had to make her way through a mob of neighbors who had gathered to see the twins. It is hard to say which of the principals was more surprised, Katie, the mother, the grandmother, Dr. E——, or the father when he returned from his work and found he had two new children for the price of one.

Kate's delivery of twins created a sensation at school. She was called repeatedly before obstetrics classes to describe the delivery step by step, and each time she reached the point where the afterbirth failed to follow, her bewildered face brought down the house.

There is something indescribably comic and lovable about Kate's expression when it goes completely blank. Immediately afterwards it crinkles into her jovial grin, but that look of complete bafflement which precedes the grin is worthy of the comic hall of fame.

"Here Lies Love"

GRADUATION was drawing near. Pat stood at the head of the class, and Kate, with becoming humility, remained a few points behind. Their Sunday meetings continued and it was time to begin making plans for their future. Pat told Kate he had something definite in mind and she was eager to hear about the project he had been mulling over for several weeks, waiting until it was concrete before he told her about it.

Now he was ready to share the plan with her and Kate listened with her eyes, ears and heart receptive to whatever Pat felt would be best for their happiness together. But as he spoke, her enthusiasm gradually began to fade. She could scarcely believe what she heard.

Pat wanted to begin his career as a country doctor. His plan was that they should settle in Canandaigua, a small community about twenty miles from Buffalo, where they would put down their roots and start raising their family while Pat served his internship. Kate would remain at home.

"But what about *my* internship?" Kate asked in bewilderment.

45

"Oh, you'll have plenty to do at home," Pat replied. "One doctor in the family is enough. You can help me when I begin to practice. Or you could take a temporary job doing desk work in a doctor's office or a laboratory to help out until the children start coming."

Katie stared at him. Surely he could not mean that she was to give up her own career, abandon her dreams of becoming a doctor in her own right, and merely become a country housewife or an office assistant, after her years of study and her lifelong passion to practice medicine?

But that is exactly what Pat *did* mean. What kind of a home could she make for him if she had to attend to her own practice? Wouldn't it be enough for her to help him become successful, and look after his comfort, and bear his children? If she loved him, that should be her chief concern.

Kate remained silent. This was something she had not remotely expected. Pat knew how much medicine meant to her. His proposal was a stunning blow, and before she could give him her decision she would have to think it over carefully. She loved him, of course, but the love of her life had always been medicine, and she had fought bitterly to accomplish the training which he now asked her to set aside as though it were of no consequence.

Pat seemed surprised and disappointed that she should hesitate even a moment about accepting his proposal. But he agreed to give her time to consider it.

The week that followed was a tormenting one for Kate. The idea of giving up Pat was all but unbearable. Yet the idea of giving up her profession was equally unbearable. What would her father say? He had gone to considerable expense to educate her.

As the days passed, Kate found it more and more difficult to make a decision. She decided to talk her problem over with Dr. E——. Needless to say, the good doctor was indignant over Pat's proposal. How could he even suggest such a thing?

"I warned you that this kind of an entanglement would come to no good!" fumed Dr. E——. "Believe me, Kate, if you accept this outrageous proposal, I'll wash my hands of you. You belong in medicine, and in *distinguished* medicine. I have watched you for eight years, and you are a born doctor. It's up to you to make the choice. You can either go to the top of your profession, or bury yourself in a country town and take care of Pat's babies. I've had my say. You must decide for yourself."

When they met for their Sunday visit, Kate told Pat her decision. It was a clear, sparkling spring day, fresh with new leaves and melodious with the nesting notes of birds. She told Pat she was going to become a doctor. She still hoped he would be able to see things her way, but if he could not, their future together was impossible.

Pat was stricken. How could she make such a decision if she really loved him? She asked him the same question. How, if he really loved her and cared for her happiness, could he ask her to give up her profession, knowing how much it meant to her? They quarrelled for the first time in the four years of their happy relationship. Neither would yield. Their visit was cut short and Kate returned home alone, a desperately unhappy girl. She knew she would see Pat again in class, but there would be no joy in their meetings. There would be no joy in life for her ever again, she told herself. Love was not to be her portion.

A lonely road stretched out before her. Behind her were the happy years with Pat at her side. She was over thirty. Her youth was gone. Grandmother Pelham had once said Katie was probably cut out to be an old maid. One thing was certain—she would never love again. The hurt was too deep. No, love was not meant for her.

The ensuing weeks were crammed with the excitement of exams. Kate worked hard to improve her rating. In her bitterness, she no longer cared to keep Pat in the lead. Now they were rivals, both honor students, and Kate intended to show him that her ability was equal to his, though he had considered it inconsequential in his selfish plans.

The results of the examinations were posted and Kate found that she had come out second, only one tenth of one per cent below Pat's top marks.

She graduated "cum laude," but it was a hollow victory. The festivities were empty without Pat at her side. The commencement exercises seemed to her more like a funeral service than the thrilling celebration of the achievement of her ambition. There were times when she would have been glad to throw it all away, just to see Pat's eyes light up with the old familiar glow as he looked at her. But she knew that light would never shine on her again. She felt cold and empty and incomplete.

Cum Laude

KATE'S next move was to secure an interneship. Because of her unhappiness over Pat, she decided to put as much mileage as possible between herself and Buffalo. An opening was promised her at the Women's Hospital in Detroit, but that would not be available until fall, and her immediate problem was to secure a temporary post.

Through the influence of Dr. E—— she obtained a temporary externeship at the New York Infirmary for Women and Children in the lower East Side of Manhattan.

Her work involved deliveries at the homes of patients who had come to the Infirmary's Maternity Clinic for pre-natal care. She lived at the hospital and made calls at all hours of the day and night, traveling on foot, by subway, street car or elevated.

The small, slender "Lady Doc," carrying her bag and hurrying through the swarming streets of the tenement districts by day, and their lurking darkness by night, became a familiar figure on the East Side that summer. Smiles greeted her as she passed, and the children, who came to know her, pulled each other out of her path and sometimes walked beside her to show her the way.

"Hello, Lady Doc," they would call, lifting their grimy faces to her smile.

"Hello," she would answer shyly, and her heart ached at their cheerfulness amid the squalid misery of their surroundings. Another and yet another would be born to crowd the teeming streets and the dank, ill-smelling cubicles of the tenements. She thought of her own childhood in the wide sunlight of the prairies, and she often wished she might gather them all in some green and open place where the freshness of country air would bring color into pale cheeks and brightness to lack-luster eyes.

Most of her patients were Italian and Armenian immigrants, and since many of them spoke little or no English, it became necessary for her to learn some of the essential words in their own language to make them understand her needs.

"*Bacino*," the Italian word for basin—"*tovaglia*," for towel—"*acqua calda*," for hot water—"*subito*," immediately—and many others. She mastered a glossary of terms for use in her practice and her patients were overjoyed to find that the young "Lady Doc" had a knowledge of their language. At first they had been mistrustful of her youth and the fact that she was a woman. Such a slight, immature little mouse could not be capable of taking on the great responsibility of bringing their offspring safely into the world. The local midwives, feeling slighted and jealous of their own authority, were inclined to be hostile to this "foreign" woman, who presumed to know more than they about the mysteries of birth.

One incident which converted the skeptics of Little Italy occurred in a crowded cold-water flat late one hot night about two weeks after Kate's first appearance in the

New York slums. An Abruzzese midwife, asserting her authority, insisted that she was far more capable of handling the delivery than was the insignificant little externe from the hospital. Her motive may have been economic, since the "Lady Doc's" services were part of the Infirmary's gratuitous maternity care, while the midwife exacted a substantial fee.

The delivery did not go as smoothly as the assertive midwife had expected, and when hours passed and the mother's labor continued with no sign of the child, the frightened father called the "Lady Doc."

It was two in the morning, and Kate had been in bed only an hour after returning from another case in the sweltering dead end of Barrow Street. The buzzer rang beside her bed and Kate rolled off the hot mattress and crawled into her clothes, wondering whether all the other externes had dropped dead. She was in for a night of it again, and it looked as if she'd never have a chance to catch up on her sleep. Well, she wanted to be a doctor, and this was it. She could take it, but she wasn't at all sure she liked it, especially at this hour.

The frantic father met her on the street, and in broken English he told her of his wife's strange condition. Why hadn't they called her earlier, she asked.

He raised his eyes and hands, "*La levatrice.*" The midwife. She had insisted she could handle the case. Dr. Kate's lips tightened. She warned him that she would not be responsible for the midwife's bungling. The man, almost hysterical with anxiety, pleaded with Kate to save his wife.

They went up the reeking stairs to the fourth floor and as Dr. Kate entered the small, airless bedroom, she noted that lighted candles were exhausting what little oxygen had penetrated the close sweltering room. She asked that the votive candles be removed. There was a hostile silence.

"*Aria*," she explained. "Air. She can't breathe. The candles take all the air. Please remove them."

The husband made the sign of the cross and a slight genuflection before the plaster statue of the Virgin, and extinguished the candles.

Dr. Kate examined the patient, who was dripping with agonized perspiration. She quickly administered a mild sedative by hypodermic to relieve the tension of fear that was making delivery of the child even more difficult. She spoke to the woman soothingly while placing on the floor the clean newspapers she always carried with her to cover the area around the bed as a sanitary precaution. The midwife looked on resentfully, and Dr. Kate, realizing that she must either win her or send her packing, decided to make a stab at gaining an ally.

"It's all right, *signora*," she said, patting the woman's arm. "You have done the best you could. It is the position of the child that makes it difficult. I will need your help."

The midwife's glowering face cleared. Her hostility vanished. Dr. Kate gave her a fold of newspaper and asked her to fan the patient.

"She will relax in a moment," she said; "she is tightened up with fear." As the laboring woman relaxed, the tension in the room slowly disappeared. Dr. Kate palpated the swollen body and gently pressed the oversized infant into position. The prayer that never failed to rise to her lips asked for strength and knowledge from the Great Source of all life. Dr. "Roxy's" formula would surely see her through.

As the labor pains began again, Dr. Kate spoke to the

moaning woman on the bed. "Now, Carolina," she said soothingly, "do not be frightened any more. Everything is *molto bene*. Just help the baby to come. If you do as I say, there will be no difficulty. Come now, you must be brave and strong—*forte*. . . . Good, *bene, bene, . . . molto bene!*"

Encouraged by the reassuring voice of the doctor, Carolina rallied all her strength and the child came at last. It appeared alarmingly black in the flickering gaslight. Was it alive? Dr. Kate held it up by the feet and shook it, spanking it briskly. Its cry filled the room, a lusty shout of victory. The father's sob of joy followed as Kate handed the enormous eleven-pound boy to the babbling, weeping midwife.

Now the mother. Kate quickly received the afterbirth. The woman was young, and apart from the exhaustion of her long ordeal and the hysteria of relief that followed, her condition was normal..

"You should not eat so much next time, Carolina," warned Dr. Kate as she prepared an additional sedative for her overwrought patient.

"No more, no more," cried the father. "Five kids, that'sa 'nough!"

Five children in this airless tunnel with the elevated trains thundering outside the window! Another urchin on the seething, littered street. Dear God, how can they live like this?

The "Lady Doc" was escorted to the elevated station by rejoicing relatives, who would have gladly carried her all the way on their shoulders. She boarded the train with relief, embarrassed at having her hands kissed and being called a saint and an angel. All she wanted was sleep. In fact, she fell asleep on the train and went past her station.

She walked the ten blocks back to the hospital as the first light of another scorching day outlined the black, crouching gargoyles of the chimney pots.

Well, at any rate, she'd have no more back talk from the midwives in *that* neighborhood.

Danger Zone

ONE night, during her rounds, Kate heard footsteps following her and her blood turned to ice water. She hastened her steps, but the pursuing footsteps finally overtook her. Her medical bag was heavy enough to provide a formidable weapon. She stopped dead and turned, ready to fling it at the head of her pursuer.

" 'Evening, Lady Doc." The deep baritone voice of a policeman met her ears, and her eyes fell on the gleam of brass buttons. Her pounding heart slowed down.

"Hope I didn't scare the wits out of ye?" The brogue rippled through her icy blood like a soothing drug.

"Good evening, officer," she gasped with relief.

"It's kind of late for a little lady to be walkin' through these streets alone, miss. We try to keep an eye on ye, just to make sure ye're all right."

"Thank you," she breathed gratefully.

"On yer way home, are ye?" asked the law, falling in beside her.

"No, I'm on my way to a case. Six fifteen is the number. It's so dark. Sometimes I pass right by the address."

55

"It's right down the street, miss." The big officer escorted her to the address. By the time they reached it, she knew his name, that he came from County Cork, had three children, and was trying to get off the night beat.

"I'd better see you up them dark stairs," said her escort as he flashed his electric torch into the gloom of the hallway.

"Ees de doctor?" a voice called from the first landing. Her patient's husband took over from the chivalrous policeman and showed her up the narrow, metal-edged stairways, through ill-smelling halls where toilet doors stood open, filling the air with the horrible fumes of sewage and disinfectant.

This was an Armenian family, and before the night was over, Kate had reason to wish for the reassuring presence of the big kindly policeman from County Cork.

It was another difficult delivery. Kate saw at once that the child was so badly placed it would be little short of a miracle if she could deliver it safely. Its position was completely inverted and again careless overeating had produced an oversized child. This, combined with the abnormal position, made the odds extremely heavy.

The small, ill-lighted flat, hung with Oriental tapestries, was crowded with relatives, dark, heavy-featured people who stood around as the doctor made her preparation, laying out the newspapers and asking for "*dak joor*," hot water. "*Adgabari!*" she urged. Hurry. Then she asked that the room be cleared. It always bothered her to be surrounded by a gallery. The husband and one older woman, evidently the patient's mother, remained in the room. They stood by anxiously as she examined the woman, awaiting her verdict. She turned and her brown eyes met the husband's dark questioning look.

"It is not good," she said gravely. "A very large child and a bad position. I'm not sure I can save the baby." The man and woman looked at each other, exchanging a few words in Armenian which Kate did not understand. Then the father thrust his glowering face toward her and muttered, "You take care. If baby die, *you* die!"

Kate's pulse pounded. Could he really mean that brutal threat? This was the first time she had ever encountered such an elemental and unreasoning attitude. She had an impulse to take flight, but her responsibility to the patient outweighed her terror.

"I will do the best I can," she replied as calmly as she could. She could feel the hair bristle at the nape of her neck. Inevitably, she prayed. The chances were against her through no fault of her own, and the brawny, dark-browed father's threat did not add to her self-confidence. The situation really called for a Caesarean section, but that was out of the question without the necessary equipment of the hospital surgery. She must do the best she could in a bad contingency. Perhaps, if the head were small, she could bring the birth off safely. If not——? Would the man really kill her, or was this just an outburst of hot-blooded panic?

The child came feet first, and to Kate's dismay, the enormous head remained tightly locked in the pelvic aperture; the infant's body was dark with strain. How to release the head before the baby strangled?

Perspiration poured down Kate's face and streamed down her body. Her clothes clung to her skin as she manipulated the position of the screaming mother, trying to extricate the resisting head.

"Please, God," she prayed silently. Tears stung her eyes and the heavy breathing and muttering behind her told her that the room had filled again. She had the momentary illusion of being surrounded by beasts of prey, waiting to spring on her and tear her to pieces. Her stethoscope picked up the feeble pulse of the child. She applied lubricants around the head and saw that her hands were shaking. All her efforts seemed hopeless. She urged the mother to help her, trying to keep her voice steady and reassuring. Then, suddenly, for no apparent reason, the child's head came free, and even without the usual spank, its voice announced that it had won its first fight for life!

Kate felt faint as she heard the chorus of exultant cries behind her, and after cutting the umbilical cord and handing the baby to the waiting grandmother, she clung to the foot of the bed to steady herself before completing her work.

By the time she had finished attending to the mother, the stubborn-headed baby had been washed and dressed, and now she saw it in its beaming father's arms, arrayed in the beautiful and elaborate embroidery which these intense, colorful Armenians always had ready for such occasions.

The doctor whose life had been threatened shortly before, now became the heroine of the night. Although she felt tired and unfestive after her grim ordeal, nothing would do but she must sit down at the banquet of sweet cakes and wine which had been spread to celebrate the event which had almost become a tragedy. She accepted some of the black, sweet coffee and rich cakes, declining the wine they tried to press on her. They drank to her health and the remorseful father insisted on pressing a ten-dollar bill into the pocket of her dress, apologizing profusely for his rudeness.

"I go almost crazy, Doc," he explained contritely. All was forgiven and Kate shook hands with all the guests and took her leave as quickly as courtesy allowed.

The hot, foul air of the East Side street had never seemed so fresh to her. A deep sense of gratitude and humility swept over her as she acknowledged the Power that had performed what she herself certainly could not have accomplished without Its help.

To this day she cannot explain the sudden change except as a miracle. A child that should not, logically, have survived strangulation had come into her hands alive and screaming.

"Maybe I've just been lucky," she reflects, "but I really believe that 'Roxy's' formula has had a lot to do with my luck. There are times when a doctor realizes he is no more than an instrument of some greater force, some greater wisdom than science will ever possess."

Destination Detroit

TOWARD the end of that sweltering New York summer of 1917, Kate received word that the Detroit interneship would be open for her in December. She gave the necessary notice to the administration office at the Infirmary, and made plans to visit with her family in Boston before returning to Buffalo to take leave of her friends.

Some weeks later, at the station in Detroit, Kate hailed a taxi and told the driver to take her to the Women's Hospital. He bustled her into the cab, jumped in behind the wheel and drove like fury. When the taxi pulled up at the hospital entrance, the driver jumped out and opened the door, exhaling a breath of relief. "Made it!" he said.

"There was no hurry," Kate assured him. "I'm signing in here as an interne."

The driver looked sheepish. He thought he'd been racing the stork.

Kate was delighted to return to the comparative quiet of a Detroit interneship after the hurry and confusion of New York. Women's Hospital provided immaculate surroundings, the luxury of up-to-date equipment, and a fine group of people to work with. It was with a feeling of rising spirits that she approached her new job.

The hospital was given over to general practice, but Kate still specialized in obstetrics. One of her most interesting and unexpected assignments involved a section at Dearborn, donated by Henry Ford, for the care of unwed mothers. Here they spent the pre-natal period at a comfortable home, which also provided a social service for the husbandless mothers and their babies. The superintendent of the home, Miss Eleanor Hutzel, became one of Kate's closest friends.

There were three other women doctors at the Women's Hospital at the time who had a marked influence on Kate's life. They were Dr. Anna O'Dell, Dr. Grace Clark and Dr. Mary Haskins, who gave of their time and knowledge to the new interne from Buffalo. As Dr. Kate tells it:

"Dr. O'Dell used to invite me over on my once-a-month Sunday off, and I had breakfast in bed. That was really *something*, for this was 1917, 1918 and 1919—war times and war rations. It was slim eating for us at the hospital, and very little free time. Internes were scarce, and we were terribly overworked. So those Sunday breakfasts in bed were mighty welcome. Cereal, eggs, bacon, buttered toast and jam, and the best coffee I ever tasted."

Dr. Grace Clark became Kate's intimate friend during the years of her internship and residency at the Women's Hospital. The two young women were together constantly, and a staff wag dubbed them "Kate and Duplicate."

Once again, Kate's quiet, inconspicuous but obviously compelling charm found favor in masculine eyes. One of the staff doctors began to take a more than professional

interest in the new interne who helped him with his o.b.
surgery. Kate was very much impressed by Dr. G——'s
competence, and by his polished professional personality.
He began to ask for her assistance in cases which were not
exactly in her field, and she welcomed the opportunity to
train in general medicine, experience she would eventually
need in her private practice. It did not occur to her that
Dr. G——'s interest might be personal, until her friends
began to ask her about him. Then she tried to avoid him,
determined that she would never again become involved
in any romantic attachment. But the more she eluded him,
the more the distinguished Dr. G—— sought her out.

One day he stopped her in the corridor outside the
commissary and asked her to have dinner with him that
night. Kate made an excuse and Dr. G—— asked her point-
blank why she disliked him.

"Oh, but I don't," Kate protested, blushing with her
usual readiness. Without further circumlocution he declared
that he found her company agreeable and intended to cultivate it.

Kate blinked. "What's so special about my company?"
she asked bluntly. "I'm certainly not much to look at and
I'm a terrible conversationalist."

Dr. G—— laughed. "That's just what I like about
you," he replied. "You're quiet and a good listener, and
you generally seem to know what I'm talking about. As
for your looks, they're the kind that appeal to me. Now, will
you have dinner with me tonight or not?" His tone was
masterful, and he seemed determined not to let her get
away without giving him a definite answer.

"If you'll let go of my arm and stop attracting attention," Kate murmured, "I might consider it." She had
caught sight of Dr. Clark and another of her friends linger-

ing at the end of the hall with "I told you so" grins on their faces.

So Dr. G—— took Kate to dinner. She admitted to Grace afterward that it was an agreeable evening and that Dr. G—— was an interesting talker, but an awful tease. He had asked endless questions about her, and he also said some nice things about her professional ability.

The last thing Kate had expected to find in Detroit was a new admirer. The hurt of her first two romances made her wary of exposing her emotions to another entanglement. Romance and a career did not mix as far as she was concerned, and she told Dr. G—— as much when his attentions became too ardent. Unless they could remain merely friends, she said, their pleasant dates for dinner and an occasional movie would have to come to an end. Dr. G—— sulked for a time under Kate's edict, but they soon resumed their meetings on Kate's terms.

Kate benefited greatly from Dr. G——'s brilliant scientific mind. His practical solution of the many problems which confronted her during her interneship and residency were of invaluable help to her, not only then, but in the future. As the months passed, Kate realized that this comfortable companionship might well be the basis for the kind of marriage best suited to a woman in professional life. Although she still insisted upon maintaining their platonic status quo, she began to take a less adamant view of Dr. G—— as a potential husband.

The time came for Kate to enter private practice. She had trained in pediatrics under Dr. David Levy, an accredited Viennese specialist in children's diseases, who was a member of the hospital staff. He was one of the finest doctors in Detroit at the time and had been a wonderful teacher.

Kate began her practice in association with her three friends, Dr. Grace Clark, Dr. Anna O'Dell and Dr. Mary Haskins. They took offices together and from the very first Kate was able to carry her share of expenses and make a comfortable income. As their practice thrived, Grace decided to buy a car to facilitate making her rounds. She studied catalogues and went to various salesrooms to inspect the latest models. She found the Paige most to her liking, and as she sang the praises of the car she had decided to buy, it became evident to Kate that her friend referred frequently to the "very nice" young man who had demonstrated the Paige to her. Apparently Grace had found not only the car of her choice, but a personal interest as well.

The process of learning to drive included numerous luncheon engagements with the agreeable "demonstrator." Kate cheerfully took over some of Grace's calls, glad to see her friend so enthusiastic over the acquisition of an automobile. She caught a few glimpses of the "demonstrator" when he drove Grace's new car to the front of the office building, and she agreed that both the car and the instructor were extremely presentable.

During her internship and her residency at the Women's Hospital, Kate had made several trips back to Boston to visit her family. Her father's business associates had given her a handsome Chase motor robe as a present, suggesting that Mr. Pelham might give her the car to go with it. This he decided to do, and Kate elatedly told Grace the good news. Grace insisted that Kate make the purchase through the same "nice young man" who had sold her the highly satisfactory Paige. The two friends went to the agency together, and Kate met "Bill" Newcomb. She found him most accommodating, well-mannered and even handsomer than her fleeting glimpses of him had revealed.

Kate bought her car from him and the inevitable driving lessons followed. Kate was slow to learn and terrified of traffic. Her instructor patiently taught her all there was to know about handling the car, and when he thought she was ready to drive it alone, he took her to a downtown section, got out and told her she would have to get back as best she could. It was a drastic measure, but it was the only way he could force her to overcome her timidity at the wheel. She returned without mishap, and from then on she used the car on all her calls and wondered how she had ever got around without it.

Kate was now living at Grace Clark's home where she had rented a room as soon as she had finished her hospital residency. It was a large, comfortable house and she was treated as one of the family. Grace was a vivacious companion and they spent much of their leisure time together.

"I had a wonderful time in Detroit," Kate recalls, "and a good practice. I paid expenses from the very first. Of course, I had the benefit of the overflow from Dr. Levy's office. He was in enormous demand and was glad to have me take some of his cases.

"One point that I'd like to make is that never, either in college or in practice, did I have to struggle to gain equality with the male doctors. They always treated me as an equal, simply as a fellow practitioner, and if they resented the fact that I was a woman, they jolly well kept it to themselves.

"Of course, neither was I a long-suffering martyr. If I didn't agree with their findings, I talked it out, doctor to doctor, and all was well."

Kate, Grace Clark and Bill had become very friendly through the purchase of the two cars and the subsequent driving lessons, and Bill often asked the two young doctors to dine with him. At first Kate demurred. She did not want to intrude upon what she believed was a budding romance between Bill and Grace. But Grace insisted she go along, saying that propriety was better served by including Kate in the party. The threesome spent many enjoyable evenings together, although they were inevitably interrupted by calls for one or the other of the doctors.

Bill was an entertaining companion. He told them stories of his adventures in the Michigan woods where he had spent his boyhood, and some of his escapades reminded Kate of the irrepressible Huck Finn and his rambunctious comrades on Cardiff Hill. Bill was skilled in aviation and motor mechanics, but Kate thought that some of his prognostications were highly exaggerated. He assured them that someday transportation would take to the air and ground travel would become as obsolete as the horse and buggy. He also had a crazy idea that someday images, transmitted through the air, would appear on a screen in the form of motion pictures, which Kate considered entirely fanciful and absurd.

Bill had worked in airplane construction at a defense plant during the war years, and he was in full agreement with the controversial General "Billy" Mitchell who contended that air power would inevitably become the dominant factor in military supremacy.

It was not until a long time afterward that Kate learned something of Bill's family background. He had been a woodsman from his earliest years. He was born in Ottawa County, Michigan, in February, 1886. His parents soon moved to Belding where his father, of a farming family, bought acreage and started raising crops for the market. Bill was taught forest lore by "Med" Foreman, an old Chippewa Indian who gathered herbs and roots in the forest and was an expert guide for sportsmen. At eight, Bill began to guide fishing parties to the lakes and streams he knew down to the last eddy and ripple. He had explored them all, and they were mapped in his mind with indelible familiarity.

He attended the local school at Belding where he took a keen interest in history and geography. He had a flair for words, was sharp of wit and alert of memory. His father recognized his capabilities as a scholar, and his mother longed to give him the advantages of a complete education. But farming was a hazardous business in those days. There were no government subsidies to pad crop failures and poor prices, so his parents' dream of an education for their son went by the board. It was no disappointment to Bill. The schoolroom had held no charms for him. His idols had been the lumberjacks who had moved into the Michigan wilderness to float the great logs down the rivers, rugged men who had filled the woods with their lusty curses.

Bill finished grade school and worked on his father's farm until the need for a more reliable income sent him to work in a shingle mill. Nothing was too difficult or too strange for Bill to tackle in those days. He could be a lumber worker, or a barber, or a baseball player, as the need arose, and when the "horseless carriage" made its appearance, he developed into a skilled mechanic through the simple process of taking an engine apart and putting it back together so that it ran even better than before. Machinery became his second love, without displacing his first. Gun and rod were his favorite implements, and the machine shop never replaced the forest in his affections. Books he learned to respect and value, and he read widely—history, travel, biography and philosophy. He loved adventure—Kipling, Melville and Stuart Edward White were among his favorite writers. But John Audubon was his idol. He would have liked to emulate the great naturalist who devoted his life to the outdoor world.

But there was a living to be earned. Bill moved from the woodlands into the cradle of motor manufacture, the rapidly growing city of Detroit. Here his talent for machinery found profitable soil. His understanding of the moods of the new unpredictable "go wagons," and his ability to put his finger on their ailments in short order, and set them right, won him outstanding recognition among the often-bewildered manufacturers. Bill became known as a "trouble shooter" for the automobile plants. Whenever something went wrong that needed a knowing eye and an expert hand, Bill was sent to the grumbling purchasers, and he not only set things straight, but he brought back observations on motor performance which were invaluable to the designers.

Always a conspicuous target for feminine attention, Bill was wary of the wiles of city charmers. Big, handsome, quick with a quip, women pursued him and laid snares for him, but he was not one to be easily trapped into matrimony. He was deeply devoted to his mother, whom he visited as often as he could between trips to distant places on "jobs" for the plants, and he knew he would not be content with any woman who did not measure up to her saintly qualities.

Bill never lost his love for the country. He insisted that the city-bound doctors needed an occasional jaunt to the woodlands around Detroit to refresh their lungs and rest their eyes from the narrow confines of office, hospital and sickrooms.

Kate thoroughly enjoyed the Sunday picnics with Bill and Grace, and the stories Bill told of the loggers in the

Michigan lumber camps. To him, the forest was home, but his observations on men and books were shrewdly penetrating. Kate, with all her schooling, found her mind no match for his keen, well-balanced intellect. Her respect for the unassuming, self-taught "mechanic," as Bill insisted upon describing himself, increased immeasurably as his endless store of infinitely varied information unfolded for their entertainment.

He often asked them questions about their work, expressing his admiration for a profession that was dedicated to the relief of human suffering. He made them feel that they were honoring him by their friendship, and that it was a privilege to share their leisure hours. He seemed to like them both equally well, showing no partiality to either of them. He treated them both with perfect deference, and one day at the office Kate and Grace discussed their friendship with Bill. Grace made a remark which led Kate to believe that her friend was disappointed in Bill's lack of interest in either of them beyond this fraternal and impersonal relationship.

"I wonder if Bill has a secret romance in his life," Grace said. She was putting on her hat to start out on her rounds, and Kate noted the soft, chestnut waves of her hair, glinting with russet lights, her large hazel eyes and the creamy texture of her skin. Grace was extremely handsome, and Kate took it for granted that if Bill did have a preference, it would certainly be for Grace.

"A secret romance?" Kate repeated, puzzled. "What makes you think that?"

"Well," Grace replied reflectively, "he's certainly all man. And he seems to like us, but neither one of us seems to appeal to him except as—sort of—sisters."

"Three is a crowd!" exclaimed Kate emphatically.

"From now on, I'm not going along any more. If I hadn't horned in, he probably would have popped the question to you long ago!"

"Don't be silly!" Grace protested. "If he'd been interested in me, he wouldn't always ask us both."

Nevertheless, Kate decided that she would give romance a chance. Grace obviously liked Bill a great deal and Kate saw no point in playing chaperone to a pair of full-grown adults, much as she might enjoy their companionship. Besides, she had been neglecting Dr. G——, and a woman in her thirties had better keep her fences mended or she would certainly find herself on the shelf.

Of Grief and Love

FROM then on, Kate accepted more of Dr. G——'s invitations. Encouraged, he resumed his courtship with renewed persistence, and while she did not find him as entertaining or as attractive as Bill, Kate realized that, if she intended to marry at all, Dr. G—— was the man she should select. He had proposed to her not once, but repeatedly, and Kate kept postponing her decision for a paradoxical reason. Dr. G—— did not arouse the baffling and exhilarating emotion she had experienced in the past. While she was sure it would never happen to her again, she shrank from marrying a man she could not love, but only admire and respect. This thoroughly feminine dilemma kept her long-suffering suitor in continual suspense, though it did not dampen his ardor.

The more he pressed for her answer, the more Kate circled around the problem, unable to reach a decision. She told herself firmly that a marriage based on compatibility and mutual interests was the best possible kind. She appreciated the qualities and the talents of her admirer. Yet she could not bring herself to give him the answer he fretted for. Sometimes she wondered whether it was marriage itself she was evading.

Suddenly all these considerations were swept from her mind, for Grace Clark became seriously ill. For some time Grace had been suffering from exhaustion and had been under the care of her family physician. She had been urged to enter the hospital for a thorough examination, but she would not give in to what she believed was merely a passing indisposition. She carried on her practice in stubborn defiance of her own poor health and not until she was literally struck down would she stay in bed. Kate remained with her friend constantly, watching her grow weaker, yet powerless to help. Her malady seemed to be an acute blood condition, a destruction of the red corpuscles, and no remedy was of any avail.

On the third day after her collapse, Grace told Kate that she knew she was going to die. Kate fought back her tears and tried to deny the awful prognostication, although she had already guessed Grace was nearing the end. Twelve hours later, Grace Clark breathed her last.

With Grace's family, Kate stood at the bedside, despair flooding over her as her dearest friend slipped out of reach of further medical intervention. To this day she is not sure what was the real cause of Grace's death, although she believes her ailment was the dread leukemia. Again the specter had robbed Kate of one she loved, even though she was now equipped with medical knowledge which should have armed her against the relentless enemy. Beside her grief, she felt a deep sense of failure and frustration as she closed Grace's eyes, her tears falling helplessly for one who only a few days before had been a laughing and fearless fellow warrior against the illness of others.

Bill had kept in touch with Kate, telephoning frequently for news of their friend's condition. Her heart was heavy as she notified him of Grace's death. He could not believe that she was actually gone.

Grace's death brought Bill and Kate together in mutual grief. No longer gay and talkative, they were now united in bereavement. It seemed impossible that Grace's vivacious presence could have been snatched away so quickly. They shed tears together, remembering her kindness, her enthusiasm, her devotion to the poorest and most humble of her patients. Bill recalled how, late one night, he had driven Grace to a tumble-down Negro section where she had remained for hours, attending a sick baby, until she brought it safely through the croup.

Bill railed at the injustice of fate. It had struck down a woman who was dedicated to humanitarian work, while gaudy, useless "butterflies" frequented *thé dansants* and squabbled over alimony in the divorce courts. This was a new side of Bill. He had seldom let serious topics weigh upon the lighter moods of their meetings. But now he revealed a depth of sentiment which had not been apparent to Kate before. She began to look at him in a different light. She found her heart being taken by surprise, and she struggled against the current that was sweeping her toward an emotion she recognized all too well. Where could it lead? Bill's life and hers ran along different channels. She had her career to think of. Yet she could not deny that the hours she spent with him filled her with quiet happiness.

Their meetings were interrupted by a visit from her friend Mabel Walters, who had become Mrs. Del Curran. She had married one of the members of the old Buffalo group, and while Del was away on business, she decided to visit Kate in Detroit. Kate had left the Clark home and taken an apartment, and the two old friends spent as much time together as Kate could spare from her practice. There was not much time left to see Bill, as Kate now had many of Grace Clark's patients on her list.

Mabel stayed two weeks, and when Bill telephoned shortly after she left, Kate accepted his invitation to dinner. When she saw him again, there was no longer any doubt about the way she felt toward him. Being with him gave her a sense of completeness. She sensed instinctively that he felt the same about her. They spent several evenings together, and he finally told her in his blunt, almost gruff way that, if he were not a simple, run-of-the-mill mechanic with little to offer, he would ask her to marry him. Kate was not surprised, but his self-deprecation angered her. She replied that he was the most interesting and intelligent man she had ever met, and that he could do anything he made up his mind to do.

"Well, then," he chuckled, "I've made up my mind to marry Kate Pelham. How's that for a start?"

Kate kept her eyes lowered. She knew that if she looked into the keen gray eyes across the table, her fight for reason would be lost. She must keep her head. Much as she liked him, she realized Bill was not a suitable husband for her.

"I—I can't give up my career, Bill," she said, pressing fold after fold in her napkin and avoiding his eyes. "I've fought too hard for it, and I'm just beginning to make a name for myself."

"I didn't say anything about giving up your career," Bill replied quietly. "Doctors marry and have their careers as well, don't they? Or are women doctors an exception?"

She looked up. Did he really mean it?

"You mean—you wouldn't expect me to give up my practice?" she asked.

"I'd be pretty selfish if I did," he said, and waited, watching her as she stared into her water glass, almost as though she were trying to read in a crystal the answer she must give. Her heart was beating wildly, but she must hold fast to the reins of logic. She must pull in the runaway emotions that her scientific mind had been schooled to curb.

"Don't decide now, Kate. Think it over." It was Bill's voice speaking her own thoughts. The restaurant was filled with people, yet she felt as alone with him as though their corner table had been transported to another planet.

"It's late," he was saying. "You should be getting home." He beckoned to the waiter and paid the check.

As he drove her home, Bill told her he had been in love with her from the first moment they'd met. The close friendship between her and Grace had posed a problem. If he showed a preference for Kate, it might have impaired the friendship between the two young doctors. And there was another reason for his reticence. Grace had told him of Dr. G——'s attentions to Kate. He had been in constant fear that she might decide to accept the doctor, who would be by far the better match for her. As for himself, he had not thought he stood the slightest chance. But he had to know.

So this was the "secret romance" in Bill's life. Herself! Kate was touched by what he had told her. His sensitiveness, his thoughtful analysis of what would be best for her, finally overcome by his need to know if he stood a chance— his humility—his willingness to let her continue her work. "Don't decide now, Kate. Think it over."

He held her hand for a long time as they said good night. He told her that if she decided to refuse him, he would understand, and he hoped they would still remain friends. Kate tore herself away, knowing that if she lingered

75

she would tell him, then and there, that he had won her heart. And above all, she must think—she must think.

She climbed the stairs to her apartment in a daze of conflicting thoughts and emotions. Dr. G—— was the man she should marry. She knew it, and yet, why was her heart bounding and the blood singing through her veins? "Think, Kate, think," she told herself. "You're not a child any longer. You're a woman of thirty-three! You're a doctor. You have a scientific mind. You cannot allow yourself to be swept away by a mad impulse."

She lay awake most of the night, tussling with the question: Bill or Dr. G——? She lined up the arguments on both sides, and came to no decision. Her previous dilemma, far from being solved, had now been multiplied by two.

By the next morning she had made one decision. She would put off her choice entirely until she could get a better perspective on her two suitors.

To Love, or Not to Love . . . ?

THAT was the question. Whether it would be better to choose the older Dr. G——, who would add much to her career. Or to fling aside all practical considerations and link her life with Bill's.

Reason battled with sentiment. Dr. G—— had a thriving practice. They would work together, each handling cases in their own field. She in obstetrics, gynecology, pediatrics. He in surgery and internal medicine. It was an ideal combination. And yet——

Bill's face and Bill's voice haunted her thoughts. Bill had added facets to her existence which the somberness of her professional years had lacked. He made her feel—well—more like a woman than a doctor. The thought of putting Bill out of her life gave her a pang, while Dr. G—— remained a remote if dazzling figure on the heights.

Another question: Was she the right wife for Bill? No. Definitely not. Her practice would take most of her time, and she would be forced to relegate the care of their home to servants. Whereas, with Dr. G——, their lives would be spent together, consulting and progressing in their profession.

Kate was torn by indecision. She found it difficult to resist seeing Bill whenever she had a free moment. What she needed was a change of scene. Total detachment from the familiar surroundings might give her the perspective necessary to consider her problem objectively. She would take a trip to Buffalo and to Boston to see her friends and her family.

She told Bill of her intention to go East. In fairness to him as well as to herself, she wanted time to think things over. She warned him what his life would be like, married to a busy physician whose first duty was to her patients, regardless of consequences to her private life. Bill seemed unperturbed by her warning. He knew what to expect. But he agreed that she should take time to think. He felt such a trip would be an excellent idea.

Dr. G——, on the other hand, was opposed to it. He wanted Kate to take her vacation simultaneously with his, and to make it a honeymoon. He protested that she had had plenty of time to consider his proposal, and he could not see why she needed a trip East to make up her mind to marry him. Their parting interview nearly ended in a quarrel. He reproached Kate for having kept him dangling for over a year, when they might have been working together and having a normal, happy life.

Kate replied that she could not be rushed into a decision. If he felt that he had waited long enough, he was free to make other plans. He had no choice but to resign himself to her trip.

Kate left Detroit in a state of morbid exhaustion. She would not let Bill see her off at the station, nor did she accept Dr. G——'s invitation to have breakfast with him before she left.

She relaxed gratefully once the train was under way,

speeding her from the scenes of her emotional harassment. This was the first real rest she had had in months. No jangling telephones summoned her to sickrooms or delivery rooms. For the moment, her problem was behind her. She almost wished the train would rumble on forever, taking her out of reach of the pressures and conflicts of the past weeks.

She had written to Mabel announcing the hour of her arrival, and when the train reached Buffalo, Mabel's beaming face and open arms welcomed her at the gate.

Kate felt like her old self again as she unpacked in her friend's apartment. Mabel bubbled over with questions. How long could she stay? Did she really intend to remain in Detroit? Wasn't there any chance of her opening a practice in Buffalo?

Almost immediately, special-delivery letters and telegrams began to pour in from Detroit. Both Bill and Dr. G—— were pressing their suits across the miles. Sometimes these impulsive missives arrived at unseemly hours of the night, much to Kate's embarrassment. She confessed her dilemma to Mabel, who wanted to know all about the two men. Kate had snapshots of both Bill and the Doctor. Mabel inspected them carefully, and decided in favor of Dr. G——. He looked so distinguished and intelligent. Bill was younger, of course, and handsomer by far. But the prominent, successful doctor seemed exactly right for Kate. By all means, she must marry Dr. G——. Kate was inclined to agree. However, she replied to the letters and wires with noncommittal impartiality, telling her suitors that she would soon leave for Boston to visit her family.

Again, in Boston, the doorbell pealed continually with messages for Kate. Grandmother Pelham was visiting her son at the time, and she was quite surprised to learn that her "mousey" granddaughter was the object of a romantic rivalry between two men. At sixty-nine Emily Pelham was as sprightly and handsome as ever. Her hair was as thick and long and brown as Kate remembered it, and her tiny feet were shod in the daintiest of shoes with heels so high that Kate could not imagine how she walked on them. Her son indulged her unstintingly, and she wore the most fashionable clothes his charge accounts could provide. It delighted him to have his mother petted and admired by his friends.

Grandmother immediately set about trying to wheedle Kate out of her dull clothes and into more colorful plumage. But Kate resisted all her efforts. To Grandmother's horror, Kate appeared at dinner parties in high-necked dresses, and with a shiny nose—a tiny gray wren in the midst of bejeweled birds of paradise. High heels, low-cut gowns, perfume and ornamentation of any kind were distasteful to her. Grandmother Pelham gave up trying. She wondered what manner of men could lay their hearts at the feet of such an unfeminine young woman as Kate.

Kate accepted the challenge and told her grandmother about Dr. G—— and Bill. Looking at their photographs, Grandmother could not deny that they were both fine-looking men, though what they saw in Kate was still a mystery to her. After quizzing Kate about them both, she emphatically declared that Kate must marry Dr. G—— and forget "that other one." After all, he was merely a mechanic. Kate would be "throwing herself away." How could she hesitate for a moment about accepting the doctor? Dear me, girls' heads were filled with silly romantic notions nowadays. Grandmother blamed the movies. Kate laughed and asked whether the "romantic notion" of eloping with grandfather at fourteen and being married to him on a river boat in the middle of the Mississippi had been inspired by the movies.

Grandmother plumed herself like a bright-eyed hummingbird and exclaimed, "Oh, but my dear, *that* was *love!* We were like Romeo and Juliet. Such things happen only once in a thousand years!"

(However, a few years later, grandmother "Juliet" divorced her "Romeo." She married twice after that and died at eighty-nine, outliving her first husband by ten years.)

Grandmother Pelham discussed Kate's suitors with her son, and urged him to persuade Kate to accept the distinguished Dr. G——, who would make a most suitable son-in-law. Mr. Pelham's experience with Kate's determined character made him wary of interfering in her personal affairs. However, he did broach the subject to her one evening when they were alone at dinner. Grandmother had been invited to a dinner party and a concert, and had departed in a flurry of lace and velvet, leaving a trail of delicate sachet in her wake.

Kate and her father sat in the huge paneled dining room with its damask upholstered chairs and somber oil paintings gleaming in the subdued light of wall sconces and candelabra. Kate thought of her modest apartment in Detroit and smiled to herself at the contrast.

"Well, Kate," her father asked, "have you made up your mind which of your admirers you are going to accept? The question seems to be giving your grandmother some concern."

Kate flushed. No. She hadn't decided.

Then her father surprised her by saying something which had an important influence on her decision.

81

"Kate," he said, when the phantomlike butler had left the room, "don't marry a man unless you love everything about him. Marriage can be the most wonderful thing in the world or it can be a hell on earth. It's a matter of chemistry, both mental and physical. You're not a child any longer. Be sure you choose a man who gives your life something it has lacked—companionship and joy. I know what your childhood was like. My heart ached for you many and many a time. You've worked hard to achieve your profession, and you've been successful at it. I'm proud of you, Kate, but more than anything else, I want you to be happy. That's all the advice I'm going to give you."

Kate felt her throat tighten, and the tears surged up into her eyes. Her father was proud of her success as a doctor. Now he wanted her to be happy as a woman. His understanding moved her beyond words. She nodded and smiled at him, and from that moment she knew what her decision would be.

"Dearly Beloved . . ."

KATE'S sixteen-hour trip back to Detroit seemed endless. When her train finally pulled into the station, she stepped to the platform and scanned the throng at the gate for the face that had hovered in her mind's eye, waking or sleeping, since the moment she had left Detroit.

There he stood, lean and broad-shouldered, and as he caught sight of her, he lifted his hat and waved it, his white teeth flashing in a broad smile. She waved back, and her body tingled with a million bells. He looked so handsome. Was it possible that he could love a plain little "mouse" like her? But there he was, and now she was going through the gate, and he was taking her bags from the porter and smiling down at her in a way that told her he must know it would be as he had hoped.

"Hello, Kate."

"Hello, Bill."

That was all. Their eyes said the rest. His, gray and warm with the joy of seeing her again. Hers, wide, brown and bright behind the prim glasses. They walked through the crowded station side by side, their glances seeking each other.

83

"You look wonderful," Bill said. "Did you have a good trip?"

"Oh, fine. But it took forever."

"I know. It seemed years. I thought you'd never come home."

Kate walked on clouds. She could not remember afterward how they got to the car, but, seated beside him as he drove uptown through the traffic, she knew that she had really "come home," and it was more than a geographical location. As the car stopped for a traffic light, Bill turned to smile down at her and reached for her hand. She placed hers in it. A thousand sonnets could not have said more. That brief gesture said all that needed to be said between them. This was one of the things about Bill that made him so right for her. They needed few words to understand each other. Kate claims she never did give Bill her answer in actual words. Everything was said in that one wordless moment on the clanging Detroit thoroughfare as the lights were changing.

They went to their favorite restaurant, ordered lunch and let it get cold as they sat side by side, holding hands and looking at each other. This kept them occupied well past the end of Bill's lunch hour. Suddenly he looked at his watch. Where had the time gone? He was due back at the plant.

Kate went directly to her office. She knew her two associates, Dr. O'Dell and Dr. Haskins, were heavily overburdened with work, and there was no question about their being glad to see her back. Kate immediately took over as much of the schedule as she could to relieve them. There were rounds to be made at the hospital. A couple of her own patients had checked in. One baby had come the previous night, and the other was expected at any moment.

84

Kate nodded. She'd attend to it. Suddenly the neglected image of Dr. G—— flashed into her mind. The hospital. Dr. G——. He would probably be there. Kate dreaded the ordeal of breaking the news to him. Well, she may as well face it. He would have to be told sooner or later, and there was no use in prolonging the agony.

She finished with the last of the office patients, scribbled a final prescription and made ready to leave for the hospital. As she walked the short distance to the hospital buildings, carrying her bag, she wondered how she would tell Dr. G—— of her decision. Perhaps he would not be there after all.

But Dr. G—— was there, and what's more, he seemed to have no intention of waiting another moment for her answer. They met in the corridor as she headed briskly for the maternity ward.

"Kate!" he cried. "Home at last!" He took her arm and walked with her down the hall. His pleasure at seeing her made the coming ordeal more difficult.

"Well, Kate?" he said after a few preliminary questions about her trip.

"Well, what?" Kate parried for time.

"Have you made up your mind?" he asked ironically, "or will it require another trip before you decide to refuse me?"

"Oh, no," said Kate, "I've already decided."

It was quick and blunt.

He looked at her sharply. "You mean—your answer is 'no'?" He had stopped in his tracks, and she turned to look up at him. His face was white.

"I'm sorry," she said. "I'm—I'm going to marry someone else."

It was done. Cruel, perhaps, but unequivocally final.

He stared at her. "You're *what?*" His tone was incredulous.

"I'm marrying someone else," Kate repeated. Her heart was thumping. It was the first time she had actually said the words that bound her irrevocably to Bill.

"Someone else—after all this time!"

She saw the quiver of hurt in his eyes, and she felt deeply and painfully sorry for him. Sorry, but nothing more.

"Who, for pity's sake?" he demanded bitterly.

"You don't know him," Kate replied.

"Did this happen in Buffalo?"

"No. I met him here."

"Is he a doctor?"

"No. He's in the motorcar business. A mechanic."

"A ——?" He stared at her. A look of disdain and disappointment swept over his face. "I hope you're not making a mistake." His voice was cold, cynical.

"I'm sure I'm not," Kate replied. "I'm in love with him."

He stood there looking down at her, his long, intelligent face with its high forehead and narrow aquiline nose almost comic in its plunge to pathos. Gradually, it recovered its composure.

"Well," he said finally, "I suppose all I can do is wish you luck." He held out his hand, fine, sensitive, supple—the hand of a skilled surgeon, the hand she was rejecting. She put her own in it. His touch was cold. "You're a good doctor, Kate," he said. "I hope this doesn't mean the end of your career." He looked down at her competent, long-fingered hand and released his hold on it.

"It doesn't," replied Kate. Even the touch of their

hands—so different. Her hand belonged in Bill's, that she was sure of.

"If you make as good a wife as you are a doctor, he's lucky."

"Who knows? Maybe *you're* the one who's lucky," Kate said drily.

"Who knows?" He shrugged, and with a bitter smile, turned away from her. She watched him walk back along the hall, then went on to her first patient.

The busy schedule of the next few days left Kate less time than she would have liked to spend with Bill. It seemed useless to delay their marriage, since it was the only solution to this problem of having time together. Why wait? A week after her return, they found a minister and were married, as Dr. Kate puts it, "without any folderol." A honeymoon was out of the question. Kate had already taken her vacation.

They had dinner together and, prophetically enough, Bill spent the better part of their wedding night waiting in the car while Kate attended an unexpectedly premature birth. The patient would have no other doctor, and when the delivery was safely over, the weary bride rejoined her bridegroom in the car.

"Well, Bill," she sighed as she slipped into the seat beside him, "You've had your first sample of what it's like to be married to a doctor."

Bill chuckled. "I'm not complaining," he said. As his arms encircled her, the weariness vanished and Kate forgot everything except this new miracle of happiness which would always be waiting for her when her rounds were over.

There was no need to look for an apartment. Kate's

quarters would do for both of them. Bill moved in from his hotel, and Mr. and Mrs. William Newcomb began their married life with a minimum of readjustment.

The only visible signs that Kate's life had undergone a major change was the bright new wedding ring on her finger and the new cards she had printed, adding "Newcomb" to her name. "Kate Pelham Newcomb, M.D." She liked the sound of it. News of her marriage circulated quickly, and presents began to arrive at the apartment. Friends, doctors, nurses, patients, family, all sent gifts, most of which Kate had to store away to keep their small quarters from becoming as cluttered as a gift shop. Then, as now, Kate was surprised to find that so many people regarded her with affection.

Her letters to her father left no doubt in his mind that Kate had made a happy choice, although he had some difficulty in convincing her grandmother that she had not "thrown herself away" on that "*Bill* person." However, Grandmother Pelham never went shopping without finding something thoroughly impractical and feminine to send the bride.

"She sent me crepe de Chine nighties and cobweb lingerie, and silly little slippers." Dr. Kate wags her head as she recalls Grandmother's determined efforts to arouse the feminine spark in her tailor-made granddaughter.

"Did you ever wear them?" It was a natural question between women. Dr. Kate looked up cautiously, thrusting out her full underlip and narrowing her eyes.

"Hm . . . hm . . ." she nodded, and her face crinkled into a Puck-like smile.

"Be sure you love everything about him," had been her father's advice to her, and Kate wondered how she could ever have entertained the thought of marrying any-one but Bill. They were "together" in every way. She re-gretted the years she had spent without him, and yet, it was as though they had never been apart.

Complete happiness carries with it the dread of change. Could she make Bill happy in spite of the pressure of her professional life? He had accepted this condition without question, but it remained to be seen whether their marriage could maintain its initial bliss on this erratic basis.

"Bill must have something of the saint in him," says Kate on this subject. "I doubt if many other men would have put up with the haphazard domestic life that went with being a doctor's husband. But Bill seemed to take it in his stride. Our evenings at home were often interrupted and I had to make calls regardless of time or weather."

Bill insisted upon accompanying her on night emer-gencies and the comfort of having him along made her wonder how she had ever endured the long excursions through the dark city alone. They sometimes stopped at an all-night diner for a snack before returning home from a case. With Bill at her side, the night calls took on the flavor of adventures. They met home-coming musicians, taxi drivers, theater ushers, policemen, newspapermen, as these denizens of the restless city's nocturnal life paused at the counter for coffee or a sandwich. Kate and Bill heard many lurid tales of night-life happenings from these casual acquaintances. Police news, political intrigue, green-room gossip—a half hour at a diner provided more inside news than could be found in the next morning's papers.

The all-night diner habitués soon discovered Kate's profession, and she doled out many a gratuitous headache tablet and verbal prescription over the coffee cups. Quite a few Detroit babies had these lunch-counter meetings to thank for their safe conduct into the world under Kate's supervision.

The Newcombs sometimes entertained their friends on Sunday afternoons, and Bill received the unqualified approval of Kate's circle, men and women alike. His good looks and ready wit dispelled whatever doubts may have existed regarding Kate's choice of a husband. Even Dr. G——, who was finally persuaded to join one of the Sunday gatherings, could not deny that his successful rival was a man it would be hard to hate. When they met, Bill told Dr. G—— quite frankly that he had been amazed when Kate accepted him. He wasn't at all sure, even now, that she shouldn't have married the doctor instead. They were soon talking away about hunting and fishing like old friends. The next time Dr. G—— met Kate at the hospital, he told her she was "a good picker." He had only to look at her to see that she was supremely happy.

It was a triumphant year for Kate: to be in love, to be loved, and to be successful in her profession as well. It was more than she had ever dared to hope for. She had recently been appointed to the staff of the Women's Hospital and still another upward step was to mark the favorable turn of her fortunes.

Dr. Levy, Kate's old mentor, had been urging her to join him in his office. He was engaged in important research in children's diseases, and he needed capable assistance so that he might spend more time in the laboratory. He offered to make Kate his associate.

Kate talked over Dr. Levy's offer with her colleagues. Much as they would regret losing her, they realized that this was an opportunity she could not afford to miss. Dr. Levy was considered one of the finest pediatricians in Detroit, if not in the country. Being connected with him would place Kate at the top of her profession. And Bill was in favor of the change. He was proud of the fact that the brilliant Viennese doctor, who could have had his pick of the best men in the city, had singled out Kate to share his practice. She decided to make the move, and when she announced her decision to Dr. Levy, he insisted upon celebrating the news with a dinner party in Kate's honor. He invited a select list of guests, and the dinner, held in the Levys' handsomely furnished apartment, was a gala affair.

It was the first formal function Kate had attended since Boston. She wore a becoming dinner dress with a lace bodice, the most "daring" she had ever worn, although its transparency was merely an illusion. The lace was lined with substantial crepe, and the sleeves covered her arms to the wrist. Bill looked so handsome in his dark business suit (he had balked at a tuxedo) that Kate could hardly take her eyes off him. She couldn't see why he had to be seated at the other end of the table instead of at her side. It is difficult to say which of them was prouder that night. Bill of his distinguished wife, or Kate of her handsome husband.

Kate was surprised to find how little of her former shyness remained. She found herself joining in the general conversation and making remarks that evoked gales of laughter. She wondered what her father and Mr. Ulrich would say if they could see her now.

Dr. Levy announced to the company that Dr. Newcomb was becoming his associate, and when their joint success was toasted in champagne, Kate never batted an eyelash. While she left her own glass untouched, it no longer dismayed her to see others drink in moderation.

She noticed, during the dinner, that Bill coughed a few times, and as the evening wore on she saw that he began to look pale and tired. She made a mental note to prescribe a tonic for him. Long hours at the plant, interrupted sleep, and possibly a slight bronchial congestion from hours of waiting in the cold night air, she decided.

There was music after dinner, Strauss and Schubert, played and sung superbly by a talented pianist and a concert singer who were among the guests. Bill was completely absorbed in the music, but Kate's entire attention was centered on his face. That wan and weary look troubled her. As the last *lied* ended, Kate went to Bill's side and whispered that she thought they'd better be getting home.

"Whenever you say," he agreed. They took their leave and on the way home Kate asked Bill if he was feeling all right.

"Just a little tired," he replied.

"In Sickness and in Health . . ."

KATE'S association with Dr. Levy surpassed her expectations. Their relationship was harmonious and profitable, both clinically and economically. Working with this talented doctor was a thrilling experience, and his approbation filled her with pride and confidence. Dr. Levy looked forward eagerly to the day when he could place his entire practice in Kate's hands and devote himself exclusively to his laboratory work.

The only thing that marred Kate's complete happiness was her increasing concern for Bill's health. His appetite and his vitality had been declining at an alarming rate. He had lost weight and his color was bad. However, he resisted all her attempts to get him to submit to a thorough examination, insisting that there was nothing to worry about. But Kate's practiced eye could see that the condition was no passing indisposition. Tonics seemed to have no effect on him, and his cough grew worse.

She finally put her foot down and insisted that he see a specialist. She suspected a blood condition, and wanted to make sure through a competent diagnostician. Bill agreed to the examination and it revealed a low red-corpuscle count and an irritation of the lungs. The doctor prescribed plenty of rest, fresh air, a diet of liver, red meat and green vegetables. He suggested injections of iron which Kate administered by hypodermic.

Bill submitted to the odious monotony of liver, eating his meals without relish. Whenever possible, Kate drove him to the country for the fresh air which seemed temporarily to revive him. He drank in the country freshness like a thirsty man at a spring, but when they returned to the city, the color would go out of his cheeks, the brightness fade from his eyes, and the torpor return to his limbs.

"If I could only stay there, under the trees," he would say unhappily. "It's this city air—full of fumes. There's no life in it. I can't seem to breathe."

When Kate returned home from her rounds, she would find him stretched out on the couch, exhausted from his day's work, his face startlingly pale. The sight and smell of food had become repugnant to him, and no tonic or medication had the slightest effect. He grew so weak that he was finally forced to abandon his work, and this added to his depression.

Kate's anxiety preyed constantly on her mind. She dropped in at the apartment as often as she could during the day, and while she knew that Bill would be better cared for in a hospital, she could not bring herself to suggest this step to him. What was the cause of his peculiar malady? To see a hale, robust man reduced to limp inertia without knowing the basic reason for it was more than she could endure. Remembering Grace Clark's sudden collapse, she grew more and more apprehensive. To satisfy her, Bill went through another series of tests, and this time the trouble was identified.

She heard the diagnosis over the telephone from the

specialist who had just finished examining Bill. During the war years, when the defense plant was turning out planes and tanks, Bill had been engaged in work that required the use of potent acids to mold and condition the heavy metal parts under high pressure. Noxious fumes had filled the working areas. The need for protective masks was not realized at that time, and the poisonous gases, filled with microscopic particles of metal, were inhaled by the men who operated the compression machinery. Bill's entire lung area had been permeated by an accumulation of these irritants, and his present condition was the consequence of that toxic inhalation. Until now, his extraordinary vitality had resisted the effect of the irritants. But the tissues had become so inflamed that the lungs were no longer able to absorb the necessary oxygen for the replenishment of red corpuscles in the blood stream. Unless some way could be found to clear up the pulmonary tissue, his condition would grow worse, and it was only a matter of time before the acute anemia which resulted would become fatal.

As she hung up the receiver, Kate felt the chill of despair settle over her. She knew now that her alarm had not been exaggerated. She had no choice but to stand by and watch Bill slip away from her without being able to do anything to save him. The doctor had said there was no known way to alleviate the condition, except with blood transfusions, and these would be no more than a temporary measure.

Bill was going to die. She was at the height of her career as a doctor, but she could do nothing to prevent it. She dropped her head onto her arms and wept. What was this relentless shadow that pursued her, snatching away those she loved? What good were all the years of study and experience, if she was to be confronted by a blank wall of defeat? The ringing of her phone recalled her to the duties of her practice. Yes, yes, she would be there. But how could she—how could she go through the day? She must, of course. As a physician, she must place her own trouble second to the needs of her patients. She heard Dr. Levy's step outside her office door and she pulled herself up from her chair. Her body felt heavy and numb.

"Come in," she answered to his polite knock. Dr. Levy stood in the doorway, a look of surprise in his dark, somber eyes behind the thick glasses.

"Kate, what it is?" He came to her side and peered at the tear-stained face of his usually calm and capable associate. As quietly and coherently as she could, she told him what she had learned. He listened gravely and shook his head. Then he took her hands and told her that she must not despair. Nothing was hopeless nowadays. There had been many new discoveries in the treatment of poison-gas cases since the war. Surely, some cure would be found for Bill. He would try to find out something about it. She must not despair. His kindness comforted her, and she allowed herself a gleam of hope that saw her through the day.

When she returned home, she found Bill in his usual place on the couch, whiter and more languid than ever. The ordeal of the examination had tired him. He wanted to know what the doctor had told her. She lifted his wrist and felt the slow unsteadiness of his pulse.

"Your lungs were affected by the fumes at the war plant," she said, assuming her best professional manner to cover the tumult of her emotions. "You'll have to have some special treatments. Dr. Levy is going to look into it."

Bill sighed deeply and shook his head.

"Kate," he said, "if I could only get to the woods . . . if I could stay there awhile, I know I could lick this trouble without any medical help. I'd be out of your way, and——"

"Out of my way?" It was almost a cry. "Do you think I'd let you go off alone in this condition?"

"Why not?" he insisted. "I'd loaf around the woods and breathe some clean air, and it would make a new man of me in no time. Let's face it, Kate. I'm getting worse every day. I'm no good to you here. You have your work, and I don't help it any. I can't even go with you on the night calls any more."

Yes, the night calls were lonely again. For two years they had been companionable forays into adventure.

Kate summoned every ounce of control to keep back her tears. Bill, who had given her the gift of happiness, was begging to be allowed to crawl away to the woods where he could die without being a burden to her. The thought of it was more than she could endure. No, they must try to find some way to purge his lungs of the poison. That small gleam of hope still lingered. Perhaps Dr. Levy would find a cure.

But the good doctor's inquiries produced no encouraging answer. Medical science had not found a cure for Bill's malady. Kate told him of Bill's longing for the forest.

"Why not send him, Kate?" Dr. Levy suggested. "We could find a good nurse to go with him, a man who could look after him and cook his meals. You say he is always better when you take him to the country. Who knows? It might work."

"Either that, or he might die there—alone—among strangers. I'm sure he wants to go because he believes he's a burden to me——" Her voice broke and Dr. Levy reached out a steadying hand and gripped her shoulder.

"I think a hospital is the only answer. A good sanitarium, a place in the country where they handle lung cases. You can't go on like this, my dear girl. You practice all day, then you go home to a sick man. It's too much for you. The sick take a lot of our strength. And when they are close to our hearts, it is disastrous. You will break down, Kate. Be practical. Put him in a sanitarium, not too far away, where you can go to see him. That's all you can do. Think about it. I will help you select a good place."

Kate nodded and dried her eyes. But her thoughts were taking a different direction. She knew that a sanitarium would be the worst possible environment for Bill. He would feel caged and fret himself to death. If he wanted to go to the woods, if that was his wish, perhaps his last wish, she could not refuse him. At least he would be happy there—until the end. But could she send him with a stranger?

Bill made the decision for her that evening. He decided to go to Milwaukee to stay with his parents. They lived a few miles outside the city, and the change of air might alleviate his condition. It was worth trying. They telephoned his father and made arrangements to have Bill met at the station in Milwaukee. Kate put him on the train with fear clutching at her heart. Would she ever see him alive again? She returned to her office and carried on her work with a troubled conscience. How could she have let him go off alone?

She received a cheerful letter from him, telling her that he was making plans to go on a trip to northern Wisconsin. He was determined to discover if that invigorating climate would have a favorable effect on his condition. She was not to worry. By the time the letter reached her and she telephoned, he was gone. She waited, fearful of receiving bad news. But his letter from the northwoods reassured her. The climate agreed with him, and he was now sure it was the only answer to his problem. He was returning briefly to Milwaukee and then going back north.

In the two weeks that Bill was gone, Kate realized that all the meaning and purpose had gone out of her life. Being separated from Bill reduced her to a tormented fraction.

She took the weekend off and joined him in Milwaukee. He seemed better. The joy of being with him again told her what she had already guessed—that her life meant nothing without Bill. He had missed her as much as she had missed him, and she told him that she intended to return to the northwoods with him.

Did she mean that she would give up her practice, he asked, troubled by her announcement. Yes, for as long as it would take to recover his health. What about Dr. Levy? He would have to find someone to replace her.

He knew what her association with Dr. Levy meant to her as a doctor. This was a sacrifice that proved, beyond any shadow of doubt, that the woman he had married was more woman than doctor. It was hard for him to find words to tell her what her decision meant to him. He did not try to put his deep emotion into words. He took her face in his two hands and kissed her. When could she be ready? In a few days, she said. He suggested that they spend the Christmas holiday with his family and then go north. They would equip themselves in Milwaukee for the heavy winter of the Wisconsin northwoods. He warned her that it would be bitter cold and very primitive. She smiled. "We'll be together. If you can take it, I can."

Bill returned to his father's home and Kate left for Detroit in her car.

Dr. Levy received the news of her decision without speaking, but she could see that it was a blow to him. Then he asked, "When are you going?"

"There's no time to lose. If I wait too long—the lake air doesn't agree with him. In one day, I could see the difference."

"Go right away, Kate," Dr. Levy urged. "Don't worry about me. I'll manage. I hate to lose you, but if I were in your place, I'd do the same. When you return, come to see me and we will arrange something. Meanwhile, if you need anything, let me know. Money, anything at all. And be sure to write to me often. Let me know how he gets along. Run along now. You have a lot to do." He paused. "You are a fine woman, Kate," he said gently.

Kate could not speak. Dr. Levy's dark, heavy-featured face had suddenly become one of the most beautiful she had ever seen.

She had been with him just ten months. The last she ever saw of him was through the grille of the elevator, a thin, stoop-shouldered figure with graying black hair, rubbing his glasses with his handkerchief.

Northwoods Pilgrimage

THE pulling up of roots in Detroit was a painful wrench for Kate. She had a thriving practice, the reward of years of study and effort. She had made many friends, a busy and profitable life. And now she must leave everything behind and journey to the wilderness. Where would that strange road lead? Only the hope of restoring Bill's health allayed the misgivings which loomed in her mind as she prepared for her pilgrimage.

Any prospect of continuing her medical career was out of the question. The sparsely settled region which was their destination was not an environment in which she could hope to establish a practice. Besides, Bill would require her constant care. His mental depression, increased by the realization of the sacrifice Kate was making for him, was as difficult to fight as the illness which was consuming his body. She had done her best to convince him that she was glad to be "taking a vacation." To please her, he had pretended to believe it. Between them, they played a brave game, each assuming a cheerfulness they were far from feeling, and trying to give their departure the appearance of a belated "honeymoon."

Kate wound up her affairs, resigned from the hospital staff, said a few brief good-bys, and as the December wind whipped through the streets, she set out to meet Bill at his father's home.

Already his condition was impaired by the heavy dampness of the lake climate. The holiday was shadowed by anxiety. Bill's hacking cough, the agonizing headaches caused by his inflamed sinuses, his waning energy and cadaverous color indicated a severe relapse from the gain he had made on his trip to the northwoods.

They outfitted themselves with all the necessary cold-weather gear: woolen underwear, heavy outer garments, lumberjack windbreakers, boots, gloves, blankets. They stocked up with a month's supply of provisions.

Their destination was Eagle River, Wisconsin, a lumber-camp station on the Chicago and Northwestern Railroad. As they boarded the train, Bill found it difficult to lift any but the lightest pieces of luggage.

It was a slow train, and the heavy snows made its progress even more tedious. Dark skies, crawling wheels, primitive tracks—bitter, bitter cold. Kate wondered if Bill could endure the endless grind of that sluggish train, its long, intermittent stops, its jerking, rattling departures only to slow down again as snowdrifts blocked the tracks.

After an all-night journey, they arrived at the Eagle River station, a rude log structure almost covered by snow. It was early morning on the first of January of the year 1922. The cheerful New Year's greetings exchanged by the station hands and the train crew fell on Kate's ears with a hollow sound. Huge piles of logs banked with snow shut away the landscape. The wind howled and the snow blew in their faces as they made their way to the dismal hotel across from the depot to rest from their journey and chart their next move into the wilderness.

For several days they remained at the hotel, their room heated by a small old-fashioned wood stove. Kate inquired about resort accommodations and learned there was a place eighteen miles from the station where they could rent a furnished cabin. How to get there? A station hack could take them part of the way, but the forest roads they would have to traverse were not navigable by car at this time of year. The hotelkeeper telephoned the resort to make sure they would be met at the highway with a sleigh.

They piled into the hack with all their belongings and started off along the icy highway which had been cleared by snowplow. The going was slow, and at about half the distance, they found the horse-drawn sleigh waiting to carry them through the wintry woods.

By this time, the cold, clear air of the pine woods had restored Kate's spirits, and the majesty of the snow-laced wilderness filled her with silent awe. The sled skimmed over the packed snow behind the pounding hoofs of the horses, their harness jingling with cheerful bells. Through the dark tracery of the trees, lake after lake, white with snow, stretched in a white expanse to the forests beyond. Bill inhaled the clean air in deep, hungry breaths and color appeared on his sharp cheekbones.

They stopped at a friendly home for lunch, where the horses were replaced with a team of mules. That eighteen-mile journey took an entire day, and it was nearly dark when they arrived at the two-room log cabin which was to be their first dwelling. It was warm and clean, but strictly primitive, heated by a wood stove and lighted with kerosene lamps. The bed was hardly more than a cot, and the furniture was a haphazard collection of crudely constructed odds and ends. Nevertheless, Kate was grateful for a place where they could unpack their belongings and feel a sense of permanency. Around them in the twilight stretched the white and dark green silence of the forest, and just beyond shimmered the frozen surface of a lake, rimmed with the ghostly outlines of snow-laden trees.

This, then, was their new beginning. Or was it only the beginning of the end? Bill was so sure this change would cure him, but Kate realized, from her scientific viewpoint, that the odds were heavily against him. As he lay on the cot, spent from the long ride, Kate heated water on the stove and refreshed her tired body with a sponge bath. Here she was, in a rustic country cabin, despite her determination to be a "city doctor." Compared with this, life in Canandaigua would have been a sinecure. She wondered what Pat would say if he could see her now.

She brewed some tea and brought Bill a cup to stir him from the lethargic somnolence that never failed to strike terror in her heart. She was always afraid he would slip away from her in his sleep. Bill roused himself and came to the kitchen where he washed and shaved the two-day growth of beard, while Kate prepared their evening meal of canned beans and bacon. They ate in silence, and then set about putting away their belongings.

After a good night's sleep, they both felt refreshed, and Bill began to initiate her into the routine of rustic life. There was much for her to learn, and she blundered through her first lessons with many a splinter and burn and bruise on her unaccustomed hands. But let her tell it:

"My culinary repertoire to date had been cake, fudge and salad dressing, so you can imagine the extent of our menu during those first weeks. Canned beans, and more canned beans—bacon, eggs, coffee. I had to learn to cook on that wood stove with the most primitive equipment. I had brought a Boston Cook Book along, but the cooking facilities for such recipes were limited. Most important of all, I had to learn not to let the fire go out—which I did, several times. But I grew more careful when I realized it meant the difference between keeping warm and freezing to death. Necessity is a good teacher. I managed to keep Bill fed, and though he did not have a very healthy appetite at first, it began to improve gradually, and before long, even my sketchy cooking tasted good to him. Fortunately, there were kind neighbors who helped with the heavy work. As Bill grew less limp, he began to take on quite a few of the chores. The first time he filled the wood box, I was so elated I nearly cried with joy. It was the first milestone on the road to his recovery.

"It wasn't easy for a woman who was accustomed to the conveniences of a city apartment to take hold and keep a home going under such primitive conditions. I was a hopeless tenderfoot, and I would be concealing the truth if I did not admit I missed the hot and cold running water and the steam heat and the modern bathroom of our Detroit apartment. Hauling water from a well and building a wood fire were not exactly my dish of tea. The basic facilities of an outhouse were a far cry from city plumbing. That gruesome structure was colder than the North Pole on a winter night. But when I began to see the color return to Bill's lips, and watched his eyes lose their deathlike dullness, I decided there were more important things in life than inside plumbing and steam heat, and I endured the discomforts with a lighter heart.

"Medicine wasn't the greatest thing in the world, after all, I concluded. Where science had failed, the woods had won. Science lost much of its vaunted prestige in my estimation that winter. I realized that there was a mighty healing power in God's natural environment which science could only emulate, but never replace. With this philosophy to console me for my lost career, I entered into the spirit of backwoods life with a zest that surprised even Bill. I was so elated over Bill's improved health that I began to love the woods with a fanaticism almost equal to his own. The winter was a severe one, and my work was gruelling, but in spite of discomforts and physical exertion, (or perhaps because of them), my own health blossomed and my spirits soared.

"I learned to handle one end of a crosscut saw like a lumberjack. I enjoyed hiking with Bill through the snow, and I finally worked up the courage to take my first lessons in navigating on snowshoes. Of course, I had some fine falls at first, but as I look back now, I'm sure I had a lot of fun mastering those tricky tennis racquets.

"One day, when we ran out of bread—and there was no running down to the corner grocer for a loaf—I ventured to make some from the recipe in my Boston Cook Book. Bill insisted it was far better than store bread, and I got quite a thrill out of it. There was something satisfying about making my own bread. Taking the fine golden loaves from the oven is a pleasure that simply can't be described. And I don't believe any perfume on earth can compare with the aroma of freshly baked bread. I recommend bread-baking as a therapeutic hobby for bored or restless women.

"Despite my distaste for cleaning and washing and ironing, and the dozens of other tiresome chores involved in keeping a crude cabin livable, I was amazed to find that I was supremely happy. For the first time in years, I knew what it meant to enjoy nights of uninterrupted sleep. I missed the challenge of my practice, but I cannot say that I missed the round of sickrooms, and hospital calls, the smell of anesthetics, the emergency calls in the small hours of the morning. As for being bored, how could I be with Bill around? As his health improved, his vivacity returned. He was always sending for new books, and bundles of newspapers came from Milwaukee, Detroit and Chicago.

" 'What more could a woman want of life?' I asked myself. The man she loved being restored to health, a snug home in a beautiful forest, good neighbors who lent each other a helping hand, spring on the way, and what was more—I discovered that I was pregnant with my first child!

" 'Sweet are the uses of adversity' may be a threadbare proverb to some, but to me it had become a living truth. Adversity had brought me gifts that no worldly success could have matched. Peace of mind, strength of body, and a baby on the way!

"Bill was deliriously happy over the coming child. He was glad it would be born under the clean sky and would draw its first breath in the pure forest air. His only anxiety was for my happiness. He asked me over and over whether I missed Detroit. I assured him I was perfectly content where we were, and my answer never failed to bring a look of relief into his eyes.

"My father's letters did not share Bills' satisfaction. Papa was concerned over the fact that I had abandoned my practice. How long did I propose to remain in the wilderness? Was Bill's health improving? Was I comfortable? When would I return to my work?

"When I wrote him the news about his expected grandchild, his attitude changed. He was delighted. If I needed anything, I must let him know. He could well afford to help. His very best to Bill. We laughed over the sudden reversal of my father's frame of mind. He had news for us, too. He was going to marry again! His bride-to-be was a Miss Gertrude Kinney of New York. He sent us some pictures of her and we agreed she would be an ornament to his glamorous social life. She brought him the happiness he had long missed—and two more children.

"When I discovered I was pregnant, Bill and I decided we had better make a change in our residence. Bill had friends in Crandon—Mel and Leona Kenaga—and we felt it would be best to have friends close by when my time came. They were willing to rent us a part of their cottage near Stone Lake, a vast improvement on our primitive resort cabin. Their place was only seven miles from the town of Crandon, and while it was still not what you might call 'the lap of luxury,' it had a few conveniences like 'pumped-up' gasoline lamps and acetylene stoves for cooking, which were luxuries compared with our crude facilities.

"The cottage was about a mile and a half from the lake, which would be navigable by boat in good weather. But during the winter months the men had to go on foot to replenish provisions, which meant a fourteen-mile hike, seven with heavy packs on their backs. In bad weather, that was no joy ride. Never will I forget the time we got really low on food, and the men took advantage of a break in the weather to hike to town. Imagine our dismay when they returned with empty rucksacks! The explanation? It was Sunday. We had lost track of the days of the week. Oh, yes, that can happen when one lives far from the accuracies of city life.

"There were lumber camps nearby, and one of our diversions was to trudge over for a meal and a visit with the lonely lumberjacks who were always delighted to see us.

As spring came on the mosquitoes were terrible, and we had to wear headpieces of netting as we went through the woods to keep from being devoured by those bloodthirsty pests.

"It was a wonderful experience to watch the spring move into the forest. As the snow melted and the forest floor turned green, I went with Leona and her two children to explore this new, fresh world. I did all the things the natives did. I dug dandelion greens, picked berries as they ripened and even tapped the maple trees for their syrup. Everything smelled so sweet and clean, and the warmth of the sun made the blood race in our veins. The dogs scurried around, sniffing everything with a zest that I could well understand.

"We had quite a pack of dogs by then. A colony of Kentuckians lived in Crandon, and they had come out with their hounds to hunt. Bill acquired a pack of hounds for hunting which it was part of my job to keep fed. Bill's hunting expeditions had yielded a good income that winter, as the state paid a bounty for the wolves and foxes that were plentiful, and their skins sold for a handsome price at this time. The hounds were a nuisance to feed, but I'll say one thing for them. They appreciated the mash of corn meal, cracklings and kitchen scraps that I prepared for them.

"One of the major advantages of the spring weather was that I didn't mind the outside plumbing so much. It rained a lot, but nothing could down my spirits as the trees turned green and the lake ice melted and the birds began to nest in the branches overhead. My heart sang with them and I came to know them all by name, for Bill was a devoted bird-watcher. He would call me to see any new kind of feathered visitor that held still long enough. . . . The shores of the lake stirred with sparkling new life as the days grew longer. We saw chipmunk, squirrel, cottontail, otter, and we placed a salt lick within sight and watched the deer come with their does and fawns to savor it. We would walk to the lake shore and watch the loons ride their young on their backs from their nesting places in the rushes. The turtles crawled ashore to lay their eggs in the sand where they would be hatched by the warmth of the sun.

"It was all new to me, and I enjoyed learning the ways of the forest creatures that surrounded us. The deep satisfaction of carrying a new life made the spring seem even more wonderful. I felt so much a part of the blossoming and growth that, looking back, I wondered how I could have endured the narrowness and the noisomeness of the city. It seemed to me that I was an entirely different being than the hurrying, brooding doctor who trudged through the corridors of the Women's Hospital, carrying a heavy medical bag.

"That summer we made a trip to Oshkosh where we acquired a battery radio and a new supply of records for our phonograph, and we did some exciting shopping for the expected baby. Then we went on to Milwaukee where we visited with Bill's family for a few days to show them how much better he was. We then picked up the car, which we had stored in Milwaukee, and drove back north, glad to return to our woodland home.

"Without a doubt, that spring and summer were the happiest of my entire life."

The Modern Touch

APPROACHING fatherhood had had an exhilarating effect on Bill. His health improved visibly each day, and his spirits were heightened by the two-fold victory. New blood was coursing through his veins and in Kate's keeping was another life which would bring fulfillment to their marriage.

Kate knew that Bill would be a good father. She had watched his gentleness toward the animals of the forest, and soon discovered that her "mighty hunter" was more inclined to stalk the predators that threatened the helpless creatures than to hunt the harmless wild life which attracted the seasonal sportsmen. An injured animal could always find refuge and medication in the Newcombs' woodshed. Bill carried scraps from the table to a spot in the forest where he sometimes sat for hours watching his protégés come to carry off their rations. Birds, chipmunks, squirrels, rabbits, even precarious skunks, banqueted within a few feet of Bill's observation post. Yes, Bill had a way with small creatures, and Kate smiled as she imagined him holding a toddling "hunter" by the hand.

Her letters to the family and to her friends in Detroit and Buffalo brought back copious mail, messages of delighted anticipation and packages containing gifts for the layette. Dr. Levy took time from his crowded schedule to write her long scholarly letters in a meticulous hand, giving her the latest medical news and bewailing the difficulty he had had in replacing her. He rejoiced over the news of her approaching maternity and marveled at the miracle of Bill's improved health. He hoped that she would eventually be able to return to her medical career.

Bill and Kate made plans for the baby's future, engaging in all the happy speculation that expectant parents indulge in at such a time. Bill's only anxiety was that Kate might want to return to the city too soon, for he wanted his child to have its start in the forest. But as Kate watched the tint of health return to Bill's cheeks, she knew that she would not exchange this blessing for all the success the crowded city had to offer. She was content with the bargain she had made and had no intention of rescinding it.

The fresh northern summer passed quickly and September painted the forest with a blaze of brilliance. The crisp air filled their veins with vigor and the crackling of wood in the stove was a welcome sound as they returned from their slow evening walks around the sun-burnished lake.

The baby's crib, which Bill had built himself, stood in a corner of their room, waiting for its occupant.

As the time drew near for her confinement, Kate decided to consult a competent physician and make arrangements for her delivery. She knew the importance of expert care, and selected a doctor who made calls in the vicinity and had weekly office hours at Crandon. They kept their car at Bruss' Landing at the north end of the lake and made the trip by boat as far as the landing, then by car to the doctor's office.

The doctor found her in excellent condition. When he learned that she was a physician, he talked to her about the latest methods of painless childbirth known as "twilight sleep," which were being used successfully by some of the most progressive obstetricians. Kate was not inclined to favor unnatural methods to avoid pain. All she wanted was expert attendance at her confinement, and the doctor assured her he would be on hand to see her through when the time came.

The Kenagas had gone to Indiana to visit Leona's family, expecting to be back in plenty of time to be on hand when Kate's baby arrived.

But before they returned, Kate felt the first pangs of labor, and Bill hurried to the boat landing and headed up the lake for the doctor. More than an hour had passed before he returned with the doctor. The cottage was a mile and a half from the landing and could be reached only through a forest trail on foot. The second phase of her labor had begun, but there was no telling, at that point, how soon the child would be born. The birth might still be hours away, and the prospect of making the long trip again, on foot, by boat and by car, to and from Crandon, or remaining there to await the delivery, was one which the doctor faced with some uncertainty. He decided to make a thorough examination to ascertain the approximate time of birth, and he administered a sedative which Kate took without question, confident that the doctor had the situation well in hand, and grateful to be relieved of the responsibility which she herself had taken so often for others.

The drug was more powerful than she had expected, and Kate slipped into oblivion.

When she regained consciousness, she was amazed to find that the doctor had delivered her child by version and extraction, which means that he reversed the position of the baby and produced a delivery without waiting for the natural course of labor. It was a boy and apparently sound and normal. She had suffered no pain.

Kate was somewhat bewildered by what had occurred. Still dazed by the effects of the sedative, she examined her child and saw it was perfect, though it seemed unnaturally quiet, which she realized was due to the drug. Bill's happy face bent over her and she drifted off into a torpescent sleep, marveling that after the second spasm of labor, there had been no more pain.

Below the surface of her somnolence, her mind struggled to touch solid ground. Troubled dreams began to loom on the horizon of her drugged consciousness. She seemed to be reaching helplessly for her child, unable to grasp it securely in her arms.

By the time the sedative began to wear off, Kate's subconscious anxiety for her baby showed signs of being more than a narcotic nightmare. It was an alarming reality. The child seemed to be failing.

Bill hurried to fetch the doctor, while an hour dragged into a terrifying eternity for Kate. When they returned, the doctor's frightened face belied his assurances to Kate that there was no cause for concern.

Within forty-eight hours of its "painless" birth, Kate's baby was dead.

Black Sky over Eden

KATE stared blindly into the face of her greatest tragedy. Once again death had reached its icy hand into her life. How could this thing have happened? To her, of all people, whose whole devotion had been given to the safe delivery of so many mothers and their babies, had come the misfortune she had held at bay for them. She had lost her own child. Her bitterness against "scientific progress" verged on hatred. Her mind remained fixed on the strange circumstances of her delivery. Wordless rebellion seethed under the icy impassiveness of shock.

The forest cottage, now lashed by autumn rain, held a despair so abysmal that its two stricken occupants seemed like prisoners in a dungeon from which they had no will to escape.

The Kenagas returned to find two hollow-eyed ghosts instead of the happy couple they had left behind. The tiny coffin was carried to the Crandon graveyard and there Kate's brightest dream was laid in the sodden earth. With it lay all her years of faith and courage, her belief that men of science could conquer death. She was convinced now that medicine was a delusive snare. Even in this remote refuge of nature, it had reached in and betrayed her.

"Bitter—bitter—bitter," she says, reliving the agony of those days. "I was so bitter that I could not taste, feel or hear—or even escape into the relief of sleep. My face became a stiff mask that reflected the warped bitterness of my emotions.

"Bill swallowed his own grief and did his best to comfort me. We would have other children, he said. What would he have done if *I* had been taken from him? He used every wile of his loving heart to lure me back to a semblance of human warmth. I felt as completely shut away from life as though I had been buried with my baby.

"The Kenagas and our other friends came to offer their help. They tried to comfort me and to draw me out of the blank-eyed silence that had enveloped me like a shroud. Nothing seemed to have the slightest effect. Bill began to fear for my reason. In fact, I did actually entertain the thought of ending my life. Even in normal births, women are known to go through a phase called 'post-partum psychosis.' The loss of my child intensified this condition to an alarming degree. I was convinced that God and man were against me. In my shocked state, I could not see any reason for my continued existence. The emptiness of my arms was an actual physical ache that words cannot describe. My breasts, fevered with useless milk, were a painful reminder of the child that had been snatched from them.

"As a doctor, I had guessed how much the living child meant to those happy mothers whose babies I had placed safely in their arms. But now I knew the full significance of that relationship.

"Was this my reward for the care and precaution I had taken to safeguard others? I turned my face bitterly away from God as I had done when I was a small child, refusing to believe He was good, refusing even to believe He existed."

The cold rains turned to snow and the early northern winter with its knifelike winds closed in around the somber cottage. Bill and his friends watched Kate constantly, hoping for some sign of recovery from her trancelike condition. She moved through the house like a wraith, answering in monosyllables, if at all, attending to her household duties like an automaton. Would she ever be normal again? Would this tragedy scar her mind forever? Was she lost to the happiness she had found in the forest Bill had taught her to love?

The answer came unexpectedly. One morning the cottage had a visitor. An elderly man made his way up the snowy path to the door and knocked. Bill told Kate it was a minister who had come to see her. He had heard of the tragedy and had come down the icy lake and through the forest trail to bring what consolation he could to the bereaved couple. Kate shook her head. She wanted to see no one. Leona urged her to see the man. He had come a long way. Kate shrugged. Leona left the room and returned with the minister. He was an elderly man, and he spoke sympathetically of Kate's loss and asked her kindly about her health. There was hostility in her attitude as she replied that she felt quite well, thank you. Her reaction to the minister's visit was one of cynical resentment. She did not want to hear about the mercy and consolation of God. She just wanted to be let alone. But the minister did not attempt to console her with sanctimonious quotations.

He simply said that he knew what it meant to lose a child. He had lost a son, a grown boy of twenty. His only son. He had struggled hard to give him an education. Then the war came and his son enlisted. He had not waited to be called. He was so alive, so full of idealism. There was a fight to be won and he must do his part. As the man spoke, he took out a worn wallet and from it he drew his son's photograph. Kate looked at the snapshot of a handsome blond boy in army uniform. A young, smiling face, a tall, strong body.

"He's buried somewhere in France," said the minister. He had a picture of the grave with a white cross and a small American flag marking it, and others—so many others stretching beyond.

Kate looked up into the minister's face. It was calm. Resignation had wiped away the marks of grief that surely had been there. Suddenly she felt the frozen springs give way. Tears broke through the icy numbness that had gripped her since that terrible September night. She wept for the quiet father and for his son who slept under that white cross on a foreign battlefield, and for all the other sons under the other crosses. This man had come through the wintry snows to share his courage with her. Kate wept, and the warm tears washed away her bitterness.

"Those tears saved me. I felt ashamed. I had thought only of myself, of my own sorrow. I had let Bill grieve without comforting him, and, what was worse, without letting him comfort me. All around me there were others with heartaches as great as mine, and I had given no thought to them. How I had changed! My life as a doctor had been lived for others. But here, instead, I had built a mausoleum of stone and had buried us both in it to mourn perpetually for the child which had been given us and taken from us.

"I dried my tears and went about making coffee and preparing a table for the visitor whom I had first resented as an intruder. We sat and talked of many things, of the lumber camps and the lonely men in them; of the Indians living in squalor and poverty on the reservations; of the need for a proper church in the community. Bill watched my face, as though he could hardly believe this was really Kate. His look of relief made me realize what a terrible ordeal he had been through. I reached out and pressed his hand and he knew I was asking him to forgive me.

"When our visitor left, we stood in the snow and watched him trudge off through the forest. Then we walked slowly back into the cottage, and I savored the crystal air of the winter afternoon as though I had just regained consciousness after a long sleep. Although I never saw that good man again, I have always remembered him. I'm sure his visit saved my reason.

"But it was many a long year before I could endure the sight of a doctor, even the one who looked back at me from my own mirror.

"My loss was just one of the many tragic casualties of an abortive experiment with 'twilight sleep.' The practice was condemned by the medical profession when it was discovered that this method of avoiding the pains of normal labor resulted—if not in actual death—then in an impairment to the nervous system of the child, sometimes for its entire life."

This was one lesson in obstetrics which Kate Newcomb learned the hard way, and she never forgot it. She leaves the plans of creation to the wisdom of Him who designed them, adding only her vigilance and precautions, and her invariable prayers.

The Ordeal of the Snows

AFTER the minister's visit, Kate's improved condition made it possible for Bill to talk things over rationally with her. The Kenagas had decided to return to Indiana for the rest of the winter, and Kate and Bill agreed that a change of scene would be best for both of them. A spell of clear weather made it possible for them to go house-hunting while the snow was still traversable, and they found an abandoned logging camp on the south end of Stone Lake which offered several advantages. For one thing, it was more spacious than their present quarters. Then too, it was situated directly on the shore of the picturesque lake, which would make it ideal for swimming, fishing and boating when the good weather came around.

It consisted of a group of buildings of primitive construction, made of whole logs sealed with moss and oakum. Beside the main house, which had served as a bunkhouse with an adjoining cookshed, it had a log barn which would make a snug shelter for the dogs during the winter weather. It had even fewer conveniences than the Kenaga cottage, no sink and no pump. Water had to be drawn from a well, and there was, of course, the ubiquitous out house, complete with crescent vents, and the best that could be said for it was that it was well calked against drafts.

They made arrangements with the logging company who owned the camp, rented for something like twenty-five or thirty dollars for an entire year, and began transferring their belongings immediately so as to be settled before the inevitable cycle of heavy snows set in.

They had made the move just in time, for they were no sooner ensconced in their new quarters than a violent snowstorm whipped over the countryside, piling the drifts high into the branches of the trees, and locking the new tenants away from further circulation for the rest of the winter.

At this point, Bill began to show signs of a relapse. The emotional strain of their child's death, coupled with the exertion of the move to the lakeside camp was taking its toll. Kate spent many nights assuaging Bill's sleeplessness with back-rubbing and hot packs to relax his tension and stimulate his circulation. She sometimes read to him until he dropped off to sleep, and then she would crawl cautiously under the blankets beside him, anxious about the sluggishness of his pulse and wondering, as she drifted into fitful dreams, whether she would still find a pulse when dawn touched the frosted windows with its eerie light.

The first Christmas in their lakeside home was by no means a happy one. Kate performed the candle-lighting ritual faithfully, with her friends' and family's Christmas cards and presents arranged around the votive candle, but she could not bring herself to sing the carols. Her thoughts dwelt more on the little grave under the snow at Crandon than on the eternal Christ child in His stable manger.

New Year's Day was the anniversary of their arrival at Eagle River. It had been a crowded year, first filled with happiness, then with anguish. Looking across the table at Bill's wan, hollow-eyed face in the lamplight, Kate wondered what further trials the New Year had in store for them.

As the clock pointed to midnight, Bill came to her and put his arms around her.

"It's a new start, Kate," he said. "Let's hope it will be a better year." She rested her cheek against his rough lumberjack shirt and felt his body shake with an answering sob as the tears rolled silently down her cheeks. Where would the next New Year's Day find them? Still together? She shivered and clung to Bill until the weakness passed. Then she composed herself and wiped her eyes.

"You should have been in bed two hours ago," she said briskly and set about warming his bedtime drink.

Through that grim winter, with the ghostly drifts looming high around the camp and the wind keening over the frozen lake, Kate struggled between the deeps of despair and the cheerless shallows of resignation. The emptiness of her arms still haunted her and many heavy tears soaked her pillow.

Winter is long in the northwoods. It begins in October, and well into May the bluster of snow and wind grips the woodlands in an icy paralysis of sub-zero cold. The drifts piled high above the level of the roof, so that a space had to be dug at the windows to admit air and, from the door, a ramp had to be cut in the snow so they could move about on snowshoes for air and exercise. Kate helped with the shovelling, fearing that Bill would overtax his strength and suffer a further relapse. But the exercise in the cold air and the strict rest which Kate imposed on him after his exertions seemed to improve his health rather than impair it. Obviously, his instinct as to what was best for his health had proved sound.

Kate did a lot of thinking about this phenomenon of the human potential for self-cure. If Bill had been a less intuitive man, he would have died, since no scientific methods had been available to cure him. Was civilization so impairing the natural instincts of the human species to do what was right for itself that science had become merely a compensatory measure, advancing less rapidly than man retrogressed? She thought of the minister's boy. Was man being safeguarded from disease only to be destroyed by the progressive mechanization of war? Where would it end? How could she have believed that science was an exalted calling?

Held fast in a prison of snow, Kate went through periods of dark, unreasoning fear: fear that Bill could not possibly survive the hardships of the unending winter; fear of the stalking timber wolves that prowled hungrily through the surrounding forest, mingling their howls with the shriek of the banshee wind; fear that she was hopelessly lost in this spectral labyrinth of snow and lamentation.

Between the rise on which the camp stood and the white sheet of snow which marked the lake ran the tracks of a logging line. All winter the heavily loaded log cars, drawn by a "peggy engine," rumbled along the lake shore to a siding where the cars were switched to the main line and sent down to the mills. The engineer would salute them with a double toot of his whistle as he passed their camp, and Kate welcomed that greeting, for it seemed their only link with the outside world. When there was mail, which the friendly loggers brought down for them from Crandon, there would be three blasts on the whistle and Bill would go down to the tracks and pick up the welcome bundle.

Kate went doggedly about her household tasks, keeping the fire going and the wicks trimmed, cooking and putting things in order with a watchful eye always on Bill.

They had seen no one, except a pair of lost hunters and an itinerant lumberjack who had strayed into their camp for food and shelter. They longed for the sight of their fellow men, needing reassurance that there were still other members of their kind and that they were not doomed derelicts, trapped in the isolation of an interminable ice age.

One morning, when Kate heard the raucous cry of the first pioneering crow, she knew that the worst of the winter weather was past. Soon now the spring would be on its way. Soon the icy walls would melt, and they would be freed from their captivity. She shook off the coils of dread that had wound themselves around her heart and began to look forward to release.

When the lake ice broke and the snows thawed, they could go to Crandon by boat, pick up their car at Bruss' Landing, and replenish their dwindling supplies. Impatiently they watched the temperature rise, fall again, taunting their eagerness. The jagged ice floes, which had promised to thaw, froze again in rough crests. It was already May and the lake was still impassable by boat. Another snowstorm, chill with sleet, prolonged the winter weather.

"The battery radio played an important part in our lives during the months of isolation," Dr. Kate relates. "We never missed a news broadcast. We became ardent Amos and Andy fans, and we were enormously grateful for the many fine programs which the networks broadcast. We came to know them all through the years. Major Bowes and his Amateur Hour, Lum and Abner, Jack Benny, Fred Allen and many others were as much a part of our lives as our daily bread. They fed our imagination and made us laugh. They gave us something to look forward to in our tedious isolation. The blessing of such entertainment to those who are cut off from intercourse with their fellow men is beyond calculation. I wonder if these talented people realize how much they mean to the lonely souls marooned in the snowbound wilderness? I hope these words will convey my gratitude to them for the happiness they brought us in those winters of exile.

"We also read a lot during the bad weather. I caught up on Scott, Dickens, and Kipling and Thackeray, and many of the classics which I had always wanted to read but never had the time for when I was practicing medicine.

"My taste included everything from poetry to murder. What I didn't read, and, in fact, studiously avoided, were medical books. Medicine, which had been my very life-blood, had lost its fascination for me. I condemned it to oblivion for having failed me when I most needed it, and I was convinced that I would never practice again."

Cooking had become another absorbing interest in Kate's life. She took to it as she had once taken to laboratory work, and, having equipped herself with a wider range of cooking utensils, she explored the authoritative pages of the Boston Cook Book for recipes that would relieve the monotony of their necessarily limited diet. She became something of an expert at Boston-baked pork and beans with molasses. The excellence of her corn bread was evidenced by the fact that no matter how much of it she made, there was seldom any left over for the following day. She says:

"Flapjacks with bacon or sausage and good maple syrup was a popular item on our menu. And rutabagas! We hauled them in by the bushel and ate them until they very nearly came out of our ears. Canned tomatoes were a blessing. I stewed them and used them with macaroni and cheese and

I even made salad of them with some cooked dressing made of corn oil, vinegar and egg yolks. Potatoes, of course, were a good old stand-by, and I found plenty of ways of cooking them though we finally decided that roasting them on the stove was the best way of all.

"I made good vegetable soup, when vegetables were in season, and as for my beef stew, well, I was proud of it. A neighboring farmer supplied us with venison, still frozen solid, and I must have been meat-hungry, because I actually ate it, though I have always disliked anything in the line of game. I can't say that I did this so-called delicacy justice by my cooking, but it was edible and it was meat, so we were glad to have it, even if it did require some extra hard chewing.

"I took to culinary experiments with enthusiasm at first, but after a while, cooking three meals a day, with extra rations for the twelve dogs we were also feeding, began to take the thrill out of this art for me. Certainly, it balanced the books for the years in which I had avoided this domestic occupation. There were times during the summer when we had twenty people for company, and I did the honors over the cookstove on these occasions. Twenty people and twelve dogs for supper a few times during the season, plus three meals a day and twelve portions of dog-supper to prepare all year round amounts to a lot of cooking. I will admit I got rather sick of it, and the less cooking I do nowadays, the better I like it.

"One of the other domestic chores which appealed to me even less was the washing. However, it had to be done, and as there were no laundry services (or Laundromats!) in the neighborhood at that time, I had to wash the hard way, with a galvanized tub and a washboard, and at first I didn't even have a wringer. Hauling and heating water and rubbing clothes on a washboard and then wringing them out by hand was a far cry from the beautiful porcelain toys women use to wash and dry with nowadays. I certainly hated to see the dirty clothes pile up, and I often thought of the linen press at the hospital, with piles of snowy, sterilized linen always on hand. What would the staff say if they could see me now, at my backwoods washtub?

"Of course, Bill helped me all he could, and when the clean clothes were finally hung on the line, I had a certain sense of accomplishment—something like swimming the English Channel or climbing the Matterhorn, I guess—until the time came when they had to be ironed. Flat irons, heated on the stove, rubbed on sandpaper and paraffin and held with a thick pad—they were my friends and my enemies. What is the irresistible affinity between a hot iron and the human epidermis, I wonder? Oh, I learned to be more careful as time went on, but even now, I have a definite allergy to any kind of an iron, even if it's an electric one that isn't connected!

"And while we're on the subject of fire, I remember a frightening incident that occurred one winter day as I was peaceably doing my laundry in the main room of the cabin, my arms deep in suds. I had smelled smoke a little while before, so I had inspected the stove and found everything in order. I decided there must be a wind that was blowing the chimney smoke back against the house and it was seeping in through the chinks. But as the smell persisted, I heard a crackling sound overhead. I looked up and saw, to my amazement, that the roof boards were on fire! There was no ceiling, of course, just the supporting beams and the rough boards that formed the roof of the house. The snow was kept pretty well cleared off the roof so that its weight would not cave it in, and—as Bill explained to me later—it seems the creosote from the chimney had set fire to the logs where they were dried out from the heat of the pipe. At that critical moment, Bill was nowhere in sight. After a moment of dumb panic, I climbed on a chair and began to throw pails of my soapy wash water up from the inside. That helped a little, but it didn't quite do the job, so I ran outside, grabbed the ladder we used to clear the snow from the roof, picked up a broom, not knowing exactly what I intended to do with it, and climbed up the icy rungs. The boards were blazing merrily, and I began to push snow on to the fire. That did the trick. The fire went out.

"When it was all over, except for mopping up the suds-soaked kitchen, Bill came strolling back over the drifts on his snowshoes with the dogs yapping after him and I said the usual wifely things to him about a man never being around when you need him, and then, to prove I am no less a woman than any of you, I had a good cry.

"We had to let the fire go out so Bill could clean out the chimney, and it was touch and go whether it was better to burn or freeze to death.

"That wasn't the only spat I had with Bill, although considering the 'solitary confinement' we went through, we got along pretty well as a general rule. Spring brought some uninvited guests to the camp, some lumberjack-sized rats that began helping themselves to our stores. Bill set traps around the house, and without telling me, he also set one in the kitchen cupboard. You guessed it. I was the first 'rat' to be caught in any of Bill's traps, and although my language, due to my upbringing, remained fairly orthodox, my opinions of the blundering and incompetence of the male sex in general (and Bill in particular), may have been colored by the pain in my bashed fingers.

"These diversions probably helped to relieve the monotony of backwoods life, but I doubt if anyone could have convinced me at the time that it was the best form of entertainment."

Toward the end of May the thaw really set in, and now another problem presented itself. The boat trip to Bruss' Landing was very pleasant, but when the Newcombs took off in their car, they found that the unpaved roads had turned from icy slush into rivers of slippery clay. Their first trip to replenish supplies found them marooned in a quagmire of mud. They always carried emergency equipment, but the process of getting the car out of the treacherous muck was a tedious and difficult one. Bill jacked up the wheels one by one and made a blocking of poles from trees he cut at the roadside. Then he filled the ruts with twigs, and after many attempts, they succeeded in moving on— until the next deep rut forced them to repeat the process. Needless to say, this discouraged frequent expeditions through the melting countryside.

Gradually the roads dried in the increasing warmth of the sun and they were able to get their car as far south as the Steffens' resort which was about a mile and a half by trail from their camp. They pitched over the rutted clay roads to call on their neighbors, thus enjoying their first social diversion in many months. Their elation was short-lived, however, for heavy rains flooded the roads once more, and they had to resign themselves to remaining at home until the weather made circulation possible again.

It was mid-June before the weather settled, and as spring brought back the birds and the chipmunks, and, of course, the mosquitoes, Kate's spirits soared. Bill's health had taken a good turn, and they began to enjoy the advantages of their lakeside camp. She recalls this period with relish:

"On the first warm, sunny day I took a swim in the icy waters of the lake and treated the fish to some copious soapsuds as well. It was wonderful to come out into the warm sun after a bath in the fresh rippling water. I guess it's the contrast that makes rustic life enjoyable. When the sun finally warms up, it seems more sunny than any other sun you've ever seen or felt.

"Spring is more springlike after a bitter winter, and summer is the nearest thing to heaven you can ever hope for on this earth. A row out on the lake to catch some fish for dinner becomes an idyllic experience and the tug of the line is a thrill that satisfies some deep basic instinct in human nature.

"One of our neighbors was a queer old bachelor who had come to the woods to die of tuberculosis, and had lived instead to a ripe old age. His name was Ted, and he was a funny old fellow, eager for companionship, but not accustomed to listening to others. He often came to fish with us on the lake, and kept up an incessant stream of chatter, more to himself than to us. I suspected that his monologues were just a continuation of his solitary talks to himself in the loneliness of his snowbound cabin during the winter. He told us he baked biscuits and hid them from himself so he wouldn't eat them up too fast!

"I have found that people who live in the wilderness and are isolated for long periods by the deep snows and heavy rains without the relief of human companionship, sometimes become eccentric in their ways. The northwoods people describe this condition as 'cabin wacky.' It is a very real and painful state of mental starvation which is recognized by physicians who practice in these parts. It sometimes produces physical symptoms, actual ailments, most of them imaginary to some degree. Modern medical parlance calls such symptoms 'psychosomatic.'

"Ted had taught himself to sew and knit and was very proud of the garments he fashioned. Shirts, pants, socks, and even sweaters that I am sure I have never duplicated, even though I did eventually learn to knit.

"Ted was profoundly religious, and deplored the fact that there was no church in the community. He predicted that the children in the district would grow up as heathen. Years later, when Ted had long since gone to his eternal rest, I remembered his anxiety and hoped he would know that churches had been built throughout the northwoods area.

"He played an important part in an incident which was nearly disastrous to our lakeside camp, and his faith produced a miracle which had no small effect on my own flagging belief in the protection of Providence."

Trial by Fire

IT was late in May of the following year and there had been no rain. The thaw had come early and had been dried away by the steady sun. The roads were ruts of dry clay, and the woods were in peril from that dread enemy which is the scourge of the timberlands— forest fire. Campers and fishermen were being constantly warned to take precautions with their campfires. Thus far there had been no trouble in the area, and it was hoped the rain would come to wet the forest and avert disaster.

Then, late one afternoon, a spark from an unscreened "peggy engine" started a fire. For three days the clear blue of the cloudless sky had been veiled with smoke. Crews of fire fighters were trying to keep the blaze under control, but it seemed to resist all their efforts to extinguish it, changing its direction with the variance of the wind, and advancing into the deep forest like a hungry dragon snorting orange flame and black smoke into the sky and roaring loudly as the dry woodland turned to a smoking ruin in its wake.

The Newcombs' camp appeared to be at a safe distance from the fire, and while the sound of the crackling flames could be heard and the smoke stung their eyes and nostrils, Kate and Bill knew that precautions were being taken to keep the fire from spreading and a drift of mare's tail clouds on the horizon brought hope that rain would soon put an end to the conflagration.

Bill got word that the flames were threatening the resort cabins of their west-shore neighbors, the Steffenses, and he hurried over the lake by boat to join the crew that was fighting to save their buildings. Kate remained at the camp and decided to calm her jittery nerves by doing a little quiet fishing for supper. As she was rowing ashore with a good catch of pike in her sack, she saw old Ted come running to the wharf, waving his arms and calling to her. She could not make out what he was saying until she reached the wharf and began mooring her boat. As he helped her up, he gasped, "The fire!" and pointed to the forest to the south of the camp. Kate saw a burst of flame emerge over the treetops and realized that the fire was now headed directly for their camp.

"The horror of the situation came at me so suddenly that I just stood there, clutching the sack of fish, unable to move or speak, while Ted gibbered and wrung his hands, telling me to hurry and get my belongings out of the house.

" 'But where?' I managed to croak. 'Where can we take them?'

" 'In the boat!' he said, with more sense than I could muster at the moment. I rushed to the house and Ted followed. I could hear the dogs howling and scratching at the door of their enclosure, frightened by the smell and sound of the approaching fire.

"I began gathering up everything I could lift, and putting things down again, not knowing what to take first. Ted seemed to have more presence of mind than I did, for he laid out blankets and began piling things into them, making a heap of our clothes on one, and of whatever came to hand on the other. I gathered up my good silver and put it in the blanket with pots, pans and cutlery, wailing over Bill's absence and wondering if the place would be burned to the ground before he would get back to help us.

"We do incomprehensible things in a moment of panic, and I remember trying to rescue some of the disreputable china I had long since been planning to discard.

"We carried a load to the boat and went back for another. As we reached the shore, Bill came back in the boat and I heaved a sigh of relief. His hair and his eyebrows and lashes were singed. His clothes had holes burned in them and he was as black as a stovepipe, but he had never looked so good to me as he did at that moment. He assured us that the fire could not possibly reach us for several hours, and that eased my panic a little, although the flames seemed to be roaring too uncomfortably close to count on any substantial period of grace.

"By this time, several other boats came chugging down the lake carrying a contingent of the National Guard, headed by Major Hines who owned the lumber camp, to help us fight the fire. They came ashore and helped us to pile the rest of our possessions into the boats. Bill got the dogs out of the shed and pushed them aboard one of the boats, where they whimpered and shook with fright.

"Into the clearing came dozens of terrified wood creatures, seeking refuge at the water's edge. Birds with scorched wings settled around our buildings; rabbits, chipmunks, grouse, pheasants, even fox and deer scrambled out of the thicket in panic-stricken confusion, with no regard for their age-old enmity, united in their flight from the common foe that had besieged their forest.

"There were still some things to be salvaged from the house, but the boats were full and we pushed off across the water, headed for the Steffens place, which was now out of the path of the fire.

"I had salvaged my phonograph records, although what use they would be without the phonograph, which we had left behind, I did not stop to consider.

"It was a pathetic regatta, loaded with chairs, lamps, mattresses, dogs, bundles—moving across the lake with the sound of roaring flames and the showering of cinders and sparks and billowing smoke all around us. Words cannot describe my emotion on that flight. The chances of saving the camp with the bucket brigade that was hurling pails of lake water on the buildings and the surrounding brush, seemed hopelessly slim. I was sure that only the water's edge could stop that hungry fire.

"We landed across the lake and unloaded our things, carrying them piecemeal to the Steffens place where we stored them in a woodshed Bill had just saved from the fire. Mrs. Steffens, who had been alone in the place while her husband was away getting provisions for their summer resort season, told me later how brave and resourceful Bill had been in fighting the fire. Some of the cabins showed scorched spots of fire that Bill had extinguished by standing on the neatly readied beds and throwing water up from the inside. Singlehanded, with only Mrs. Steffens's help, he had managed to save the place as well as the livestock, locking it up in one of the sheds to keep it from running out into the blazing field behind the buildings.

"Bill left me at the Steffenses' and went back to fight the fire which was now threatening our own place. The wind was the worst factor in our situation. I have heard the expression 'as changeable as the wind,' but that did not apply to the wind that was moving the flames steadily in the direction of our camp.

"Bill solved that problem by building a backfire against the blaze in the forest. All that night the men battled the flames, while Mrs. Steffens and I supplied coffee to the weary fighters who came over the lake for a few moments of respite and refreshment.

"By morning, the men had our camp pretty well safe-guarded and I went back to see how close it had come to destroying us. I found our camp surounded by charred and smoking stumps. It was sad to see our lovely background of trees turned into a charred ruin, but I knew it couldn't be helped. We could hear the ring of the axes as the fire fighters chopped down smoldering trees to prevent them from spreading sparks into other parts of the forest.

"All that day and all the following night, and for that entire week, from Monday until Saturday, Bill and I carried pails of water from the lake to put out burning stumps. They would smoulder down and seem to go out, but then they would blaze up again at the first puff of breeze. We snatched what sleep we could in the boathouse, and for a whole week we never once took off our clothes.

"Then, on Saturday evening, it began to rain. The sound of that rain, pouring down on the forest, sizzling into the flaming treetops and extinguishing the flames, was the sweetest music I have ever heard. We stood there, right out in the downpour, and listened to it as though we couldn't hear or feel it enough. Then we went into the house and washed away as much of the soot as we could. I put pads of healing emollient on Bill's scorched eyes. Then we dragged ourselves into the bare bunks and slept—and slept —and slept. I never hear rain on the roof without remembering that terrifying fire.

"The scenery was sadly wrecked, but our home was safe. The loss of timber was enormous. The carelessness of one lumberjack in neglecting to put a screen on the 'peggy engine,' which hauled a log train, had brought about all this devastation and had nearly cost us our home and all we possessed.

"When the rain let up, we got our belongings back into the house, but the smell of smoke lingered over everything and the tragedy was not easily forgotten. After thirty years, the scars of that fire still remain in that once beautiful woodland, although the log buildings have long since fallen into ruins."

In fact, the scars of such fires are visible in many places in the northwoods. In other sections, the reckless cutting of lumber has reduced acres of virgin forest to desolate graveyards of rotting stumps. The scars of fire and thoughtless greed will always remain to mark the invasion of man into the peaceful security of the wilderness.

"What about Ted? Was his cabin burned down?"

"No," answers Kate thoughtfully. "Ted's place wasn't touched although it was almost directly in the path of the fire. We went there to see, and the fire seemed to have gone around Ted's cabin. Bill figured that the wind must have shifted at that point. Ted declared firmly that his home had been protected by his faith in the Almighty. That seems as logical an explanation as any, for is there any other power that can change the direction of the wind?"

The Forest People

To celebrate the saving of their home, and to show their gratitude to those who had helped save it, the Newcombs gave a party, complete with square dancing to the tune of a squawky fiddle. They had plenty of baked ham and beans, potato salad, good Wisconsin cheese, with cake and coffee for dessert. All their neighbors came and brought their children, and several of Bill's Indian friends came from Crandon to congratulate them on their escape from the fire.

Kate was fast becoming a typical backwoods resident. She entered into the social life of the community with far more enthusiasm than she had shown for the polished elegance of Boston society. She found these rustic people much to her liking. Their friendship had warmth and a simple human directness that brought them close to her heart. Their problems had become her problems, and their courage in the face of the primitive hazards of the wilderness won her admiration and respect. They were always ready to lend each other a helping hand, and there was a genuine community spirit among them that would be hard to find in the more competitive circles of city life, where envy and self-interest were the driving force. This was the bedrock of human survival, and it brought out the strongest and best in human nature.

"We had two good Chippewa friends," Kate recalls. "One was Paul Maray, and the other was old Jimmy Hardhead. They were brothers, although they bore different names, which is frequently the case among Indians. Some of them were brought up in white families and took the names of the people who had been their foster parents. Paul and Jim were guides. They had taken a great shine to Bill, and what little he did not know about forest lore, his two Indian friends soon taught him. Old Hardhead was evidently a member of the Midewiwin lodge, which is the Chippewa society of medicine men. He knew every herb and bush and root in the forest, and their medicinal properties. I explored a new phase of pharmacopoeia through him, for when he learned I had been a 'medicine woman' among my own people, he shared some of his knowledge with me.

"His prescriptions may have been somewhat involved with superstition, but they were evidently based on an ancient herbal science, and I had proof that they were not just fantastic notions of tribal legend. Once, when I had a miserable headache which my own nostrums did not seem to relieve, Old Hardhead brewed me an herb tea which I took somewhat skeptically, more to avoid hurting his feelings than with any confidence in its effect. I was surprised to find that my headache soon disappeared. He was delighted with the success of his remedy, and he brought roots and herbs which he claimed would help Bill's blood condition, and which Bill insisted upon trying. He swore that the concoction, brewed under Old Hardhead's gimlet eye, made him feel much better. He took it whenever he was threatened with the sudden exhaustion which was one of the most persistent symptoms of his ailment. I accused him of letting his imagination run away with him, but I could not deny that the brew seemed to give him the pickup he needed. I know that one of the ingredients was wild sarsaparilla root, but I never could get the rest of the formula from Old Hardhead. He gave me some Indian names for the queer-looking fragments he steeped to make the concoction, but I would not be able to spell the words, much less identify them.

"Paul taught Bill the finer points of setting traps for the wily fox and wolf that menaced the peaceful existence of the wood creatures. Bill did not care for traps. He preferred the quick dispatch of his gun to the cruel and painful misery of trapping even the predators. The Chippewas are known as a 'timber people,' expert in the handling of skins, and Bill gained profitable knowledge in skinning and tanning hides from his Indian friends.

"They also taught him to build a birchbark canoe and showed him how to keep it watertight and limber. This canoe was later borrowed for an Indian exhibit. Unfortunately, on the way up the lake to be shipped, it was inexpertly grounded on some sharp rocks and ruined for further use. It takes real Indian skill to handle a birchbark canoe and keep it intact.

"I fast became an expert woodsman, and learned to follow a trail in the woods and to read weather from the clouds. I could never bring myself to handle a gun, however, although my father sent me an expensive .22 rifle for my use. I became a good fisherman, and learned to clean and filet the catch, and to put up ducks for the winter as well. Who would have believed that I, Kate Pelham, who had complained about going outside the city limits for a suburban party when I lived in Buffalo, could acquire woodland skills I'd never dreamed I could learn, much less like?

"Old Hardhead told me the story of the otter, and how it had brought the wisdom of healing to his people when they were helpless against the evil spirits of disease. One day he brought a birchbark chart which depicted symbolically the legend of Gitshi Manito and the otter. Gitshi Manito is their name for the Great Spirit, and it is their belief that it was through the otter that the Midewiwin, or 'Grand Medicine Society,' was developed. Old Hardhead's grandfather had been a member of high degree. I asked him if he were also a medicine man of high degree, but he smiled and said, 'I am Christian,' which was neither affirmation or denial. I let it go at that, knowing that these reticent people preferred not to be questioned too closely about their beliefs. Many of them had accepted the Christian faith, but their tribal traditions were too old and too strongly rooted to be completely abandoned. As I came to know them better, I discovered that they still honored many of the beliefs of their forefathers."

After the "fire-party," Bill and Kate talked over the project of building a home of their own. The blighting of their woodland impelled them to make a change, and Bill had been looking around for a suitable site. Kate's only requirements were that it should be on the shore of one of the many lakes that dotted the region, and easily accessible to a center where they could replenish supplies.

The Mel Kenagas had returned from Indiana, and Mel and Bill did plenty of building that summer. Between jobs they guided fishing parties and they were sometimes gone for days at a time in their quest for the best fishing waters. On one of these trips, Mel had run across a

141

piece of property which he thought might suit the New-combs as a site for their new home. It was some fifty miles northwest of Crandon in an area known as Boulder Junction. One of its main attractions, according to Mel, was that it seemed to be entirely free of mosquitoes. It was on a creek above Island Lake, which was fed by the waters of the Manitowish River. Bill had gone to look at the property and agreed with Mel that it was an ideal spot.

It had some drawbacks, however, being accessible only by water. There was an old "tote road" leading to an abandoned railroad bed that went through the property, but that ancient logging trail was too overgrown to be usable without clearing.

Kate hesitated. She wanted, above all, to avoid being isolated in an inaccessible spot, but she agreed to go with Bill to inspect the land and they set out in their car over the rough roads toward Boulder Junction. The trip, though it is an easy one in these days of paved roads and connecting highways, was then an overnight excursion, as they sometimes had to cut their way through the narrow forest roads that led from the dirt highway into the thick woodlands.

They stopped at a resort overnight and continued their journey in the morning. At the La Fave resort on Island Lake, they took an outboard motorboat from the landing and skirted the lake, entering the narrow neck of Rice Creek and heading northeast until they came to an elliptical island in mid-channel. The property was directly opposite the island on the east shore of the creek, and the island was included in the acreage. The property consisted of four "forties," which meant four parcels of forty acres each, a sizable tract, and, without question, it was a beautiful location.

At the northern outlet of the creek, an abandoned railroad trestle spanned the flowage as it entered Big Lake, the next link in the chain of lakes that led back into the Manitowish River.

A slight knoll rising from the creek shore presented a perfect site for a house, and a high rise of land beyond the cove promised shelter from the north winds. The surrounding forest, though it was second growth, was already heavy enough to form a rich background of fir, poplar, birch and scrub oak, with leaves beginning to turn red and gold from early frost.

Kate agreed that it was the loveliest spot they had seen thus far, and Bill sighed with relief as he confessed that he had already made a down payment on the property, since some resort people had been dickering for the site and he had been afraid of losing it. With Kate's approval, he could now complete the purchase.

They returned to the La Fave resort, where they remained for a week on the wooded island which gave the place its name. The La Faves were a hospitable couple. He was the son of Abe La Fave, a fabulous giant of French Canadian descent who had pioneered in the area, and his wife, Sye, was a pretty Norwegian girl whose charm and fine cooking had helped make the resort one of the most popular in the Boulder Junction district. They were delighted at the prospect of having congenial neighbors and the two couples formed a solid friendship that has endured through the years.

The Newcombs resumed their homeward journey, again stopping at the resort where they had stayed on their way up, and here they met a vacationer who also became one of their closest friends. His name was John Roosink, and he was a Milwaukee attorney who spent his summer holidays in the lake country. They met on the resort verandah and exchanged greetings in the free and easy manner of the northwoods. The topic of conversation was, prosaically enough, the plague of mosquitoes which had all but ruined the season and was threatening to continue well into the fall. From this beginning they launched into a discussion of comparative climates, and Kate mentioned the fact that one of the things she missed about the Eastern seaboard was the shellfish, especially the good Eastern lobster that was so plentiful in the waters of northern New England, and which had been one of the main attractions of the gay "shore dinners" during her Buffalo years.

They exchanged names and addresses and expressed the hope that they would meet again. Kate thought nothing more of the chance encounter and it was with considerable surprise that, a couple of weeks later, she received a bulky package by railroad express from Milwaukee, and found that it contained several handsome boiled lobsters, carefully packed with dry ice, and containing a card from John Roosink. Kate was overwhelmed by the thoughtfulness of their new acquaintance. She wrote him a cordial note, expressing her thanks as well as her amazement, and assuring him that the lobsters had won him a lifelong friend. As it turned out, this was no "blarney," for all that Kate's maternal great grandfather, it may be noted here, had been for many years the custodian of Blarney Castle.

Every summer thereafter, and during the holidays, John Roosink visited his friends the Newcombs, and throughout the years he has played an important part in the life of the Newcomb family. Casting his lobsters upon the woodland waters has brought John Roosink many joys of family and community life which he values so highly that to miss one of his bi-yearly trips to Woodruff and

Boulder Junction would be unthinkable. As for the New-combs, their family circle would seem incomplete without the regular visits of "Uncle John."

This cosmopolitan gentleman, with all the suavity and sophistication of his high standing in the legal profession of Milwaukee, finds the simple life of the Newcombs and their neighbors rich in enjoyment and relaxation. He cheerfully "bunks" wherever they happen to have room for him, whether in the Woodruff "rumpus room" or in the roughhewn "boathouse" cabin at Rice Creek, where he peels off his city cares and goes fishing with an enthusiasm equalled only by that of the traditional small boy with a worm on a bent pin.

When there are problems to be solved which require a practiced legal eye Dr. Kate summons her staunch friend, John Roosink, to advise her and rests assured that everything will be as it should be, right down to the last punctuation mark.

For some time, Kate's family had been urging her to take a trip home and early that winter she decided to go East for the Christmas holidays. Bill agreed that the change would be good for her. He had never felt better, and since the Kenegas were remaining in Wisconsin that winter, he would be well taken care of and Kate could leave without being concerned about him.

So she left by train from the Woodruff station, with Bill and Mel and Leona waving good-by from the snowy platform.

On the long trip through cities and plains and factory areas Kate thought of the poetic Rice Creek property and imagined the home that they would build there, their very own home at last.

The low bay climate of Boston seemed penetratingly

chill compared with the crisp winter of the northwoods. The holidays proved exciting and merry with her family around her, all eager to hear about the wilderness, but hoping they could persuade her to return to "civilization." She announced with smiling finality that there was no chance of it. She and Bill were going to build a permanent home in the northwoods.

The family received the news with stunned amazement. Did she mean that she actually *liked* the place? Of course she did. She loved it. Hadn't she told them so in her letters? They agreed she had, but they had thought she was only putting a brave face on an unbearable existence. Kate grinned and assured them they had been quite mistaken. She was "sold" on the northwoods and nothing could ever "unsell" her. They shook their heads and looked at each other in baffled incomprehension. How could anyone prefer that primitive life to the comfort and excitement of Boston?

"Ring Out the Old"

KATE and Bill settled into the Stone Lake camp with happy tranquility, looking forward to spring and talking over plans for their new home. Kate dreamed of having some of the comforts they had lacked so far, and, of course, one of her most cherished dreams was inside plumbing. But that luxury was still a long way off.

They spent many evening hours with their heads together over the sketches Bill and Mel had drawn, the lamplight shining on their absorbed faces as they traced each wall and window and door, sharing such happiness as only they can know who have created a home from its first rough outline to a finished reality. There was still a long road ahead, to be sure. Building a house on an isolated lake shore in the wilderness is not accomplished by waving a magic wand.

The "pulp" had been ordered and was being gradually accumulated at Keith's siding where spruce, cedar and balsam logs were being carefully matched for the Newcomb house. Cement, gravel and other materials had to be ordered and shipped. It took the entire summer to make preparations. The actual construction would begin the following spring. They planned to pitch a tent on the shore of their site and live Indian fashion while the house was being built. Kate looked forward to the experience, though Bill was not sure she could take the roughness of camp life and suggested that she might stay at the La Fave resort if it got too rugged for her. But Kate scoffed:

"Nothing is too rugged for me any more!" she assured him. Bill chuckled and wagged his head. The metamorphosis was complete. He was even prouder of the woman Kate had become than of the doctor she had once been. His forest had put her to the test and found her stalwart. Watching her at work over the stove, her glasses steamed from the bubbling pots, he would sometimes say, "I wish the Detroit crowd could see you now, Kate!"

"Wouldn't they just about *faint?*" Kate would reply with an answering twinkle. Yes, she wished some of her old hospital cronies could see how things were with her. It would be fun to see their faces as she mixed them a batch of corn bread, or went out to split some extra kindling to hot up the stove.

"How Dr. G—— would squirm if he could see my unmanicured fingernails!" she thought to herself. Dr. G——, elegant and urbane, polished to his finger tips, fussy about his tailor. She conjured him up in her mind's eye, wearing imported tweeds and a London ulster, his faultless Borsalino at that just-right angle—standing in the middle of that rough camp kitchen-living room with his eyes popping as Kate rubbed a soapy union suit on the washboard in her galvanized tub!

The letters from Detroit continued to plead for her return. "For pity's sake, Kate, when are you coming out of the wilderness? Dr. Levy will take you back with him any time you get ready to come home. How awful for you to be doing all those terrible chores!"

Kate, it must be confessed, had delighted in writing and telling them how she sawed and chopped wood and shoveled snow. She would finish a letter: "Well, I'd better close now. My bread is ready for the oven and I still have the ironing to do." Or else: "I hear Bill coming with the dogs and I suppose he's shot another of those pesky timber wolves, and we'll have to get busy skinning it." She knew perfectly well that Bill would do the skinning in the shed, but she took a mischievous delight in treating her city friends to the best possible goose flesh, and giving them something to bemoan and begroan about. She could hear them discussing her sad fate over their coffee cups in the hospital commissary:

"Poor Kate. Who ever dreamed she'd wind up as a backwoods drudge? That marriage—a terrible mistake, my dear—ruined her life—wrecked a brilliant career."

Kate poured molasses into her bean pot and tasted the mixture with her finger. Hmm-mmm! Now, plenty of lean salt pork. Bill never could get enough of it. Boston had better look to its laurels. Her baked beans were leaving even the Boston Cook Book recipe behind. Lots to be done. Tomorrow would be Christmas Eve. Last year she had missed the northwoods Christmas festivities. They were having company this year. They had invited their neighbors for the traditional Christmas Eve ceremony.

They came on foot and on snowshoes through the snowy trails and over the frozen lake, the Kenagas, the Steffenses, the Paquettes, with their rosy-cheeked children. The supper was at five. Just before seven a Christmas poem was read. Then Kate lighted the Christmas candle, made from the candles of past years. The youngest member of each family was then given a candle in a candlestick, and they marched in and lit their candles from the votive flame. They placed their candlesticks on the window sills to light the way of the Christ child and everyone sang "Silent Night." Kate knew that in many parts of the country, at this exact moment, other friends would be performing the same ritual, and it gave her a feeling of oneness with the other celebrants.

For the next half hour they sang Christmas carols, and then the songs became light and festive. Cake and coffee was served and the guests sat around chatting for a time and then said their good nights, returning to their homes early to prepare for the next day's celebration.

It was a good Christmas this year, Kate reflected as she tidied up after her guests. Bill was a healthy man again. As for herself, she had never felt so well, so strong and tireless. She realized now that in her city years, she had been only half alive. Body and soul, the forest had made her a complete woman.

New Year's Eve was spent at the Kenagas' with a lively group of neighbors. Kate thought of their first New Year's Eve—the long, lugubrious train ride, the arrival at daybreak at Eagle River, the long haul by sleigh through snow and wind, the gray haggardness of Bill's face on the pillow in their first cabin. And then the second New Year's Eve, with their hearts still aching from the loss of their little one. Bill's relapse. Her own wintry despair.

All that was far behind. The worst was over. Soon they would begin building their home. This year she could really say, "Happy New Year!" and mean it.

As midnight struck, Bill caught her eye across the room and she read in his look far more than either of them could or needed to express. Their fight was won. Another year was beginning.

"Happy New Year!" The cottage rang with the joyful din of improvised cymbals as frying pans and pot lids scuttled the old year on its way. Mel blew a hunting horn, and a gun was fired into the snowy sky to signal the turn of the year. Other shots answered from the distance as faraway neighbors responded to the New Year signal.

The crowd sang "Auld Lang Syne," and then the fiddle summoned them to the first square dance of the year. The couples paired off and this time Kate was not a wall flower. Here was no waltz or fox-trot on the waxed floor of a country club. This was rustic revelry, and Kate needed no prodding to learn its merry figures. Flushed and laughing, she "sashayed" and "promenaded" with the rest, her eyes shining into Bill's as they found each other in the pattern.

Outside, the wind whistled and the snow swirled through the woods, lacing the big trees with ghostly white. Another storm. Best to be starting home before the going got too difficult. Good night and Happy New Year!

Kate and Bill tramped the mile and a half homeward through the stinging snow, their lantern throwing a dancing, snow-speckled light against the trees.

Safe in their log house, they piled wood into the stove and heated bricks to take the chill from their bed. The thermometer had dropped to thirty below, but what did that matter? They had weathered another year and they were still together.

The shining ornaments on the Christmas tree reflected the lamplight and the red isinglass window of the wood stove. The bright Christmas fruit, red, blue, green, gold and silver, danced as the howling wolf-wind shook the cabin walls, but the two people who sipped their cups of steaming milk beside the stove listened without alarm.

And now to bed. The lamp goes out. The clock ticks in the first hours of a new year. Victory is not always a pageant with flying banners. Sometimes it is a warm, quiet room in the heart of a storm-swept winter wilderness.

Kate Pelham, aged four. This picture was taken in Leoti, Kansas, and is one of the few pictures of young Kate Pelham that survived the fire which later destroyed her northwoods home.

Dr. Kate as she appears today. She still calls on patients day and night, despite the bad weather and icy roads.

On impassable roads, the Snowmobile was often the only answer.
Here is a picture of Dr. Kate, taken at the wheel of an early
model. The year was 1927.

When Snowmobiles weren't available, Dr. Kate resorted to
more primitive methods of travel over snow. Here is a picture in
which she demonstrates her ability on snowshoes.

(Andrew Pavelin, Chicago Tribune)

William Newcomb and friends (the tiny spot to his right is a kitten) taken in front of the Newcomb home.

Bill Newcomb displays an old flintlock, one of several which he has collected.

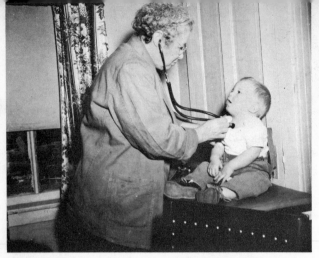

(Vic's)

Dr. Kate listens to the chest of a very important
patient. She has delivered hundreds of babies in
her years as a country doctor.

The roll-top desk, the leather chair, the photographs and the
medical books are all familiar to those who know backwoods
doctors. What doesn't show in this photograph is a quality of
heart without which they are meaningless.

The Community Church of Boulder Junction which occupies such a prominent part in Dr. Kate's story.

The Million Penny Parade in Woodruff, Wisconsin.

Indians, in their colorful costumes, celebrated, too.

Dr. Kate in the parade car on *Dr. Kate Day*.

A display of the mail response to Dr. Kate's appearance on Ralph Edwards' *This is Your Life* television program.

The Lakeland Memorial Hospital, for which Dr. Kate worked so long, begins to take shape.

The finished hospital.

A Christmas saying that the Newcombs use as a motto in their backwoods life.

Dr. Kate:
a recent portrait.

(Vic's)

A Home on Rice Creek

IT was May of 1926. The snow had been washed away by heavy rain. The charred forest around the camp dripped desolately, its bare black skeletons bereft of spring's eternal promise. The birds returned with querulous cries as they found their old nesting places still barren of leaves. Kate threw them scraps and crumbs. The sun, uncertain at first, obscured by blustering showers, at last poured down its steady warmth upon the steaming woodland. Life began anew.

The dogs, who had been whining impatiently in their shed, yelped with joy as Bill released them to pursue the spring scents of the forest.

Bill walked through the burned area and found a trail that had been untouched by the fire. He drew deep breaths of the woodland air, pungent with greening herbs, wet leaf mold and steaming balsam. The hounds tore around in a frenzy of ecstatic sniffing, their noses quivering over the earth as though held there by magnets. The young dogs, stumbling around on their thick paws, nipped and tumbled each other in their exuberance, their long ears flapping and their silky hides hanging loosely over their awkward bones.

This was living. A man could die in a city and return to life in the woods. Bill had proved it. He was not a psalm-singing Christian, and sometimes called himself an agnostic, but he walked through the spring trees as one might walk through a cathedral, for he knew the Power which had given him back his life dwelt there. He did not call it God. Gods had been many in man's time. He had touched the hand of the Life-giver, and he believed, not superficially with his mind, but with his being. Man-made death had reached for him and he had known where to run for his life. This, too, was a form of faith.

Overhead was the sun. Around him, the green things unfolding, and beneath him the stirring earth. In his veins, new blood, in his heart, conscious acknowledgment. If this was not prayer, then it would do until a better word could be found for it. The forest needed no words. It spoke in the rustle of leaves, the ripple of water, the flash of a bird's wing. Through the thicket he saw a doe leap across the winding trail and stand immobile behind a screen of white birch trunks. He whistled to the pack and they froze at his heels, whimpering. The doe turned her head and fixed her brown velvet eyes on him. Her moist nose shimmered in the filtered light.

"Come, follow me," she said, and when she saw he did not follow but stood there as if enchanted, she turned the white flag of her tail to him and vanished through the thicket. He knew she was trying to decoy him away from the hiding place where she had hidden her fawn.

Everything in the woods had significance for Bill. He was at one with the regenerating rhythm of the natural world. It was good to be alive in the forest he loved. It was good to be dreaming of the home he would build for himself and Kate.

A Home on Rice Creek

The time soon came for Bill and Kate to say good-by to their Stone Lake friends. They gave a farewell party and gaiety was mixed with the sadness of parting. Their loyal friends, the Kenagas, were moving north with them. They had taken a house in the Boulder Junction area to be on hand for the building.

Most of their heavier possessions were loaded on flat cars to be shipped by rail, then carried by truck to the site. Their personal possessions were piled into boats and they headed up the lake to Bruss' Landing where they packed everything into their car and squeezed in, Kenagas and Newcombs together, for the long trek northward. The journey over the rough roads in the crowded car, bouncing over the ruts, was a weary one. They had started early in the morning and it was almost nightfall when they arrived at the Kenagas' new place where they could rest overnight. Bill had already made the trip with the dogs, and they were safely penned in an enclosure that had been built for them, being fed by the men who were at work on the property.

The travelers had a simple meal and lay down, adults and children alike, wherever they could find a place to lay their heads amid the confusion of bundles, luggage and kitchen ware.

The next morning Kate, Bill and Mel started for Rice Creek, leaving Leona to put her house in order and look after the children. They made the trip over the "tote road," crawling cautiously over the rough, winding forest trail and stopping to cut away overhanging growth. It took two hours to cover the twelve miles from Boulder to their new land.

The end of the "tote road" met the ties of the roadbed about a hundred yards from the spot where the logs were being peeled, and as they saw the shining pile of logs gleam in the sun and La Fave's welcoming voice greeted them from the well-diggings, Bill and Kate gave a cheer and the car bumped to a stop. They got out, and with a thrill of exultation felt the soil of their own property under their feet. This time they were really "home."

The dogs were yelping and leaping in the enclosure and Bill turned them loose for a romp. They licked his face and tore around in paroxysms of joy at having their family together again, then loped off to explore the woods and leave their scent on the trees. It was a beautiful day for dogs and men alike.

Their tent was waiting to be unpacked and Bill set about driving stakes and poles and erecting the canvas walls of Kate's summer residence. He then made a hearth of stones and cut down a birch to provide backlogs for the fire that would be Kate's outdoor cookstove.

Mel was already on the knoll, measuring and calculating the exact position of the structure. There were trees to be felled and stumps to be blown out, and the surface to be leveled. Bill joined him in consultation while Kate cooked her first meal on the campfire. Their supplies had been unloaded and stored in the tent, and she drove the inquisitive dogs back to their enclosure with a pan of mash to keep them from overrunning her "kitchen."

Canned pork and beans and coffee and warmed rolls was the menu of her first lunch for themselves and the crew, with doughnuts for dessert. The relief of having no mosquitoes to torment them was proof that they had chosen their homesite well. The running waters of the creek were not a suitable breeding place for the pests that had often made their Stone Lake summers miserable.

When the day ended, Kate lighted a kerosene lamp

in the tent and they readied themselves for a night of rest, for they would have to be up at daybreak to make the most of every daylight hour. John La Fave had returned to his home by boat, taking the log-peeler with him. Mel had driven Bill's car back to Boulder to rejoin Leona and his family.

The army cots that served as beds in the sloping tent might have been luxurious feather-beds, so deep was the sleep of the two pioneers in their forest refuge.

As the summer sped by, the house gradually took shape on the knoll. The first building they would occupy would be used later as a laundry and storeroom, when the rest of their plans were carried out, for they intended to have a good-sized home before they were through building. It might take several years to complete, but it would be just as they wanted it when it was eventually finished.

The Newcombs were by no means isolated at their Rice Creek camp. Visitors came from Boulder Junction to get acquainted with the new residents, and Kate and Bill made many friends that summer. In June, John La Fave and his wife, who made frequent trips up the creek from Island Lake, planted a rosebush at the spot that would be the "front yard" of the Newcomb house, and it is there to this day. Kate and Bill visited back and forth with the La Faves and met the Larry Doolittles and the Sam Williamses. Sam was the owner of the general store at Boulder Junction, as well as the postmaster and operator of the telephone exchange, all of which were housed in one small, clapboard building. Sam's store was the community's meeting place in those days, and many a hot argument on politics and hunting volleyed around the pot-bellied stove in true "cracker barrel" tradition.

The Newcomb skies were serene until August. Then Bill received word from Grand Rapids, Michigan, where his family was living at the time, that his mother was seriously ill and longed to see him. The diagnosis was cancer. Kate, knowing Bill's deep attachment to his mother, urged him to go to her. She assured him she could hold the fort while he was gone, and Mel could certainly carry on the work with one man to help him, as the building was well on its way to completion and the heaviest work was over. She drove Bill to Boulder Junction where he got a ride on a logging train to the main line at Woodruff, and thence to Michigan via Chicago.

Bill was gone eight weeks, remaining with his mother until death released her from her suffering. After the funeral, he returned to find the Rice Creek house ready for occupancy. Mel Kenaga had done as fine a job as only his master hand could have achieved.

It was then early October, and the surrounding woods were vivid with autumn colors, but Bill was blind to their beauty. The death of his mother, especially under such agonizing circumstances, had cut deep into his heart. Kate could only comfort him with her silent understanding.

They struck camp, stripped the protecting tarpaulins from their piled-up furniture that had stood in the clearing behind the tent, and moved into their one-room home. It was a fair-sized room, sixteen by twenty, and Bill partitioned it off to form a sleeping area at one end. He made clothes closets, and shelves wherever Kate needed them. With the stove crackling merrily, curtains at the windows, their tables and benches and phonograph in place, a couple of rocking chairs for comfort, and Kate's good silver and china in the antique cupboard she had ordered from Detroit, the big, rosy cedar room looked inviting and livable and the Newcombs felt at peace with the world.

But their tranquillity was not to remain undisturbed. They received news from Crandon that fall that the bank where they had their house-building nest egg had suddenly closed its doors. Its cashier had absconded with all the bank's cash, and the authorities were searching for him.

The blow staggered them, but Kate refused to let it daunt her spirits. She still had paying investments at a Boston bank that would keep them going, and she would write her father to lend them a hand until they could readjust to the loss. In the meantime, perhaps the culprit would be apprehended and the money recovered.

Bill agreed that they could weather the storm, but what of the other depositors, the little people around Crandon who had worked hard all summer to be secure for the winter, only to have their small savings snatched away? Bill raged as the police hunted in vain. The light-fingered cashier was never caught, although his alleged body was purported to have been identified some years afterward.

That year Bill went out for deer. Legend has it that no family in the vicinity of Crandon who was in need of food lacked venison that winter—nor did they have to buy it.

Bill's hunt for predators had been unusually good that year. He more than made up the bank loss from bounty and sale of skins, and the following spring he was selected by the Boulder Junction community to represent the area at the Outdoor Show in Chicago.

Kate accompanied him, for she had had news of illness in her own family. Grandmother Pelham was seriously ill in Leoti, Kansas, where she had gone to visit a daughter. Kate's father had asked her to go to her grandmother's bedside.

Grandmother Pelham improved and Kate returned to Rice Creek to find that Bill had added a kitchen and a root cellar to the house as a surprise for her. She was delighted with the improvements and laughingly announced that she also had a surprise for him.

She was going to have another child.

"Tommy Duck"

BILL immediately began making further additions to the house. With an increase in the family on the way, a real bedroom had become a "must," and a screened-in verandah was added to the kitchen. Bill's exhilaration at the joyful news made him buoyant with energy and enthusiasm. He would have liked to install a bathroom for Kate, but the cost was prohibitive under their crippled budget. He did manage to pipe water to a sink in the kitchen and install a pump to eliminate the necessity of hauling water from the well.

As autumn painted the woods again, Kate felt the vigorous stirring of her child, and she assured Bill it would be a boy. He watched over her anxiously, urging her to rest and taking over most of her household chores as her burden grew heavier.

She was plagued throughout her pregnancy by a persistent nausea which would not respond to any treatment, and toward the end of October she noticed that her ankles were swollen and the puffiness of her face warned her that she had better look to her blood pressure.

They had made arrangements for her to go to Green

Bay for her confinement. Kate knew doctors at St. Mary's Hospital in that city, and they decided it would be best for her to make the long trip immediately as the first snow had already blanketed the countryside and there was no telling how heavy the next fall would be. Bill still had work to do on the house and there were the dogs to be fed, so Kate asked one of her friends to accompany her to Green Bay. Mrs. Kenneth Warburton, the wife of one of Boulder Junction's best guides—he was known as a "wizard on snowshoes"—gladly agreed to make the trip with Kate, and Bill drove them to the Woodruff station through a lowering landscape.

They arrived in Green Bay just in time to avoid one of the worst blizzards of the season. Kate went to see Dr. Kelly, who was on the staff of St. Mary's, and he advised her to remain in Green Bay until the date of her confinement, which would be late in January, so he could treat her for the excessive albumen and high blood pressure which was causing her nausea. After seeing Kate comfortably settled at a pleasant boardinghouse close to the hospital, Mrs. Warburton returned to Boulder, and Kate relaxed for the long wait until the arrival of her child. This time she was making absolutely sure.

Green Bay, a historic Wisconsin city with a population of some fifty thousand, is an industrial center for paper mills. It seemed like a metropolis compared with the rustic remoteness of Rice Creek. When the weather permitted, Kate took long walks, borrowed stacks of books from the library, and for the first week she luxuriated in her unaccustomed idleness. But the life of ease soon began to pall on her. She missed her home, and when Bill telephoned her, which he did twice a week, he had to use all his persuasion to convince her that she must remain in Green Bay until January. As Kate tells it:

"I'd been entirely weaned away from city living. I missed my backwoods home much more than I had expected. By that time we had a very cozy house and I had a washing machine, a hand-pumped one, of course, because we had no electricity as yet, but it *was* a washing machine nevertheless, and a great improvement over the old washboard method. Housework had ceased to be a drudgery to me, for I had learned to do things easily and efficiently, with plenty of leisure time left over. In fact, it irked me to see how much time was wasted by the help in that house. Why did people putter around instead of getting things done? I fretted.

"As you can see, I was a different woman than the one who had left Detroit the winter of 1921. I had reverted to the primitively feminine, and my sole object in life was to provide a home for my husband and raise a family. Gadgets and conveniences no longer meant anything to me. I think I rather enjoyed picturing myself as a pioneer wife battling the hardships of the wilderness. I felt out of place in the lap of luxury, with nothing to do all day but read and knit and wait for January.

"I made friends with some of my fellow boarders and they took a lively interest in the preparations for my 'blessed event,' bringing me little gifts and helping me to prepare the bassinette, quite a fancy affair for a backwoods baby, all fussy with ruffles and peach-colored quilting. Yes, it was a lot of fun.

"Bill came to Green Bay for Thanksgiving, and we had our turkey dinner at the boardinghouse table. As Christmas neared, I bought gifts and wrapped them and sent them to my friends and family, and a flood of cards and boxes began to arrive marked 'Not to be opened until Christmas.' My room began to look like an express office. Every mail brought another batch of cards and packages from Detroit and Boston and from my good friends in the northwoods.

"Bill arrived on Christmas Eve to spend the holiday with me. The house was decorated with pine boughs and holly, and having a mother-to-be on the premises gave the holiday a touch of realism. Everybody was so good to me and many of the gifts around the tree were earmarked for 'Baby Newcomb.' "

Faithful to her pledge, Kate introduced the Christmas Eve ritual to her new friends and in later years she heard from some of them that they had perpetuated the ceremony, and that it was being carried on at Green Bay and in other parts of the country as a result of its introduction into that friendly boardinghouse in 1927.

Bill returned to Boulder after Christmas, and Kate spent a quiet New Year's Eve, feeling terribly homesick, though Bill's midnight call cheered her up a little and she welcomed the New Year with gratitude for the blessing that was now only a few weeks away.

The final weeks dragged slowly by. How much longer? Had she figured wrong? It was nearing the end of January.

In the late afternoon of Sunday, January twenty-ninth, Kate began to feel the first uneasiness that warned her the zero hour was near. Her reservations were made at St. Mary's and a graduate nurse had been booked for her delivery. By six o'clock she realized she was in labor, and she made rapid tracks for the nearby hospital. Bill arrived just as she was leaving, and her landlady took them to the hospital in her car.

"I just barely made it," she recalls, chuckling. "Tommy was nearly born in the elevator! Everything went like clockwork, with one exception. My son rolled off the table while he was being given his first bath. Fortunately, no damage was done as he was caught in transit, but it made me realize, from a different viewpoint, how much responsibility rests on those who officiate in a hospital delivery room.

"William Thomas Newcomb, named after his father and his grandfather, weighed seven and one half pounds and looked exactly like a northwoods papoose! He had a lot of black hair, shoe-button eyes, and his face was as round, dark and red as a winter apple. As a matter of fact, when our friend Chief Dacoteau came to Rice Creek that summer to see the Newcombs' pride and joy, his smiling comment was, 'Him papoose for sure!' "

After six long years, Kate Newcomb was to know the overwhelming happiness of holding her child in her arms, and the terrible emptiness was filled, this time, please God, for good. The tiny life tugging at her breast fulfilled her so completely that her past seemed no more than a prologue to this supreme moment. The joy she had helped to bring safely to other women was now her own. What a thrilling reward it was for the heavy months and the few spasms of labor!

As Bill, wearing the sterile hospital gown they had put on him, held his son in his arms, his eyes met Kate's—and they remembered. They had come this way before. But the pang lasted only an instant. This time they could rejoice, and their heads bent over their new love, marveling at each detail of his minute perfection.

Kate's one thought was to return to Rice Creek, but the weather was still too severe for the trip with a newborn child. She resigned herself to remaining in Green Bay until the storms abated. Bill returned to Boulder to keep the nest warm until the day when he could bring his family home.

Kate's return to the boardinghouse with Baby Newcomb was a gala occasion.

"My room was turned into a reception hall. People came and went all day to see Tommy in his bassinette, or getting his bath, or sleeping with his little red fists curled up under his chin. You can't imagine what a new baby does to a group of lonely strangers in a boardinghouse. Everybody looked dewy-eyed, and when my son proceeded to have the colic every evening from six to nine, you never saw such running around with hot-water bottles and flannel bellybands and anxious-to-help expressions! One would have thought he was a crown prince, surrounded by a doting court. I guess both of us were pretty spoiled by the time we left that house. I'll never forget the kindness of those dear people."

It was the sixteenth of March before the weather relented enough to permit Kate's return to Rice Creek. The weather was still cold, but the worst of the storms were over, and Bill came to Green Bay to gather up his family and take them home.

Their train arrived at Woodruff at five A.M. on March seventeenth, St. Patrick's Day. They drove the twenty-five miles to Boulder Junction in their car, with Tommy bundled in his basket as snug as an Easter chick, and their hearts warm enough to keep out the twenty-below-zero cold.

Arriving in Boulder, they found that the forest road was still not navigable by car. A snowmobile was available and, leaving their car at the local garage, they started off in the clumsy "snow chariot" equipped with tractor belts at the back and sleigh runners in front. As they crawled slowly over the snow toward Rice Creek, a warm "chinook" wind came up and the temperature rose to sixty degrees. The snow turned to slush and the runners veered into a ditch and refused to budge. They were still two miles from home, and there was nothing for them to do but take to "shanks' mare," with Bill carrying the baby on his shoulder in the basket, and Kate carrying her bag and the baby's paraphernalia.

"We looked like a real pioneer family, wading through the slush, but we got home safe, and I was never so glad to see a place in my life! How marvelous my home looked to me. It was all I wanted in the wide world. Outhouse and all, that forest cottage was the most beautiful place I'd ever seen. It was *home*."

As the weeks passed, spring turned the forest green and Kate's heart felt as light as the treetops that swayed against the sun-drenched sky. The bassinette, standing beside the window, where the sunlight streamed in on Tommy's chubby, kicking legs, was the center of their lives. Bill dubbed him "Kickapoo," for his fat legs were never still during his waking hours.

June came, and vacationers began to dot the creek with their bright-colored shirts and dresses and kerchiefs, as though tropical flowers had bloomed under the warming sun. Tommy's wide brown eyes gazed at everything in delight. The skimming boats, the birds, the dogs, all the wonderful details of a brand-new world unfolded before him and filled him with excitement. He had a playpen to play in, and a "kiddy-koop" to sleep in, gifts from his grandfather, the latter a novelty in those parts.

When he was ten months old, he began walking around his playpen without holding on to the sides. One day, as Bill and Kate were having lunch at the kitchen window overlooking the creek, they heard Tommy's voice beside them.

"Here, Daddy," he said, and they saw him standing there holding the bolt from his playpen in his hand and offering it to his father.

From then on it was a merry chase to keep tabs on him. Now Kate saw her "mighty hunter" walk along the forest paths with the "small hunter" by the hand. Bill was sure Tommy would become a woodsman worthy of his father, for, he had literally cut his teeth on a Colt revolver! Although his doting grandfather had sent him a silver teething ring, Bill's son and heir had scorned that elegant device. He had taken a fancy to a .22 Colt which Bill had let him examine one day, and found it a fine substitute for the teething ring from Cartier's. Bill was delighted to find that his son displayed the rugged tastes of a woodsman.

After the first "Here, Daddy," Tommy's vocabulary increased rapidly. He repeated everything he heard, and that sometimes included some pithy lumberjack words carelessly employed in his presence when he went visiting in Daddy's car, for Bill took his new son to all points of the compass for everyone to see.

Bill had built a boathouse and a guest cottage that spring and they had many visitors, for the Newcomb baby was a marvel to behold. Some of his friends from the boardinghouse at Green Bay made the trip to Rice Creek especially to see him, and he won hearts across the map from Boulder to Boston. John Roosink came to see him on his yearly vacation, and Kate's sister Gladys came from the east with her bridegroom, braving the northwoods cold to see Kate's baby, and bringing news that a second son had blessed their father's third marriage.

An alarming incident at the close of Gladys's visit kept Kate in a turmoil of anxiety for two days and nights and brought about the installation of a telephone at Rice Creek. The visitors, who had been occupying the boathouse, suddenly decided to return east. A heavy blizzard was sweeping over the forest and Kate and Bill tried to persuade them to wait until it subsided, but they were determined to head back to Boston. Bill warmed up the car and started for Woodruff to put their departing guests on the train. The car foundered in the snowdrifts and Bill had to go for help. He finally got his passengers to the station but would not risk returning until the roads had been partially cleared. There was no way of communicating with Kate, and she waited, alone with the baby, a dozen hounds to be fed, the fires to keep up, and her heart torn with the fear of what might have happened to Bill and her relatives.

Bill finally returned to find her almost hysterical, and they decided then and there that they must have telephone communication for such emergencies. Bill made arrangements with some of his neighbors to install poles and party lines to the Sam Williams exchange the minute the weather permitted. It would be costly, but well worth the price in convenience and peace of mind.

On Christmas Eve, Kate had the joy of holding her own child's hand around the Christmas light which was placed in the window to guide the footsteps of the Christ child.

Early 1929 brought a soaring stock market and all seemed well with the world. They had their telephone and the cost did not matter. Kate's investments at the Boston bank, together with Bill's guiding and hunting income, kept their bank balance well padded, and the future looked bright for the Newcombs and their neighbors.

During his second summer, Tommy was very much taken with some neighbor girls who had several pet ducks. It was hard to say which he admired most, the girls or the ducks, and he soon began to call his little friends: "Mary Duck, Violet Duck," and so on through the entire family. They, in turn, began calling him "Tommy Duck" and from then on to this day he has been known in Boulder Junction and its environs as "Tommy Duck."

Kate continued to get letters from Detroit urging her to return to civilization and to medicine. Dr. Levy wrote to congratulate her on the baby, but still deplored the fact that she was "wasting her life in the wilderness."

"Well," smiles Kate as she tells it, "I figured that if having Tommy and Bill and being happy was wasting my life, it suited me just fine!"

Many changes took place in the lives of Bill and Kate Newcomb during Tommy's early years, but there was only wonder and delight in Tommy's forest world. He grew and thrived on the shores of the beautiful creek, learning to swim as naturally as his nickname implied. He was pestered in his aquatic enjoyment by the solicitude of the dogs, who plunged in to "rescue" him by the seat of his swimming trunks whenever they thought he was becoming too reckless for his own safety. He howled and raged at them in vain. Whenever he swam too far out into the swift waters, one of the hounds would inevitably leap in and bring him ashore.

He was a fisherman at three, with a suitably sized rod

provided by his delighted father who perceived in his budding young sprout an incipient Izaak Walton.

"Tommy Duck" was barely five when he caught his first "musky," that wily "tiger" of the northwoods waters. For some time, Tommy, who had been fishing for small fry from the dock, had been incensed over the hijacking of his catch by a large "musky" that seemed to be taunting him from the shallows. He made numerous efforts to lure the big fish to his hook, but the old reprobate continued to flip his fins derisively and bask in the sun-dappled eddies of the creek under Tommy's freckled and exasperated nose.

One day the irate youngster caught a particularly fat and tempting frog and baited his hook with it on the long chance that his elusive enemy might find it too succulent to resist. And that was exactly what happened. Suddenly, the line went taut and Tommy, tugging with all of his five-year-old might, managed to drag the big fish to the bank where he stood watching it flap, unable to believe his eyes as it struggled to get free of the hook and head back to the safety of the creek. With a leap, the youngster got astride the lashing monster, yelling for help as he attempted to stun it with the tip of his rod instead of the handle as he had been taught. Bill and Kate ran out to see what was causing the ruckus and when Bill saw his son astride the enormous fish which, by then, was heading toward the creek with Tommy aboard, he grabbed a pole and hastened to stun the fish. There stood Tommy, his eyes ablaze with excitement, beside one of the biggest "muskies" of the season, weighing twenty-two pounds and caught with a child's rod!

Needless to say, Tommy's catch was a sensation, and

it added much to the fabulous reputation of Bill Newcomb's son as a sportsman of parts. That he is a woodsman cut on the pattern of his robust father, there is not the slightest doubt. That he could hold his own in the thick of the winter forest with a well-oiled gun and on the lake waters with a rod and reel, as well as in the schoolyard with his fists, is attested to by those who have known him from the time he first began to streak through the woods and swamps of Boulder Junction on his own power.

Descriptions of "Tommy Duck" in his early years range from "chain lightning" to "jet propulsion," and his comeliness is evident from the snapshots in his mother's album. Of his liveliness, Chief Dacoteau said, "Him not born. Him spawned by muskies in lake waters."

Dr. Torpy

THE crash years of 1929 and 1930 brought disaster to the resort trade in northern Wisconsin, even as they exploded the dream bubble of Wall Street profits and rocked the foundations of the nation's industry. The recreation areas were all but deserted during those gaunt years, and while the empty northwoods larders were somewhat relieved by fish and game, the "rainy day" had come with a vengeance, and the savings of the provident were soon exhausted to provide food and warmth against the icy inroads of winter.

Government relief and public work projects began to take the place of summer earnings, for the meager trickle of vacationers made it hardly worth while to open the resorts during these years.

One W.P.A. project undertook the paving and grading of roads. By dint of gradual effort, Kate and Bill had managed to clear the roadbed of rotting ties and cut away the brush, turning the old logging line into a sometimes navigable dirt trail which led to the equally precarious dirt highway. The black topping of the highway and the grading of the Newcomb road provided some relief work for crews of local men and brought better accessibility to the Rice Creek house.

Kate was receiving assurances from the Boston bank that her investments were being cautiously handled to avoid serious loss, although the dividends that had formed part of the family income had to be used to bolster tottering stocks. Bill jumped into the breach with his gun and snowshoes, reaping the reliable harvest of pelts that never failed to provide an income, and his luck held, for the decline in "pleasure" hunters had left plenty of game for the predators and they multiplied to Bill's advantage.

The crash had been a severe blow to Kate's father, and when she received news of his failing health, she made a trip East with Tommy to visit him and bring him the consolation of seeing the grandson of Kate Callahan, his first lost love. Tommy resembled his grandmother in coloring and personality, and the baby's visit brought a gleam of cheer to Tom Pelham's troubled heart.

When she returned, Kate found that anxiety and the squeeze of economic pressure was producing more than the average quota of illness among her forest friends. She did her best to help those who needed competent nursing. Medical attendance was provided by two hardy doctors who had offices in Minocqua, the island town adjacent to Woodruff. These two men, Dr. Thomas Torpy and Dr. Gale Huber, served the vast lakeland area, covering hundreds of square miles in all kinds of weather, and generally without bothering to collect fees.

Kate knew of Dr. Torpy, having heard tales of his fabulous personality, but it was not until the summer of 1931, when Tommy was three and a half years old, that she met the man who was to catapult her back into the profession she thought she had abandoned forever.

Dr. Thomas G. Torpy, whose nickname, for no explainable reason, was "Papa Zers," had been a familiar figure in the rugged Wisconsin wilderness since 1895. When Kate met him in 1931, he had been practising in the northwoods for thirty-six years. In a newspaper article published in the *Lakeland Times* in 1949, when Dr. Torpy was eighty-one years old, we find a succinct description of this extraordinary man which is well worth quoting:

> . . . . Over the fifty-four years he has practised medicine in the area around Minocqua, Dr. Thomas G. Torpy has acquired a legion of friends and a volume of anecdotes. His patients—lumberjacks, homesteaders, millionaire resorters—all get the same treatments from eighty-one year old 'Doc' Torpy, and none of them get bills. When people drop around to pay for their treatment, Doc Torpy paws through dog-eared medical books, pretending they are ledgers, while he makes up an amount he thinks the patient can pay. The doctor's fees have become legend. . . .

Photographs of Dr. Torpy reveal him as a small, spare man, wiry and tough as a lumberjack. He is reputed to have been as proficient in lumberjack profanity as any callus-handed son of the log-mills. He had a temper as quick as a buzz saw, but no patient ever complained of neglect, for the dynamic little doctor made his rounds faithfully, by rig or cutter or on horseback or snowshoes, regardless of weather. The saga of Dr. Torpy's northwoods practice would be worthy of a volume in its own right, and it is hoped that someday that volume will be written.

"Lumberjacks, homesteaders, millionaire resorters,"

and one might add, poverty-stricken Indians—he tended them all with the same rough and ready alacrity, concealing a nature as sweet as maple syrup under a growling gruffness that fooled no one but himself. He was one of the most loved men in that northwoods outpost for over half a century, and while he was still alive, a park was named after him in the heart of Minocqua, an honor which he thoroughly enjoyed and made jokes about to his dying day, laughingly calling it his "cemetery."

This was the man who called Kate back to her profession, and this is how it happened:

Small Tommy had had a frightening mishap, getting his baby fingers slammed in the door of the family car in an experimental moment when his parents weren't watching. The frantic Kate gave him first aid and rushed him to Dr. Torpy's office in Minocqua.

When Dr. Torpy saw the professional touch of the bandage, his sharp brown eyes looked up at Kate through his glasses and he asked, "Who put on this bandage?"

"I did," said Kate.

"Are you a nurse?" inquired the doctor.

"No," she replied. "I used to be a physician."

"Used to be?" Torpy exclaimed. "What happened? Did you kill 'em too fast?"

Kate flushed. "No. I just gave up practicing," she said her anxious eyes on the child's bruised and swollen fingers.

The blunt-spoken Torpy gave her a searching look.

"You gave up—why?" he asked.

"My husband got sick and we came up here for his health."

Tom Torpy grunted and bent over the injured hand.

"Where did you practice?" was his next question.

"In Detroit. I was associated with Dr. David Levy," replied Kate. Again, Torpy looked up at her. Dr. Levy's name was significant in the medical profession.

"Pediatrics, eh?" he remarked briefly.

"I'm a specialist in o.b." Kate replied.

"What about your husband? Did he get well?"

"Yes. He's fine now. But he needs this climate."

"Why don't you get back into practice again?" asked the doctor. His tone was irritable, and Kate was equally irritated. Why was he quizzing her? She didn't want to talk about her medical career. It was over and done with.

"I'm through with medicine," she said firmly.

"Humph! Why?" growled Dr. Torpy.

"The doctors couldn't do anything for my husband. We came to the woods and he got well. I like it here, and I wouldn't go back to the city for anything. There are more important things than money and success. I've found that out."

"D—— right there are!" snapped Dr. Torpy. "But why should you be sour on medicine? You sound bitter."

"I am," said Kate. "I lost my first baby through some modern medical monkeyshines. Believe me, I'm through with all that."

"If you're through with medicine, why are you here?"

The doctor's brown eyes fairly crackled as they shot up to search her face. Kate noticed the gentleness of his long, sensitive fingers as he palpated the bruised little hand. Tommy wailed and Kate held him closer.

"Any bones broken?" she asked anxiously.

"Nope. He'll be okay." Torpy applied a salve and wound a bandage around Tommy's hand.

"Hmph!" he snorted. "An expert doctor, holed up in the backwoods doing housework. It's a waste of talent." And he swore.

"That's the way I want it," Kate replied stubbornly.

"You took an oath, didn't you?" nagged the doctor.

"Yes, but I'm not a doctor any more. I have a family to look after," Kate bristled.

"You don't do that so good, either!" said the doctor drily.

He finished winding the bandage, fixed an impressive sling and patted Tommy's tear-stained cheek. "You'll be all right, bucko! Just hold that hand still, hey? And next time, keep your fingers away from those car doors, understand?"

Tommy nodded and sniffled and Kate wiped his nose and brushed back his hair. His brown eyes looked importantly solemn as he held his hand in its bandage sling against his chubby stomach.

Kate opened her purse, but the doctor waved the gesture away.

"No charge," he said. "Professional courtesy. So you're through with medicine, eh?" He shook his head. "Too bad—too bad."

Kate thanked him and took her leave, strangely impressed by the brusque, keen-eyed man who had taken her so bitterly to task. He reminded her of the men who had poured their knowledge into her thirsting ears when she was a student. Like them, he had no glamour, but he had something she recognized—dedication. The teachings of Dr. Louise Hurrell, which she had buried away in her determination to be done with medicine, began to haunt her. Nostalgic sparks of her early enthusiasm flared up briefly. Had she lost something after all? Had the high purpose which had fired her to fight for a medical career been completely quenched? Yes, she told herself doggedly. Living for Bill and Tommy was enough. A woman has a right to her own life. Home, husband, child. What more should be expected of her? The Hippocratic oath? Service to humanity? They weren't meant for her. These were her thoughts as she drove home to Boulder Junction, with Tommy asleep against her side.

The little boy's hand healed quickly, and Kate avoided another visit to Dr. Torpy's office. Why expose herself to any more assaults on her conscience? Winter was coming, and there was much to be done before the deep snows shut them in. Stores to be replenished, warm clothing to be made ready, blankets to be taken out and aired.

Tommy grew and chattered, a constant source of entertainment to his parents and their friends. Community life was knit closer by the difficulties of the depression era. Neighbors met at the town hall for suppers and card games of Five Hundred. Kate joined a group of women who began to consider the need for better school facilities and some sort of church services. Dr. Torpy's reproaches faded from Kate's mind.

Then one night late in 1931, during a heavy blizzard, the Newcomb telephone rang. Kate answered it and heard Dr. Torpy's husky voice at the other end of the wire. He was calling her for help. His tone was desperate. Eight miles north of the Newcomb place, a woman was dangerously ill with pneumonia. He was thirty miles away and the roads were impassable. The snowplows would not clear the drifts until morning. He asked Mrs. Newcomb to take the case and told her how to reach the house.

Kate protested. She had not practiced medicine for

ten years. Besides, she didn't have a Wisconsin license. Dr. Torpy's language became unprintable.

"License be damned!" he wound up. "No trained physician has any right to play housewife at a time like this. That woman will die if you don't get to her! Dig out your blankety-blank medical bag and get over there! And by the way," he concluded, "don't put that bag away when you get back. From now on you're taking all the calls in your end of the country, understand?"

Kate mumbled a flabbergasted, "Well—all right—if you—think——" But the irate Dr. Torpy had disconnected.

Bill agreed that this was no time to dilly-dally. A human life was at stake. He drove her as close as he could to the snowbound cabin Torpy had described. From there they hiked two miles on snowshoes over the deep-packed drifts.

The cabin was icy cold. There were three small children huddled near a stove that contained only a few ashy embers. Bill built up the fire and warmed some food for the little ones while Kate attended to her patient. The man of the family, it seemed, was seeking work many miles away at the paper mills. The woman was burning with fever and gasping for breath.

Kate had kept her medical bag up to date for whatever emergencies might arise in her own family, but these were the days before antibiotics and she had to treat the pneumonia patient as best she could with what was on hand. In her own words:

"It was a case of bronchial pneumonia, so I started a vaporizer, consisting of a tomato can and some haywire to fasten it to the wall, and a kerosene lamp under it to keep it boiling. Then I put hot packs of mustard and flour on the chest, made a pneumonia jacket for her, gave her some expectorant cough mixture—in those days it really tasted terrible—and administered a stimulant.

"I went back and took care of her until she was well, and that meant looking after the children too, until we got a neighbor to come in and take that problem over.

"It gave me quite a shock to realize how little help there was for the sick in that area. I guess I responded to the need like a retired fire horse when it hears the alarm.

"When the storm abated, I drove down to Dr. Torpy's office in Minocqua and said to him, 'Doc, I guess you'll have to take over the calls up my way——' He began to go up in the air like a bundle of firecrackers, but I managed to finish my sentence '——until I get back from Madison. I'm going to take out my license.' He came down from the ceiling and pumped my hand and the look on his face was pure gratitude. Later, when I was swamped with practice, I wondered how the two Minocqua doctors had managed to cover those hundreds and hundreds of miles of northwoods territory for so many years.

"My respect and affection for the peppery little 'Papa Zers' increased as the stories of his skill and self-sacrifice came to my ears. We became fast friends and, for eighteen years, professional collaborators."

Tom Torpy was as roughhewn as the "round stuff" that rolled through the lumber camps where he had begun his practice in the days when loggers were a breed of men in a class by themselves. At that time Minocqua and Woodruff and the surrounding towns were hardly more than trading posts to provision the loggers, and "skid roads" where they indulged their lusty tastes in relaxation at the taverns and "pleasure houses" that catered to their demands. The rough nature of these original inhabitants was ingrained in the personality of the timberlands doctor.

Although the community had long since become largely a resort center, with little left of the logging element after the forests had been "skinned," Tom Torpy in his speech and manner still carried on the profane tradition of his early associations.

Many stories are told of his encounters with the "summer people" whom he privately scorned as interlopers, though he was often called to attend them. One hot midsummer day he was summoned by a summer resident who needed a physician. He arrived in shirt sleeves carrying his battered old medical bag. The patient, living in one of the luxurious homes on the shore of a lake, met him at the door and asked in supercilious surprise, "Are *you* the *doctor?*"

"Yes," snapped old Tom Torpy with his usual display of spleen, "and a d—— good one, too!"

The lady lifted her eyebrows another notch and inquired, "Do you always call on your patients in your shirt sleeves?"

This was too much for the irascible Torpy. He turned on his heel and returned to his car, taking off in a cloud of dust and fury.

Another of Dr. Torpy's summer encounters almost had tragic consequences. He was called in to examine the young son of a summer family, who had taken sick suddenly. Torpy examined the twelve-year-old boy and advised that he be taken to the nearest hospital for an immediate appendectomy. The parents, mistrustful of the backwoods doctor's diagnosis, decided to send to Milwaukee for their own physician. By the time the city doctor arrived, the boy's appendix had burst, and for several weeks it was nip and tuck whether the youngster would

Dr. Torpy

pull through the peritonitis which resulted from the delay in removing the infected appendix.

Dr. Torpy, keeping posted on the case, paced his office raging like a madman. Ignoring the offense to his professional pride, he cursed the stupidity and snobbishness of the boy's parents. It was not until the lad pulled through by a whisker that old Tom settled down to some lively cursing on his own account. His feelings were somewhat appeased by a call at his office from the city doctor before that worthy left for Milwaukee. The boy's parents realized the affront they had given the brusque but competent lumber-camp physician and had sent their family doctor to offer their apologies.

"By blankety et cetera!" exploded Torpy. "I hope you sock 'em with a so-and-so of a bill. Those (profanity) stiff necks need to learn the hard way!" But he was proud of having been right in the first place.

Kate worked closely with the two local doctors. Dr. Torpy respected her ability and never failed to call her in for a discussion on any medical problem that needed a fresh viewpoint, and she never hesitated to disagree when she felt it was warranted.

"We had plenty of hot arguments," says Dr. Kate of these consultations. "Dr. Torpy's 'mule-skinner' language sometimes blistered my eardrums. But we always managed to arrive at a meeting of the minds, for our only concern was the welfare of our patients."

This close collaboration among the three doctors was an advantage to their patients, who had the benefit of their combined knowledge.

Dr. Huber's thirty-five years of service to the north-woods districts is also worthy of an accolade. Although

183

this humorous doctor makes little of the hardships, there are stories of his long rides by rig or sleigh, drawn over the rough roads by the faithful family horse, Barbara, an extraordinarily "educated" mare who, when her master fell asleep at the reins, would stop dead at a railroad crossing until he awoke. Another of Barbara's talents was to make her own way home to be stabled when Dr. Huber found it necessary to remain with a case overnight. The next morning, hitched to the rig or cutter by Dr. Huber's father, she would return to the exact spot where she had left her master the night before.

There are other hardy wilderness doctors who have tales to tell. They often traveled by handcar or "pede" on the logging rails. One icy night the rails became so slippery that the "pede" could not be pumped any farther. The doctor and its driver had to get out and push the heavy conveyance most of the way from Lake Tomahawk to Rhinelander to get it out of the path of oncoming log-carriers, a distance of approximately fifteen miles.

The early wilderness was obviously no place for any but the sturdiest of men—and women—medical or otherwise.

Angel on Snowshoes

AS Kate puts it, "Before the ink was dry on my license, my telephone began to ring at all hours of the day and night."

Her practice soon became so widespread that she was forced to set up a circuit of offices in the town halls and schoolhouses of the various communities around Boulder Junction, with her main office at the Rice Creek house. Patients flocked to consult her at Manitowish Waters, Winchester, Winegar and Spider Lake. This meant driving about a hundred miles a day, to say nothing of the many miles she covered on snowshoes to make house calls on back roads that were inaccessible by car. It became customary to tie a piece of red rag to an overhanging branch or a fence post to indicate that the doctor was needed at some backwoods cabin. Kate knew, when she saw these "flags" along the main road, just who was signaling for help, for she was familiar with every cottage and shack and cabin that lay behind the thick growth of woodland and knew how to reach it on her trusty snowshoes. She always carried them, together with a shovel and the equipment necessary to extricate her car from roadside mishaps when the going was rough.

"Bill always went with me in bad weather," she says. "And sometimes, when we couldn't get anyone to stay with Tommy, we would bundle him up and take him along."

One day, when she was making an emergency call by snowplow, which had been sent to make sure she arrived through the heavy snow, the plow struck a ridge of ice two miles from her destination, veered off the road and into a ditch. Bill and Tommy were along on that ride, and the patient was Larry Doolittle's daughter-in-law, and they were close friends of the Newcombs. The young woman was having a hemorrhage after a sudden miscarriage and Kate knew her arrival was a matter of life and death. She strapped on her snowshoes and leaving the baby with Bill and the driver, she set out to cover the remaining miles on foot. At the Doolittle turn, some twenty yards away, she turned to wave before plodding into the thicket of snow-draped trees. Bill was helping the driver extricate the plow and she caught her breath as she saw the heavy vehicle, with four-year-old Tommy sitting alone in its cab, suddenly begin to slip down the embankment that sloped sharply to the river. Kate stood there petrified, too frightened to scream a warning. The crawling snowplow lurched down a few feet, tilted—and stopped. Kate's heart eased down from her throat as Bill jumped into the cab and lifted the little boy out. Tommy protested vehemently at the interruption of his solo ride, and Kate continued her trek over the two miles to the Doolittles' as fast as her short, sturdy legs and the clumsy snowshoes could carry her.

When she arrived, both her legs were frozen, but she attended her patient before she stopped to do anything about her own distress. Only those who have suffered the agony of frostbite can realize what that pain can be. Larry Doolittle telephoned to Boulder for help in extricating the snowplow, but it was morning before the Newcombs could return to their home. Bill snowshoed to the house with Tommy in his arms while the emergency crew worked on the plow. Tommy slept peacefully through the return journey and looked around in amazement when he woke up in his own crib.

Shortly after she began her northwoods practice, Kate came close to losing her life on a call she answered alone while Bill was on a hunting trip. Her car skidded on an undercoating of ice and nosed into a snowbank. When she tried to back it out, the wheels spun helplessly, then inched back slightly and spun again. The muffler was obstructed by snow and fumes from the engine began seeping into the closed car. Kate felt a faintness coming over her. She opened the door and staggered out, stumbling unconscious into a snowbank.

When the doctor did not turn up at the house where she was expected, the family called the exchange in an effort to learn whether she was on her way. She usually left word with Sam Williams as to her whereabouts, and he knew she had set out for High Lake in answer to the call. Sam left his wife in charge of the store and the exchange and headed out to search for the intrepid little doctor. He found her, half buried in the snow beside her stalled car, where she was in danger of freezing to death had he not come to her rescue in time. Sam aroused her, half led, half carried her to his car and took her home. She recovered quickly and the only thing that worried her was her delay in getting to her patient and the urgency of getting her car back so she could go about her business. But it was the next day before she was able to complete the call.

In 1932, the Boston bank which had been trying desperately to extricate its customers from the chaos of the crash, gave up the struggle and closed its doors. Kate's father had also suffered serious losses, and though he managed to save enough out of the wreckage to provide for his immediate family, Kate could not place an added burden upon him by asking for his help. Her practice, while it was extensive both as to number of patients and area of activity, was hardly lucrative. In these difficult years, with unemployment, illness and actual want stalking the land, Kate Newcomb's devotion to the sick and destitute made the difference between life and death to many of her northwoods neighbors. By the unfailing reliability with which she attended her distressed patients and also saw to it they received needed relief from the welfare authorities, she won the affectionate sobriquet of "Angel on Snowshoes," and she well deserved it.

Kate never gave a thought to collecting fees. Her grateful patients sometimes tried to compensate her for her services with whatever they could donate in the way of provisions or supplies. One day she was followed home by three farm trucks, one containing cordwood; another— sides of beef, mutton and pork; and another—garden vegetables. A local paper printed a ditty on the subject which fittingly immortalizes the selfless service of the wilderness doctor in the eloquent simplicity of rustic doggerel:

There's scarcely a family in these back woods
Has any amount of worldly goods,

But Doc, she treats 'em all the same
Keeps a-comin' till they're up again,
And gets her pay, when not in cash,
In green cordwood and garden trash.

This testimonial has become a part of northwoods history.

Dr. Kate's growing practice made it impossible for her to run her home, take care of Tommy and attend to her patients. "Sylvester" became a member of the Newcomb household to keep a controlling hand on the ebullient Tommy and help Bill with the numerous chores and errands entailed in running the house.

Bill and Mel Kenaga had built a summer cottage on the shore of the creek where Kate had kept house in a tent the summer they began building. Bill rented the cottage and the boathouse to occasional parties of summer people. He also worked as a guide and hired out boats to fishermen, and thus managed to keep up his end of the budget during the lean times.

Kate's shingle hung over the entrance to the veranda which had been converted into her Rice Creek office. "Kate Newcomb, M.D." in gold letters on rustic brown wood with jagged ends was the sign under which a stream of patients sought Kate's healing help during her morning office hours. She engaged an efficient young nurse to help her with her office practice. Alyce Blazing became an important member of the Newcomb household, for she lived in the house and proved as capable in lending a hand with Tommy and handling the endless detail of running the house as she was at assisting Kate in her office.

Another important figure in the lives of the Newcombs was young Norman McMahon, whom Bill engaged to help him with his summer work. He proved so able in keeping a firm rein on the dynamic Tommy that he became a permanent adjutant in the Newcomb menage. A romance blossomed between Norman and Alyce and their subsequent marriage was one of the high lights of Kate's early medical years.

The greatest handicap in Kate's practice was the remoteness of hospitals. The nearest was the Sacred Heart Hospital, a Catholic institution run by the Sisters of the Sorrowful Mother, at Tomahawk, fifty-five miles from Boulder Junction. St. Mary's at Rhinelander, under the auspices of the same order, was even more remote. In the winter, Kate tended most of her confinement cases in their homes, though she preferred hospitalization for maximum security. When the delivery gave signs of being abnormal or difficult, Kate would drive her o.b. patient to the hospital at Tomahawk. When the roads were still uncertain, she was in constant dread of some mishap which might endanger the patient. Her consistent record of never losing a mother was often placed in jeopardy by the difficulties of transportation. In a number of instances, when she found that the roads were too hazardous, she stopped along the way and took a confinement case to the nearest house, whether it was an humble cabin or a luxury resort or residence, rather than risk continuing the slow and perilous trip to the hospital. She is proud to say that she managed to avoid ever having a delivery in her car, which, dramatic and news-worthy as such contingencies might be, would be unsafe for her patient. The lives of both mother and child were a sacred trust to Kate, and she never hesitated to ask for help when she needed it to safeguard them. She always received cheerful co-operation in such emergencies, and it became something of a distinction to have given Dr. Newcomb refuge on these occasions. The thrill of having an unexpected birth under one's roof brought a fillip of excitement and pride to those who provided the hospitality for the delivery of one of "Dr. Kate's babies."

As an example of the heavy mileage required for Kate's rounds, Bill cites a day when he drove 376 miles, taking Kate to three hospitals—at Tomahawk, Rhinelander and Ironwood—stopping for seventeen calls in between, and winding up a period of thirty-six hours with seven deliveries! Thirty-six hours meant nonstop attendance at bedsides and in delivery rooms, without sleep. Bill waited for her in the car, in the foyers of hospitals, or at some wayside café, keeping awake on coffee.

As an auxiliary measure, Dr. Kate taught some of her older patients to help her by learning to give "shots" when necessary, to read a thermometer correctly, to describe symptoms accurately so that the doctor could diagnose the case sufficiently to recommend emergency treatment by phone. In obstetrics, Dr. Kate earned the confidence of her following to such an extent that young women who marry and go elsewhere to live, return to Dr. Kate to have their babies because, they say, "Dr. Kate makes you feel as though you're the most important person in the world."

Kate's activities in the Boulder Junction community were not restricted to her medical practice alone. She was determined to bring every possible advantage to the people who were her friends, her patients and her neighbors. She wanted a better schoolhouse for the children. She wanted unpolluted water. She wanted purer, fresher and richer milk, and, above all, she wanted a church to assure a good spiritual foundation for the growing youngsters of Boulder Junction, including her own Tommy.

Some of these things she was able to accomplish, with the help of her fellow Boulderites, soon after she was appointed health officer of the district. She assumed this post almost simultaneously upon her return to medicine.

Of all her projects, the church took longest to achieve. It was one of the closest things to her heart and she fought for its accomplishment with the tenacity and faith that moves mountains.

A Place to Pray . . .

THERE were practical reasons behind Kate's desire for a church at Boulder Junction. The prohibition years had brought a corrupting element into the northwoods area. While the occasional loggers were no longer the reprehensible roughnecks they had been in the days of the "big timber," some of them were still a godless and carousing lot, and not the best example for the impressionable youngsters of respectable families.

The glorification of big-time racketeers and gangsters had begun to be the subject of many movies and radio programs, and there was a twinge of fear in the hearts of good parents that, without proper teaching, their children, in their formative years, might find such characters morbidly attractive.

The school problem was satisfactorily on the way to improvement, and in this regard Bill Newcomb deserves a few lines of recognition. He had gained considerable prestige in Boulder through his astute handling of the school situation. There were three schools in the area, all of them sparsely attended and with poor sanitary and heating facilities. For four years Bill and several of his friends on the school board planned the consolidation of the three schools into one unit so that there would be sufficient attendance at one school to warrant the improvements that were badly needed. The move had to be made cautiously, for it is always the tendency of conservative country people to resist any change, even though it may be a beneficial one. So the board planted the seed and finally succeeded in accomplishing the consolidation, thus obtaining funds from the state to build an addition to the Boulder Junction schoolhouse.

The remodeled structure was planned with inside plumbing, another classroom and an adequate heating unit. Bill, having brought the school improvement question to a happy conclusion, now thought it should be carried out by abler hands than his. When the school board asked him to become its director and supervise the actual building, Bill protested that he knew nothing about public buildings and declined the honor. But the board elected him its director "in absentia" and he could do nothing but accept.

It was through Bill's canny checking that the building was finally constructed in strict accordance with the architect's specifications. His services proved so satisfactory that when he finally declined, six years later, to continue as director of school affairs, the board unanimously elected him to the post of school clerk.

Bill groaned. This, if anything, increased his responsibility, for it put him in charge of all appropriations and applications for the administration of the school and the supervision of the hot-lunch program which had been instituted. In addition to this, when Tommy was of school age Bill undertook the job of driving the school bus in order to keep an eye on his rambunctious son's safe conduct to and from the seat of learning, for Tommy began his schooling with a broken arm. He had taken off from the roof of the garage without regard for the pull of gravity and wound up with his left arm in a cast.

Now the women of Boulder Junction began to press for a religious center for the spiritual and moral fortification of their families. Kate was one of the original group of women who began the movement for church services at Boulder Junction. There had been a Sunday School in the area some time before, but it had been abandoned for lack of attendance, and the good women of Boulder felt it was time to revive a religious influence in the community.

A prayer meeting was called at the still unremodeled schoolhouse in 1931, with one of the local citizens conducting the service in the absence of a minister. About sixty-five people attended this service and a Sunday School Class was initiated under "Papa" (F. H.) Best, who had conducted the service. About twenty-five children were registered.

At this meeting a Ladies' Aid Committee was formed to raise funds and hire a minister for regular services. This group, presided over by Mrs. Minnie Doolittle, Larry's wife, consisted of Kate Newcomb, Bertha Ashton, Jennie Blaisdell, Helen Espeseth, and Florence Haag. Their names are too important in Boulder Junction history to be obscured in anonymity. By arranging weekly luncheons at their respective homes, with food contributed by the members and served at a small charge to the guests, they accumulated the necessary funds to engage the Reverend Lake of Minocqua to conduct services at the town hall, having found the schoolhouse too small to accommodate the attendance.

For several years services were held in the basement

of the town hall. It was a damp and poorly heated meeting place which sometimes reeked of the beer that had flowed freely there the previous evening, with empty beer kegs still in evidence as the worshipers gathered on Sunday morning.

Mrs. Doolittle, energetic leader of the Ladies' Aid Committee, deplored the use of this unsuitable underground hall as a place of worship. She formulated a campaign to arouse interest in the building of a proper church for Boulder Junction and her dream received enthusiastic support from Kate and the other members of the Ladies' Aid Committee.

But these were the lean years, and although the women exerted themselves to the utmost to raise funds for a church building, their endeavors were slow to bear fruit.

Money was scarcer in the northwoods than ever before. There was barely enough to feed the children, much less to buy land and materials for a church building. There is a bitter story connected with the poverty of these northwoods people. Many of them had bought land cleared by the lumber companies, under the persuasion of unscrupulous promoters, who assured them that it was fertile two-crop farming country, lying fallow until enterprising farmers should cultivate it. When the buyers came to begin their two-crop farms, they found that the "fertile farming country" would not produce even one crop because of the brevity of the growing season. Some of the swindled innocents had left the unproductive land and gone to seek better pastures, but many of these disillusioned farm folk had remained to eke out an existence as best they could in the forest, finding occasional work at the sawmills or summer resorts.

It was small wonder then that, during the depression,

the ladies of Boulder Junction found it difficult to raise a fund for their church project. So, for some years, the congregation continued to hold services and Sunday School in the town-hall basement.

One of the brighter interludes of this discouraging period began with the arrival of a towering, rosy-faced Texan minister and his wife in a house-trailer. The Reverend Sloan was engaged in Christian missionary work under the patronage of a group of businessmen, and his assignment was to travel through the country establishing new Sunday Schools and bolstering up those that needed encouragement. His time was usually limited to three weeks in each community, but he took such a fancy to the Boulder Junction area that he remained in the district for ten months, replacing Reverend Lake.

During that time he served as minister at the town hall services and his warm leadership gave the struggling congregation a new surge of Christian spirit. Their hopes of building a church were revived by his enthusiasm, but still the building fund remained static. When he left, his enthusiastic presence was sadly missed. Although the congregation realized he had far outstayed his time, they felt sure that, if he had remained, they would have achieved their dream of a church.

Two fine Christian teachers were the next leaders of the Boulder Junction Sunday School and worship services. Mr. and Mrs. George Erdman of Plum Lake, at Sayner, about fifteen miles from Boulder, took over where the hearty Texan had left off, and their attractive personalities brought increased attendance at the weekly and mid-weekly Bible study sessions for children and adults. But still the church fund lagged.

Mrs. Doolittle and Kate and fellow members of the

Ladies' Aid decided on a drive to rally the community to the church project. An orchestra had been organized by Roland Carey, the postmaster of Boulder Junction, and it had given the attendance at the town-hall services an additional boost. Mrs. Mel Kenaga, an accomplished pianist, walked many miles to bring her talents to the congregation. What with the orchestra, and the Erdmans, and better times beginning to be in evidence, Minnie Doolittle and Kate were sure the people of Boulder would respond in a body to the notices inviting all those who were interested in the church-building project to meet at the town hall.

On the night of the rally, the women arrived with high hearts expecting a capacity crowd. But only seven people arrived, and the optimistic Ladies' Aiders suffered a sad disappointment.

They huddled to discuss the reason for the failure of their meeting and decided it had been premature. The project needed more publicity, they agreed, and for the next few weeks the committee women spoke of the church project wherever they went, and then sent out another batch of notices.

This time ten people attended the rally. Mrs. Doolittle, who had counted on the support of her community, took the disappointment deeply to heart. The lack of interest displayed by the people she had worked so hard to organize into an active unit to raise money for the church came as a profound shock to her. She returned home a broken-hearted woman. That night she suffered a heart attack and died the following evening.

Minnie Doolittle's death struck at the conscience of the Boulder Junction community. Her funeral, held at the town hall, was a reproach to their indifference. This courageous and energetic woman had given of herself to the point of her own destruction.

Her favorite hymn was sung at the services and it spoke for her to many attentive ears:

> "I would be true, for there are those who trust me,
> I would be pure, for there are those who care,
> I would be strong, for there is much to suffer,
> I would be brave, for there is much to dare."

Kate wept for her friend. She had been true, pure, strong and brave, but few had followed her. Kate vowed that nothing would be left undone to fulfill Minnie's dream of a church for the community they both loved.

Syd Doolittle, Minnie's eldest son, had promised his mother on her deathbed that he would carry on her fight. Kate and Syd joined forces, and soon after the funeral, another meeting was called by the determined and indomitable Ladies' Aiders. This time thirty people responded.

The Reverend Reid Radford now assumed the leadership of the town-hall congregation and began to prepare the workers for their future roles in the church project. He schooled them as to the duties and functions of the various committees which would carry on the projected church. He never failed to refer to the church as an accomplished fact instead of a remote possibility. He was a wise leader who knew that the matrix of any accomplishment must be first fixed in the mind.

One day, at a meeting called to assemble the various committees and elect a board for the Boulder Junction Community Church, still in the form of architects' plans, Kate objected to some of the proposed ideas on the grounds that they were too costly. Reverend Radford rebuked her with a few memorable words:

"If you would stop thinking about the money, and begin to have a little more faith, you would find that much more would be accomplished."

Kate flushed, but she soon learned that the pastor's admonition was a potent formula. The prayers of that earnest little congregation brought unexpected help to their efforts.

The superintendent of one of the CCC camps in the area offered a crew of men to pour the cement for their church foundation, if they would provide the cement. In order to pour foundations, they needed land, and this was forthcoming through the generosity of Mr. and Mrs. Sam J. Williams. Another Boulder Junction resident donated the gravel for mixing the cement. Only $300 was on hand toward the church project, and $137.75 of it was invested in cement for the foundation.

On Mother's Day, in 1940, when the foundation had been completed, a ceremony was held and the cornerstone of the Boulder Junction Community Church was laid. It consisted of a crude flat stone picked up in the forest and chiseled with the date of the event by Mr. Hammond of the congregation.

The history of the church-building project was sealed in a glass jar and placed in the hollow cement block under the cornerstone. The Boulder Junction Community Church was dedicated to Christians of all denominations who needed a place to pray.

The foundation measured thirty by fifty feet and the next step was to raise a church building upon it. There was exactly $162.25 in the building fund. But at that cornerstone ceremony a generous collection swelled the coffers, and at the dinner which followed, the church-building "kitty" was given an additional boost.

Although the majority of the two hundred and fifty Boulder Junctionites who attended the ceremony and the dinner were Protestants of various denominations, there were many Catholics among those who had worked for the church building.

With the church fund moving toward its goal, the building committee began to make plans. The blueprints were ready. All that was needed were materials and labor. Volunteers stepped forward. The lumber companies co-operated by permitting the volunteer building crew to select "pulp" from their stockpiles, and regardless of the price, it was sold to them at a #3 rate, which was the minimum, although the lumber itself was actually first grade.

Other materials were donated, and the volunteer crew hired additional help to speed the work. At a cost of three thousand dollars the church hall was erected. The treasurer announced a deficit of a thousand dollars, but during the winter season the deficit was covered by contributions and the Boulder Junction Community Church became a debt-free reality.

But what about pews? Church members contributed seven dollars for the material with which a pew could be constructed in those days, and the labor was donated by carpenters in the congregation so that the church was soon ready for its opening ceremony. On Mother's Day, May 10, 1942, dedication services were held at the Community Church of Boulder Junction with Dr. Reid Radford presiding. Minnie Doolittle's name appeared at the top of the final page of the program, heading the list of three "star workers" for the building of the church, honored in memoriam. Dr. Kate P. Newcomb was listed as Chairman of the Board of Trustees.

This was by no means the alpha and omega of the determined Ladies' Aiders' plans. The next move determined upon was the erection of a parsonage so they could have a resident minister. The summer people—who had begun to return in the late 'thirties and were taking an interest in the brave little church—became interested in the project. By 1945 there wasn't quite enough for the construction, and the members of the building committee made a daring decision. Being interdenominational, they were not qualified to get funds from any church organization, so they would go to a bank. It was hardly likely that the bank would advance them money for a parsonage, but then, many unlikely things had happened. The bank made no difficulty about accepting their notes, which meant that the members of the Board of Trustees would have to sign the bank's notes personally, making them individually and collectively responsible for the return of the borrowed funds. Undaunted, the trustees signed.

The parsonage was built, but before it was completed a sad blow fell on the congregation of the Boulder Junction Community Church. Their inspired pastor, whom they had hoped to house in the new parsonage, succumbed to a heart attack and died in his pulpit at Flambeau just as he was finishing services. The Reverend Radford had been the spiritual leader of Boulder Junction, and the grief of the congregation on hearing news of his death was deep indeed. The beloved old pastor had left a memorial in their midst—the finished church itself! He would never occupy the parsonage his flock was building for him, but his inspiration and guidance would never be forgotten.

Another minister, the elderly and eloquent Reverend Olsen, moved into the finished parsonage. The fortunes of the little church were on the upgrade, for, with the help of the summer people, it was able to pay off its five-year note in two years. They also built a garage for the minister's car, as his frail health and advanced age made it precarious for him to attempt to start an icy motor that had been standing in the weather of a winter night.

But Ladies' Aiders had not reached the end of their determination. The members of the Community Church congregation were still holding their social gatherings at the town hall. The ladies of the entertainment committee were not ungrateful for the blessings that had been poured down upon their church enterprises, but they did complain to Dr. Kate Newcomb that their joints ached from climbing down the steep stairs to the basement, and up again, carrying the refreshments they had prepared below. It was a great pity, they sighed, that the church did not have a suitable social hall where church entertainments could be held—all on one floor—not a very large one. But, of course, it was out of the question. It would be too expensive, although all they wanted was a modest hall with kitchen facilities—right back of the church. The property there was really going to waste.

It took them five years to accumulate a fund for a thirteen by thirty foot hall with kitchen facilities—but oddly enough the size of the hall increased as their funds accumulated, and by the time they had seven thousand dollars, the plans for the social hall had expanded to a building thirty-two by fifty-four feet, thanks to the architect's enthusiasm. At the 1950 annual meeting, the congregation voted to secure a loan of eight thousand dollars from the bank and really do the social hall up brown!

The explanation for this seemingly reckless undertaking was that the church had a new, young minister, Reverend Wilfred Hansen, who had a golden touch when it came to raising funds, and he approved of an appealing and attractive community social hall to attract young people and make church attendance comradely and comfortable.

The building was erected with materials secured at special discounts through the business firms of Boulder Junction. Again free-will labor cut down costs, but the project ran two thousand dollars over its budget. The bank co-operated by deferring amortization on its loan until the money was collected for the deficit, which it was—for Reverend Hansen's fund-raising talent is still the talk of the community. He was a divinity student who eventually had to return to his seminary to complete his studies. If he had remained in Boulder, who knows what fabulous edifices might have arisen on the site of the modest Boulder Junction church!

The Ladies' Aiders had one more touch to add. They wanted a study for the minister, so he could have privacy while he was preparing his sermons—*and they got it!* Now they had the beautiful social hall, a fine kitchen with a "Magic Chef," indoor bathroom facilities, a library nook which also serves as a nursery (with sitter) during services, a furnace which fairly toasts the congregation, and a handsome new minister with a pretty young wife—Reverend and Mrs. Daniel Nelson.

Juveniles Without Delinquency

IN 1931, shortly after Kate Newcomb returned to medicine at Boulder Junction and its surrounding communities, she was appointed Health Officer of that district. One of her first moves was to tackle the problem of water pollution. She had run across several cases of intestinal infection which pointed directly to the contamination of drinking water from improper sewage disposal, and she requested an official *bacillus coli* count of the lake waters by the state authorities. The count was made and the pollution was verified. The contamination was found to increase as the summer progressed, and a meeting of lakeside residents was called to apprise them of their danger and advise them in the correction of their sewage situation.

It was at this time that Dr. Kate also got after the milk supply. There had been bitter dissatisfaction in the community over the quality, freshness and purity of the milk purveyed by the various distributors. Complaints seemed to bring no improvement. The new health officer did not waste time in controversy. She sent a sample of each delivery to the State Health Laboratories at Madison, and upon receiving their analyses of richness, freshness and bacillus plate count, she posted in the markets and in various public places around Boulder a typewritten chart of the findings on each company's product—and waited for the charge to explode.

The companies howled as the authorities moved in and demanded milk reform. The first sign of Kate's success was the introduction of paper containers by one of the larger distributors. The others soon followed suit. From then on the companies vied with each other to provide the finest, richest, cleanest and best-packaged milk and dairy products. The most violent of the objectors soon became the most rabid in reform measures. Dr. Kate had won the "milk war."

Her reputation for public zeal impressed many community leaders, among them "Daddy" Wones, director of the big Y Camp, Manitowish, on Boulder Lake. Twice that summer he summoned Dr. Newcomb for consultation on cases at the camp. The following year he asked her to become its official doctor.

One of her first projects was the thorough inspection of its water situation, and her official position as health officer lent the weight of authority to her recommendations. She began with an inspection of the wells and lake waters, and to make sure there would be no noxious drainage from cess pools into the wells or the lake where the children swam, she had septic tanks installed. Bottled water was hauled in for drinking until the purity of the wells could be absolutely assured.

Pursuing her policy of preventive precautions, Kate inquired about the kitchen employes. A camp kitchen, where food is handled for two hundred children, can easily become a source of contamination, unless the food handlers are rigidly and regularly examined. Kate made this inspection a requirement at the very outset of her program.

She also recommended that the Y Camp should have an infirmary adequately equipped to handle any emergency that might arise. In a camp where nearly two hundred active youngsters scramble in and out of boats, tramp over rough forest trails and fling themselves recklessly into sports of every kind, an infirmary is not only advisable but indispensable, especially when the nearest hospital is some fifty miles away.

Neither Rome nor the camp health program was built in a day. "Daddy" Wones was keenly aware of the inadequacy of the camp's medical facilities, and Dr. Kate found him a staunch ally in her plans to improve them. Manitowish was the "pioneer camp," which she dubs her "guinea pig" in the camp-improvement program, and it soon set a pattern for health measures in other camps.

One of Kate's chief difficulties was that of convincing the parents of the young campers that their children must have a premedical examination by their own physician no earlier than five days before they came to camp. The parents protested that the time was too short. But Kate insisted that the rule be observed and the forms be filled out and sent to the camp within the prescribed time by the family doctors. This was to make sure the children had no contagious infections, and also, to provide a medical record of their general condition in the event of any developments while they were at the camp. Families soon realized that this measure safeguarded their offspring, and they began to co-operate without further difficulty.

Kate found a patron for her infirmary project in a woman who had grandchildren at the camp. This cooperative grandmother, Mrs. Schrieber of Oshkosh, built a three-bed infirmary on the Y Camp grounds, complete with examination room, running water (the first to be installed in any camp thereabouts), and a bathtub. This infirmary was used for fifteen years, until R. G. Halverson, a juvenile camp enthusiast who was a member of the Y Camp committee and vice president of the Hamilton Manufacturing Company at Two Rivers, Wisconsin, interested a number of his fellow businessmen in the erection of a fourteen-bed infirmary at Camp Manitowish.

The new infirmary, built at a cost of some fifteen thousand dollars donated by these public-spirited businessmen, was a vast improvement over the old building. Besides the fourteen beds, it consisted of a large waiting room, an examination room, an operating room, a stainless steel kitchen and laboratory, toilets, bathrooms, "teletalk" and a fine office. When the need for such a large infirmary was questioned, Dr. Kate explained that she believed in "an ounce of prevention" as against "a pound of cure." Young people, especially when they romp in the woods, are inclined to run themselves ragged before they realize they are out of energy. Whenever a headache or some other symptom of overtaxed strength appeared, this cautious camp doctor prescribed bed rest, and the subsequent decline in the sick-log rate proved she knew more about youngsters than did her questioners.

Kate handled loss-of-weight cases by prescribing an extra feeding at regular rest periods during the day and at bedtime. The loss-of-weight incidence soon gave way to her sensible treatment.

When Dr. Newcomb's success with Camp Manitowish was observed, other camps invited her to act as their official doctor. She warned them that it would mean expense and constant vigilance, but some bad experiences had made their directors amenable to stricter health regulations and they agreed to give Dr. Newcomb a free hand if she would take them on. Her reputation for sound judgment on camp health was established by this time, and whenever she made it known that she needed certain additions to her medical equipment or personnel at any of the camps, whether it was an examination chair or a permanent nurse, her requirements were met without delay.

To share the responsibility of providing maximum protection for her young charges, Kate organized a consultation staff of competent doctors, who met at the Y Camp several times a year to discuss health problems and recommend measures for their solution. Nothing must be left undone to safeguard the young campers while they were away from their homes. There was the tetanus risk, for instance. The rough-and-tumble activities in the woodlands often resulted in cuts and abrasions which might easily become infected through carelessness or neglect. Kate pressed for compulsory immunization against tetanus, but it was twelve years before she could persuade the camp committee that this measure was urgently needed. They were finally convinced by an alarming incident which almost cost the life of one of the young campers.

The girl involved had stepped on a nail in the stable yard. Her file card indicated that she was allergic to horses, and the injury was certainly one which indicated the possibility of infection. Since she was the daughter of a physician, Dr. Kate telephoned to her father to ask whether a tetanus antitoxin could be administered. He suggested that a skin test be made to determine the child's reaction. Kate made the test and was horrified to see the girl go into an immediate state of collapse. The antitoxin had acted as a deadly poison, and emergency measures had to be taken to revive her. She was given a shot of adrenalin and a resuscitator was rushed from the State Forestry Office to administer oxygen. The child's father was sent for, and, fortunately, by the time he arrived the child was out of danger. Kate remained at her side until she was sure there would be no further trouble.

Had that youngster had a routine injection of the harmless toxoid used for tetanus immunization, this frightening incident would not have occurred, as there would have been no need for the antitoxin. The mishap convinced the camp committee. Kate won her fight for compulsory immunization against tetanus.

When the story reached one of the members of the camp committee, he insisted that there must be an oxygen resuscitator in the Camp Manitowish infirmary, and he donated this important piece of equipment.

The ubiquitous wood tick was another of the problems of camp life. Dr. Torpy, who was also a member of the camp's medical staff, gave his associates a thorough briefing on this annoying pest. He produced a huge model of the insect to illustrate his lecture, and his droll description of the insect's habits and the methods necessary to remove it sent the staff into howls of laughter. Someone finally suggested that they "get down to business." Dr. Torpy looked up over his glasses in his inimitable way and asked, "Well? Isn't this business?" Dr. Torpy's wood tick has become a prized relic in the camp, and the instructions he gave for thorough reciprocal inspection by the boys, from hairline to heel when they turned in at night after a day in the woods, are followed faithfully.

Skin irritations also had to be watched very carefully by the camp doctor. The distinction between chicken pox, poison ivy, measles and impetigo is no trifling matter in a camp swarming with susceptible juveniles. A story is told of one of the young campers who took a keen interest in Dr. Newcomb's medical activities. He later studied medicine and had occasion to profit from one of Kate's sound, if primitive, medications.

When this young man was interning in Philadelphia after graduating from Northwestern University, his chief of staff confronted him with a problem involving impetigo, a well-known and highly communicable bacterial condition of the skin. It had broken out in the nursery of the maternity ward, and the young interne was asked how he would go about treating this highly infectious condition which was giving much concern to the staff. The young man proceeded to paint all the tiny occupants of the nursery with gentian violet, and the infection cleared up quickly.

The senior physician was curious to know where the interne had learned of this treatment, and the young man replied, "From a northwoods doctor in God's country when I was at summer camp. Her name is Dr. Kate Newcomb."

This ardent "disciple" of Dr. Kate's methods was young Dr. John Hooker, a Wisconsin resident who has since distinguished himself in cancer research. He never fails to call on Dr. Kate when he happens to be in the neighborhood of his old camping grounds.

Today, with fifteen northwoods camps under her official supervision, Dr. Kate is conceded to be without peer when it comes to preventive medicine and sanitation in juvenile vacation centers. Her requirements have been adopted by the American Camping Association and the American Academy of Pediatrics, in the form of a standardized questionnaire. This form was arrived at by soliciting information from a national cross section of camp doctors, and was prepared by Dr. Kate in consultation with the medical staff at Camp Manitowish.

The nursing associations have also issued manuals for camp nurses based on Dr. Kate's form letter entitled: "Standing Orders for Camp Nurses. What they can and cannot do until the doctor arrives."

Kate gives much of the credit for her success with the camps to "Daddy" Wones, who has since traveled on to greener camping grounds.

But professional satisfaction is only part of Dr. Kate's reward for twenty-three years of effort. She is also an enthusiast, and the charm and spirit of her camps is a subject which she is always happy to discuss. "Daddy" Wones once said the camps gave the children a "plus" for their future life, and Kate agrees.

"The camps are my happiest workshops," she says as she relates her many experiences in the haunts of the young vacationers. "Camp Manitowish was my first love, of course, and it still heads the list, because it got me started in camp work. 'Daddy' Wones was always my staunch supporter in this work, and many a parent owes him a great debt for his wonderful care of the children entrusted to him.

"When I go to the Y Camp, I feel as though I am going home, and I would feel lost without my summer boys and girls. The boys have June and July at Manitowish, and the girls arrive in August. Of course, they grow up, and new ones take their place. But they are just as dear to me, and it makes me feel so good to watch them grow as they come back each year, and to know they are getting a fine start through the high standards of the camp teachings. The inscription on the wall beside the big fireplace in the lodge hall tells the story better than I can. It reads: 'This Lodge is dedicated to the development of that strong manhood, character and spiritual growth to which every American boy is heir.' These fine words are the expression of Mr. C. W. Nash who has given much support to the beautiful camp, along with many other far-visioned American businessmen. They know 'the boy is father of the man,' and they support the youth camps for the good of their country's future.

"The huge raftered dining and recreation hall at Manitowish is hung with facsimiles of the implements and possessions of the fabulous Paul Bunyan. The boys have a ceremony on July seventh each year, which is Paul Bunyan Day. They have a high old time commemorating the legendary lumberjack giant whose counterparts, the husky loggers of the lumbercamps, 'brought daylight' to the northwoods. On that day the youngsters have log-rolling and 'peavey' throwing contests, and they bake beans underground in the traditional lumberjack fashion.

"Then there are my other camps. I don't know which of them I love most. There's Pinemere which I took over when our good old Doc Torpy died. That's a girls' camp. Then there's Warwick Woods where the girls play hard and work hard, and yet they are taught a high standard of gentle living and good fellowship. Their supper table is set with perfect taste, lighted with candles and decorated with pine boughs by the girls themselves. The lowering of the flag at sundown brings a lump to the throats of those who watch the solemn reverence of these fresh young American girls as they bring down their flag and fold it carefully away until the next sunrise. And their 'warmth creed,' recited in unison by the girls at their meetings, just about breaks me up whenever I hear it:

'To start the day with a merry heart,
To seek the spirit of repose and patience,
To refuse to stoop to what is trivial and false,
To be a lover of truth, simplicity and honesty,
To seek happiness for others, contentment for myself,
This shall be my creed.'

I think this creed, inculcated in the young, supplies a good basis for the future of a nation.

"There is Osoha, a girls' camp founded by a man who might have been the inspiration for that magnificent poem by Kipling which ends: 'And what is more, you'll be a man, my son.' I know some people will smile at the triteness of Kipling's verse, and think I am out of date and old-fashioned. But I recognize pure gold when I see it, and I'll take the old standards of 'If' as against some of the so-called 'new' ones I have seen—any day!

"Robert Snaddon, Camp Osoha's founder, was known as 'Chief.' He's gone, along with 'Daddy' Wones and Doc Torpy. But his spirit still hovers over the camp, and his wife Emily, known as 'Nahwani,' or 'Little Chief,' carries on the tradition of Big Chief.

"I can see the closing ceremony of the camp as the summer ends. The little lighted candle-boats of the young campers drift out over the lake, carrying the wishes of the girls to one who has gone. . . . I always hear singing somewhere in that camp, even in winter when I pass that way, though the camp grounds are deserted.

"The Highlands is another of 'my' camps. It is deep in

214

the woods, a rugged place with a difficult approach through a forest trail just barely wide enough for my car. The camp lies at the end of the trail, and when one gets to it, one is amazed at the activity that suddenly bounces into view! Boys playing tennis, another sweaty team playing baseball—on the lake, boys in boats, boys hoisting sails, boys swimming, boys fishing. You never saw such a busy place! They haven't even time to wait the twenty minutes required after an allergy shot, and I sometimes have to catch them by the shirttail to remind them that I'm the doctor. The counsellors have been there many years, and each spring is like old-home-week for all of us. I love the opening of the camps. I guess I love it as much as the youngsters do.

"A year ago, a terrible storm swept through that forest at Highlands. Hundreds of big trees were struck down. A couple of the boys were hurt and the place was a shambles. Giant trees were piled up like so much cordwood, and the road was impassable by car. I drove in as far as I could and tramped the rest of the way on foot to get to my boys. Dr. Monilaw, who owns the camp and is small in stature but mighty in spirit, looked over the chaos and asked for volunteers to clear the wreckage. 'Let's carry on!' he said. 'Camp Highlands never quits!'

"Not one of those boys even mentioned going home. They went to work and cleared away the debris, stacked the logs for cutting and did the best they could to repair their buildings until the damage could be properly fixed. That's the kind of spirit that makes our summer camps a place of 'juveniles without delinquency.' Troublesome youngsters are so few and far between that I sometimes wonder if our youth isn't being sadly misjudged through bad publicity. You are more likely to find a fish with feathers in our lakes than a 'bad' boy or girl in our summer camps.

"Is it any wonder I'm in love with the camps? I could talk to you about them for days, so you'd better stop me!"

The glow in Dr. Kate's eyes and her infectious enthusiasm are too engaging to be dampened. When a busy doctor rides a hobby with such zest, the listener climbs on and goes along.

"There's Red Pines, the friendly girls' camp where every girl is the personal guest of every camper and counsellor. Each newcomer is received with such warmth and friendliness that it does your heart good to see them arrive. I see each child there weekly and get to know them pretty well, and I have yet to find one I couldn't love, although they are all as different as little individualists can be.

"Red Arrow is another of my boys' camps. It is something like Highlands, all the boys so busy with their activities, boating, hiking, canoeing, practicing on the basketball court with the next year's team in mind. These camp youngsters give one confidence in the future of our country, and if I had my way, no American boy or girl would lack the opportunity to spend some part of the summer vacation in a camp like those in our northwoods, for I am sure many of the juvenile problems would soon vanish under such an influence.

"Woodlands is a camp for small children, from four on up. They are so happy there, and so full of interest in what goes on. They sit their horses like little kings and queens, straight and proud, and they greet me so affectionately when I arrive, with no trace of anxiety about what needs to be done to keep them safe. Shots don't bother them. They know Dr. Kate is looking after them, and they see me off in my car when I leave so that their happy little faces seem to go with me on my long rides from camp to camp.

"Well, I don't have to tell you how crazy I am about the camps and how proud I am of what I have accomplished to make them safe vacation grounds for those wonderful kids. So please tell my friends about them in the book. I want everyone to get as interested in the youth camps as I am so that all Americans will support them and help to increase their number. I really think it would make a great difference in the 'delinquency' problem."

It is encouraging to report here that, although application for camp attendance has become so heavy that many thousands of youngsters must be turned away each year, the number of youth camps is rapidly increasing. In the Wisconsin directory alone 178 camps are listed, with an average attendance of 120 campers. The Y Camps, of which Manitowish is one of the three largest, number twelve thousand in the forty-eight states, and the Y.M.C.A. has done a tremendous service to the nation in its promotion of the youth-camp program.

Eldorah

KATE had always longed for a daughter. When
it seemed apparent that the Lord was not going
to see fit to bless her with another child, she began to consider the possibility of acquiring one by adoption.

She discussed the idea with Bill, but he was not inclined to approve of taking in a strange child. One never
knew—heredity was a risky business—one's own child was
responsibility enough. She'd better forget about it.

But Kate still clung to the idea. She wanted a daughter and she intended to have one. She kept a weather eye
open for a possible child and mentioned her desire to a few
of her close friends. Among them was Judge Carter, then
in charge of county welfare matters at Eagle River.

One day in March, 1936, Kate was in the judge's office
consulting with him about the homeless Vilas County children who were being cared for at the State Home in Sparta
at county expense. To clarify the assessment for this purpose which had been imposed on Vilas County by the
state, the judge showed Kate a list of the youngsters who
had been sent to the Sparta institution from Vilas.

Kate noticed one name on the register which bore the

birth date of July 26, 1934. July twenty-sixth was Kate's own birthday, and she inquired about the baby. The judge, knowing that she was interested in adopting a little girl, suggested that this one might be exactly the child she wanted. He took a picture of the baby from his file and Kate saw a tiny wisp of a girl with a tangled mop of light curls and enormous dark eyes shadowed by a look of indescribable sadness. The judge told Dr. Newcomb that, although the baby had been medically certified as normal, she had been so neglected and isolated with smaller children in the Home, that she knew only a few words, and, to add to the pathos of the case, an unexplained leg injury had impeded the child's ability to walk so that she was still crawling around long past the age when she should have been walking. Kate listened attentively as Judge Carter gave her a brief outline of the child's family background. She had been placed in the Home by a young mother whose husband had died shortly after the baby's birth. Unable to earn a livelihood for herself and her baby during the hopeless depression years, the young widow had placed the child in the State Home and signed a release for her adoption.

Kate looked at the baby's picture for a long time. Then she lifted her eyes to the judge's face. "I'll take her," she said briefly.

Returning home, Kate told Bill about the child and again he protested. Kate decided to try a different approach. She suggested that they take the baby for a short time as a medical experiment. If they gave her proper care and built up her health, she would have a better chance of being adopted by some other family. Bill shrugged. If Kate wanted to borrow trouble, she could do as she liked. Personally, he did not favor the idea.

It was three months before the Home was ready to release the little girl called "Eldorah," as she was then going through a siege of chicken pox. The pressure of Kate's practice made it impossible for her to go to Sparta to see the child, and when the time came to get her from the Home, Kate went to her friend, Mrs. Jennie Blaisdell, whom everyone in Boulder affectionately called "Aunt Jennie," and asked her if she could pick up the baby, since she was going to Madison to visit relatives and Sparta was about two thirds of the way between Boulder and Madison, on a slight detour to the west. "Aunt Jennie" gladly agreed to pick up the child.

There was a community meeting at the town hall the evening of "Aunt Jennie's" return from Sparta. The news of Kate Newcomb's baby's imminent arrival had spread through the town and the social gathering at the town hall drew a record crowd that evening.

At about eight o'clock, when the festivities were well under way, Kate left the hall with Tommy and drove to Aunt Jennie's home not far from the meeting place. Mrs. Blaisdell had just pulled up before her house as Kate and Tommy arrived; they met her getting out of the car with the baby in her arms. Aunt Jennie greeted her friend and handed her the little girl, saying, "This is Eldorah. Eldorah, this is your mamma."

The tiny, emaciated child, grotesquely clad in black stockings and a mauve jumper under the rough blanket that had been wrapped around her, went into Kate's arms. Her big eyes filled with tears as she looked timidly at the strangers in the glow of the headlights. Tommy crowded close to look at the baby, and when he saw the thin, sad face with its tearful eyes under the straggling curls, he said in an anguished voice, "Oh, Mamma, let's go back and get *all* of them!"

Kate drove back to the hall, and as she entered carrying the tiny girl, she was greeted by a burst of applause and her friends crowded around to see the newcomer. Alarmed by the sea of strange faces that closed in to catch a glimpse of her, Eldorah flung her arms around Kate's neck and buried her face in her shoulder, whimpering, "Mamma." That was all Kate needed to bind the baby firmly and permanently to her heart. The frail mite snuggled against her shoulder and calling her "mamma" was as dear to her from that moment as though she had been really her own. Kate's eyes filled as she took leave of her friends and hurried home with Tommy to put her newly acquired daughter to bed.

A warm bath revealed the neglected injury to the child's right leg, and the sorry state of her chafed, emaciated and eczema-ridden little body aroused both rage and tenderness in Kate. "How could people, even the heartless custodians of a public institution, allow a baby to fall into such a state of unspeakable neglect?" She fumed as she washed the little girl with gentle hands, then slipped her into one of Tommy's discarded sleeping suits and tucked her into bed, where she immediately fell asleep.

As for Bill, he had watched the entire process with a dubious eye. If Kate wanted to get herself involved in a responsibility like this, it was her own lookout. He wanted no part of it, he grumbled.

Slowly, gradually, with infinite patience and gentleness, Kate overcame the sadness and wary bewilderment in the baby's eyes. After a week of careful feeding and thorough bathing, the little girl's strength began to rally and she was soon walking. She trotted after Kate wherever she went, sitting solemnly outside the office door while Kate interviewed patients, or watching her new mother with great, wondering eyes from the playpen which had been restored to the place in the kitchen where it had stood when Tommy occupied it. Kate noticed that whenever the child was tired, she began to drag her right leg. She would get on the floor and crawl around, dragging the weak leg after her. Determined to overcome the difficulty, Kate massaged and stretched the troublesome leg whenever she bathed the child, until the dragging and crawling became less and less frequent and Eldorah was soon trotting around without resorting to her former device to favor the weak leg.

Tommy was delighted with his new playfellow, and Norman McMahon proved to be an expert at persuading Eldorah to eat her cereal and drink her milk. He played games to cajole her into eating her food and she allowed herself to be tricked with obvious enjoyment. It was good to hear her laughter and to see her dark eyes shine with merry mischief as their sadness vanished.

Kate sometimes took Tommy and the baby with her on her calls. When the car turned into an unfamiliar road, Eldorah would quickly slip down to the floor and crouch under the seat. Apparently she was in terror of being taken back to the scene of her unhappy past. After a few rides, with Tommy assuring her that they would soon be returning home, Eldorah's fears faded and she began to clamor to go whenever she heard the car start.

Kate soon learned that the baby had a marked allergy to eggs, which made her swell and suffocate. By a process of trial and error, she learned what to avoid in the child's diet, as malnutrition in infancy had made her susceptible to some allergies.

In July, Kate celebrated their joint birthday with an eggless cake. Kate's friends held a "shower" at the town hall in Boulder, and Eldorah received so many dresses, coats, bonnets and shoes that Kate, who had looked forward to the fun of buying clothes for her, found she would not need to buy her a single garment for a whole year.

Eldorah displayed a will of her own at an early age. One day Kate took her to Manitowish Waters where "Aunt Jennie" was visiting some relatives. Eldorah was the center of an admiring group of women and had her first taste of candy. She enjoyed the attention and the candy so much that when it came time for Kate to leave, Eldorah's brow darkened and her face crumpled in protest. She removed one of her shoes and threw it across the room. The ladies laughed appreciatively at this flattering demonstration of Eldorah's reluctance to leave them. Seeing the success of her maneuver, she removed the other shoe and repeated the compliment. From then on Eldorah became the pet of Manitowish Waters as well as of Boulder.

The indulgence of one of her Boulder admirers very nearly put an end to Eldorah's happy life. While Kate wasn't looking, this well-meaning friend gave the little girl a huge piece of cake made with plenty of eggs. Kate spent a terrifying night overcoming the suffocation and convulsions which resulted. No one ever offered Eldorah any more unsupervised refreshments after that.

Eldorah's vocabulary remained limited to a few incoherent sounds, and Kate was concerned over her failure to speak. One day, while Kate was treating a baby in her office, Eldorah, who was sitting in her accustomed place outside the office door, heard the baby cry. She pushed the door open and looked in, and with an expression on her face which was a perfect imitation of the Home matron, she enunciated severely, slowly and emphatically: "Too —much—noise!" This was Eldorah's first articulate sentence, and its significance pierced Kate's heart. She picked up the little girl and held her close, half laughing and half weeping over the baby's comic reproduction of a familiar and threatening admonition. Kate knew then that Eldorah was far from backward. In fact, she had an acute memory and was a born mimic.

Everything the child saw was new to her, as she had spent her first two years in a room at the Home and had never seen the outdoor world. Kate named all the wonders for her—the trees, the sky, the birds—and Eldorah listened, her big, dark eyes turning from these new sights to Kate as she pondered upon each marvel of her new life. Gradually she began to form sentences: "See dog?" "Dory go, too?" "Tommy come home?" Kate, with happy relief, heard her vocabulary grow.

As her speech became more consecutive and continuous and her confidence increased, so did her sovereignty over the Newcomb household. When September came and Tommy left for school each morning on the bus, Eldorah emitted wails of protest. She adored Tommy as much as she did Kate, and Norman called her "Tagalong," for she followed first one and then the other around the house, constantly at their heels as if to prevent them from ever getting out of her sight.

As for Bill, from the very first Eldorah rode on "Daddy's" shoulder and climbed into his lap as familiarly as Tommy had done at her age, and when Kate asked him, with feigned seriousness, if he thought Eldorah should be taken back to the Home, he scowled and snapped, "Why the devil would you want to do a thing like that?"

Kate smiled and set about arranging the formal adoption of their new daughter, with Bill urging her to make sure there would be no strings attached to their full possession of Eldorah for their own. Kate's "medical experiment" had proved to be an overwhelming success. That Christmas Eve it was Eldorah's hand that lighted the Newcomb candle for the Christ-child and placed it in the window, for she was the youngest member of their family.

The snow was a new adventure, and Tommy hauled her over the paths on a sleigh while she squealed with delight and her cheeks glowed with rosy health. When summer returned she ranged the shore of the creek and learned to swim as Tommy had done, by splashing into the water and paddling like a puppy. She had the same trouble with the dogs as Tommy had had. They "rescued" her persistently, for she was now a Newcomb and in their charge. From a frail infant, she had become a sturdy, sun-browned three-year-old, and Kate rejoiced in the vigor of her unfolding personality.

At four, Eldorah developed a passion for the tools in Bill's workshop. One day, when he was doing something at his work bench, Eldorah came in and demanded to be allowed to help him. Bill told her to run along and play and stop bothering him. Eldorah trotted off, deeply offended. She went to her room, took out a small valise which was among her numerous play things and put some of her clothes into it. Then she went back to the yard and said to Bill, "Good-by, Daddy. I'm going away now." Bill chuckled and replied, "Okay, good-by," and went on with his work. But Eldorah really meant it. She got on her tricycle with the valise on the handlebars and pedaled away.

Kate came out of her office and, as usual, asked where Eldorah was. Bill said she was somewhere around. Tommy was on the dock fishing. Kate went to him, asking if he'd seen Eldorah. No, he hadn't. Nor had Norman, who was tinkering with the newly installed lighting plant. Kate was frantic. Where was Eldorah? Had she drowned in the creek? Bill got the boat ready to go searching over the waters, while the others rushed around calling: "Eldorah? Eldorah!" But no Eldorah was to be found.

Kate noticed that the tricycle was gone. On a hunch, she got into the car and started down the road. Over a mile from the house she caught sight of her small daughter pedaling as fast as her fat legs could go. Kate sounded the horn. Eldorah looked back and pedaled harder. Kate caught up with her and passed her gingerly, then stopped the car to block the runaway. She got out and retrieved Eldorah and the tricycle and sped home to reassure the frantic family.

Eldorah got her first spanking. In fact, she got two spankings—one from Tommy who had been beside himself with fright. Eldorah had been in his charge and her escapade had reflected on his responsibility. She never tried to run away again, though she found plenty of other mischief to get into. Her explanation was that she had been on her way to stay with her friend Mildred, a little girl who sometimes came to play with her, and who lived seven miles down the road on the way to Boulder. Daddy had told her to go away and not to bother him, so she decided she wasn't wanted around there.

This was Eldorah. As "chain lightning" she was a perfect match for Tommy. At six, when she had just begun to go to the Boulder Junction school, she fell from a swing in the schoolyard and broke her arm. She cried and said her arm hurt, but she would not allow anyone to touch it. When she got home, her mother examined the arm, found it was broken and hurried her down to Dr. Torpy to have it set, not trusting herself to inflict the necessary pain on "her own flesh and blood," as Eldorah by this time seemed to her.

When she was seven, Eldorah was sent to her first camp. It was a farm camp where she could indulge her passion for all kinds of animals, and work out her dynamic energy in farming activities. She went to camp every year after that and became skillful at all sports, including horseback riding and trap-shooting. She was so proficient at the latter that some of her envious companions once jimmied the sights of her gun to make her miss. But before the day of the championship shoot, Eldorah telephoned Bill and complained to him that her gun had gone sour. Bill hurried to camp with his own gun. Eldorah won the shoot and Bill beamed with pride for he had taught her himself. She was equally proficient at riding and became the riding instructor at one of her later camps. She won ribbons at the shows and excelled in everything she undertook, much to Tommy's and Bill's delight. She was a real Newcomb and did justice to their renown as sportsmen.

"Oh, I'll admit we spoiled Eldorah," says Kate without a trace of regret, "but we felt that she was entitled to a little spoiling, and to tell the truth, we enjoyed it as much as she did. Eldorah brought us a great deal of fun and happiness. We loved her dearly and she loved us in return, and although she sometimes behaves in the 'wacky' manner of most modern youngsters, she is still the Newcomb pride and joy."

Sisters of Mercy

F OR many years Dr. Kate did most of her hospital work at the Sacred Heart Hospital in Tomahawk, a very old and venerable institution erected in 1906 by an order of missionary and hospital nuns known as the Sisters of the Sorrowful Mother. Their Mother House is in Rome, and there is a convent and nursing school of the Order in Milwaukee.

When the Sacred Heart Hospital was built in 1906, it stood in lonely isolation against the thick pine forests, surrounded by a few scattered homes and by the seething activity of lumber camps, then at the height of their operations in the Wisconsin timber country.

The solemn edifice of burnt-orange brick weathered by many northwoods winters, has since been enlarged until its present capacity is sixty beds. Here eighteen nuns, the older of them sent from Rome and still speaking with the accents of their German origin—for the founder of the order, Mother Frances Streitel, was of German birth—maintain the building in immaculate order. Every window gleams. Its floors are waxed and polished to a mirrorlike gloss, and its dark, ancient woodwork and painted walls are kept scrupulously clean.

There is a tranquil spirit in this place, an aura of peace and healing. In contrast to the functional steel and glass of modern hospitals, Sacred Heart seems more like an old residence, well cared for, but retaining the atmosphere of past traditions. There is the shimmer of candlelight on deep, polished wood as the devotional tapers flicker in the recessed niche under a statue of the Virgin beside the entrance door. The faint scent of beeswax and incense permeates the subdued light of the long corridors, an "odor of sanctity" befitting the religious origin of the hospice.

The Sisters are coifed in starched white muslin, and long white gowns cover the black robes of their habits. The whisper of their robes as they move silently through the halls and rooms evokes an illusion of angelic wings, and their soft voices scarcely brush the surface of the velvet silence that envelopes a visitor who comes to learn of Dr. Kate's long connection with the work of the hospital.

There are prayers in the chapel, with its stained-glass windows and glowing altar forming a rich background for the white-clad nuns who sit in twos at their devotions. Their coifs are bowed and their soft voices chant in unison from the Latin of their missals. The altar candles gleam on their snowy habits, and the picture is one long to be remembered.

Sister Mary Katherine Hedwig, the head nurse of the second floor, last year celebrated her golden jubilee, her fiftieth year as a "bride of Christ" and a hospital nurse. Her fresh round blue-eyed face, unmarked by time, was framed by the snug white wimple and the snowy coif which flowed over her shoulders. She spoke of Dr. Kate's work with the Sisters:

"Many and many were the cold, stormy nights she

came driving through the snow, sometimes with her husband, sometimes alone, to attend her hospitalized patients. Often, when she arrived, she would be at the end of her strength. We had a room for her, and whenever we could, we made her stay for a few hours of sleep when her work was over. And there were times when we had to trick her into taking a rest. I will confess that I was often alarmed at her weariness, and she admitted that she could scarcely stand on her feet. Her poor feet! They had never recovered from the terrible frostbite of her long hikes on snowshoes in the early days. How she could endure those dreary rides, and the work she did here on her burning, aching feet—it was always a miracle to us. Surely, the Lord is with Dr. Newcomb.

"This has been proved many times in our experience with her. She always knew when a delivery was going to be difficult, and she was always right. Once she said that one of her patients would have to be delivered by Caesarean section. Another doctor examined the case and disagreed. He said the birth would be normal. But Dr. Newcomb insisted that the surgery must be ready and a surgeon on hand to perform the operation. As usual, she was right. After hours of fruitless labor, the woman had to be taken to surgery and the child was delivered by a Caesarean operation. Few doctors ventured to disagree with Dr. Newcomb after that.

"One night Dr. Newcomb was held up on the way by a severe blizzard and her patient was delivered by another doctor. She was so depressed by this that none of us could console her. She felt that she had let down a patient who had counted on her. But Dr. Kate's influence played an important part in the birth. The mother had had prenatal instruction in the relaxation method known as 'childbirth without fear,' which Dr. Newcomb had been using since it was introduced in England about eight years ago. The patient remembered Dr. Kate's lessons, and the birth was an easy one.

"We have found that the women who have had this prenatal training are our easiest confinement cases, and we are always glad to have them with us. The fear of labor seems to have been eliminated from their minds. They know how to breathe and relax between the labor pains, and exactly how to help the doctor.

"But we have had our bad moments as well. Dr. Newcomb has had cases so difficult that she would look up at us over her mask, the perspiration pouring down her face, her eyes desperate with anxiety, and she would say, 'Sister, it looks pretty bad. I don't think I'm going to make it this time.' And we knew it was time to pray. I would say, 'The Lord is always with you, Doctor. He will see you through. He always does.' Some of our Sisters would go to the chapel, while others stood by to help her through the trying hours. She knew our hearts and our prayers were with her, and it gave her courage. Invariably, the crisis would break and she would hold the child in her hands. Then the weariness would drop away from her. The child and the mother were safe! Her eyes would brighten and she would smile and chat with us as though there had been no difficulty at all. But we knew that she needed rest and we would lead her to her room and bring her warm milk and persuade her to lie down. But then a call would come from Woodruff, and she would be off again, over the miles to attend another patient. We prayed for her in those days, for we knew she needed help that no human being could give her."

Sister Hedwig and Sister Pulacheri were Dr. Kate's

chief aides, but all the Sisters are her friends. Sister Pulacheri, a dark, intelligent-eyed woman from Aschaffenburg, Bavaria, who has been with the hospital for ten years, is the surgical nurse, and Sister Mary Conrada is in charge of the first floor. The rest of the Sisters are aides and hospital workers, and all of them join in their love and admiration for Kate. When she arrived at the hospital, every Sister had a greeting for her, and sometimes a little gift they had made.

Twice a year, Dr. Kate would take some of the Sisters on an outing, for their work confined them monotonously to the walls of the hospital, and she felt they needed a change of scene now and then.

One day, when she had several of the Sisters in her car and was driving along the highway, one of them caught a glimpse of some cattails in a clearing beside the road. She wanted some to decorate the hall of the hospital, and she begged Kate to stop so she could gather them. Kate pulled up along the roadbed, and the eager Sister lifted her long black robes to clear the ground and sped across the busy highway without looking to see if it was safe to cross. Kate held her breath—and as she saw her make it, with cars missing her by a hair's breadth, she heaved a sigh of relief. The cattails grew in a bog, but that did not deter the enthusiastic Sister. She gathered an armful of the cattails and scampered back to the car, again risking life and limb through the traffic. Kate blew out a long puff of breath as the Sister climbed back into the car, clutching her harvest of cattails.

"Sister," said Kate, "you certainly wanted those cattails pretty bad. I was afraid we'd be taking you back to the hospital in pieces!" The Sister, her shoes and skirts muddy, but her eyes glowing with the joy of having found her long-wished-for cattails, glanced at the speeding traffic, and it was only then that she realized what she had risked to gather them. She was all apologies for having given her friend so much alarm, and they continued their ride. They laughed for weeks over the story of Sister G—— with her skirts gathered up around her, scooting through the traffic after her cattails, as gay as a child on a holiday, and just as reckless of danger.

These Sisters are far from the dolorous women one might imagine them to be from the name of their Order. They are humorous, human and enthusiastic, and they are being encouraged by the present Pontiff to find relaxation in the outer world and to seek companionship with lay people, for the strict discipline of the Orders is being somewhat relaxed to keep pace with modern life. There is work to be done in the world, and while prayer is essential to the mystical part of their mission, the Sisters are also beginning to take an active part in social betterment programs outside the walls of their hospice.

Sister Hedwig told of her mischievous and irrepressible nature as a child. She was so lively that she wore out a pair of shoes a month, and her dresses were always torn from her rambunctious climbing of trees and fences. Her mother scolded her, saying she did not know how she would ever learn to behave in the world. When Katherine Hedwig declared that she had decided to become a nun, her family and her neighbors scoffed. She would last no longer than two weeks in a convent. She was much too naughty. But Katherine was determined to enter a convent despite her mother's objections and protests. Her family warned her that if she went to the convent she would have to remain there. They would permit no capricious going only to return home when she tired of the convent.

At fifteen, Katherine became a postulant, and at eighteen she became a nun. She studied nursing and was sent to Rome to be assigned to foreign fields by the Missionary Order. She came from the Order's Oshkosh hospital to Sacred Heart seventeen years ago presumably to stay six months, and she has been there ever since. It is hard to believe that this serene, composed Sister was once a frolicsome hoyden. And yet—there is a glint of blue merriment behind her polished glasses which the years have not entirely suppressed. And there is a flash of blue fire in her eyes as she tells of another incident in Dr. Kate's life at the hospital.

One day when the doctor arrived to attend a confinement she was suffering from what appeared to be a bad cold. She delivered her case and the Sisters insisted upon taking her temperature. It registered 104 degrees. She had pneumonia. Kate telephoned her family and told them she was remaining at the hospital overnight. This time she made no protest at being tucked into bed. She remained at the hospital for three days under the care of the anxious Sisters, with no word from her family to inquire about her long absence. Finally Sister Hedwig called them and told them of the doctor's illness.

Conscience-stricken, Kate's family arrived at the hospital and found her on the mend. Sister Hedwig took them severely to task for their negligence. Surely, she scolded, they should have felt some concern for her when she remained away so long. But, they explained, they were so accustomed to having Dr. Kate stay with her patients and not come home for days on end, that it had never occurred to them that she might be a patient herself. Kate was feeling better and she was so happy to see her children that she treated the whole matter as a joke. But the Sisters grieved at the evidence that Kate's very life was being endangered by her struggle with the elements over endless miles of hazardous roads, with little or no relief. They prayed constantly that, somehow, her burden would be lightened.

One day she arrived with a piece of news which gladdened the hearts of the Sisters. She had been summoned to attend Mrs. Arthur Rubloff, a summer resident who had been her patient for some years. Mrs. Rubloff was seriously ill. In fact, her condition was so critical that moving her to a hospital forty miles away from her summer home was out of the question. Dr. Kate treated her at her home and remained with her until she was out of danger.

As the doctor was leaving, Mr. Rubloff, who is a prominent Chicago businessman, accompanied her to the door and thanked her for the prompt and devoted attention which had undoubtedly saved his wife's life. He asked her what he could do to show his appreciation, as he knew her fee would certainly not be adequate for the service she had rendered. Kate thanked him, but said she couldn't think of anything, and then she grinned, "The only thing I really want, Mr. Rubloff, is a hospital, and that's like asking for the moon. But you can see for yourself how badly we need a hospital around here, and even a small one would be better than none."

Mr. Rubloff looked thoughtful. "How much do you think a small hospital would cost, doc?" he asked.

"Oh, maybe seventy-five thousand dollars," guessed Dr. Kate.

"I'm afraid it would cost more than that," replied

Mr. Rubloff. "But we may as well get the hospital idea started. Suppose you get some of your friends together, and we'll talk it over."

"Whenever you say," said Kate. There had been talk of a hospital before, but it hadn't got anywhere.

"How about tomorrow?" said Mr. Rubloff. Kate gulped. She knew Mr. Rubloff was a man of action, but she hadn't expected his action to be so immediate.

The following day a group of her friends met with Dr. Kate at Mr. Rubloff's home and discussed serious plans for collecting a fund for a hospital at Woodruff. Mr. Rubloff pledged one thousand dollars to get the ball rolling, and several others pledged various amounts. A piece of land had been offered, and this time the hospital project really got under way.

The Sisters were elated. Their prayers were being answered. Of course, it would take some time to make Kate's dream a reality, but the seed was planted, and the Sisters would nurture it with their faith.

"Above and Beyond . . ."

THE years that followed Kate's early struggles against the inroads of the depression were by no means lacking in challenge to her valiant spirit. Stories of her courageous dedication pour in from every side as one speaks to the forest people.

The John La Faves, who suffered acutely, as did many other resort people, from the decline in the summer business which is the mainstay of the area, tell of Dr. Newcomb's loyal care of their sick and her unfailing friendship in their misfortune.

Mrs. La Fave, who lost her first baby by suffocation at birth at approximately the time Kate's first child died, tells how Dr. Kate saved their third baby, when it appeared to be dying from the same inadequacy of breath, by clearing its bronchial passages with a suction valve and breathing life into the strangling infant's lungs.

"If she had only been there the first time," sighs Mrs. La Fave, but those were the dark days of 'twenty-three, when Kate was "through with medicine." Fortunately she was on hand for the third La Fave baby. When Mrs. La Fave had her fourth child, ten years afterward, at the age of forty-three, Kate insisted that she go to the hospital at Tomahawk, for she knew the birth would be difficult. The mother would have died of hemorrhage had she not been under hospital supervision, and Kate confessed afterward that this was the closest she had ever come to losing a mother.

When John La Fave was burning and gasping with pneumonia, contracted while he was on a relief-work project in the bitter cold of winter in order to feed his family, Kate propped him up and leaned him forward over a bed tray piled with pillows, to relieve the weight on his infected lung area. She sat at the unconscious man's bedside for two days and two nights, administering medication and helping his wife keep him comfortable until he was out of danger.

Bad luck continued to dog the La Fave family. In 1936, the pressure of economic anxiety and the grief caused by the death of two older members of the family finally led John La Fave into a serious breakdown. Kate saw to it that he was placed in a reliable sanitarium and consulted with the doctors about his treatment until he was entirely well again. Mrs. La Fave claims that had it not been for Dr. Newcomb's help and loyal encouragement at this time, she herself would have gone to pieces under the strain.

When the La Faves asked for a bill for Kate's numerous and invaluable services, she named some inconsequential amount and said they weren't to worry about it until they got on their feet again.

Mrs. La Fave tells of a night when the very sky seemed to be pouring down every torrent it had ever accumulated from the rivers and lakes, there was a knock at their door. Kate stood there, a soaking figure, clutching her sodden medical bag. It was four in the morning. Kate's car was mired in a ditch about a mile down the highway. She was on her way to the Sinnings', a mile and a half beyond the La Fave place. Mrs. Sinning, who was Mrs. La Fave's sister-in-law, was in labor. Kate thought John might not mind driving her to the Sinnings' place in his car. Mind? John La Fave would have walked barefoot on hot coals wherever Dr. Newcomb asked him to! He dressed hurriedly while his wife made coffee and found some dry clothes to put on the dripping but cheerful doctor. Then they set out for the Sinnings' where Kate remained all that day attending the delivery, while John extricated her car and had it ready for her to proceed to her next case.

Such incidents were not unusual in Kate's practice. She took them in her stride as part of the curriculum of a northwoods' doctor. Friend or stranger, her patients received equal consideration.

One night, in midwinter, she received a phone call from a frantic husband. He and his wife had just arrived at a closed resort to act as winter caretakers and his wife was about to have her child. Bill got out the car, and they drove through the snowy night to the resort cottage and found the place dark. The door was not locked and they went in. Bill turned his flashlight on the pitch-black, icy cold room. The couple's luggage was still standing beside the door, unopened. Kate called and a faint female voice answered from the adjacent room. Bill flashed his light to the doorway and Kate entered and found the woman in final labor. "Where is your husband?" she asked.

"He's gone for the doctor," the woman moaned.

"Well, I'm the doctor," said Kate, shivering in the icy darkness.

There was no kerosene in the lamps and no wood for the fire. Kate had a miner's carbide lamp with her for just such emergencies. She fastened it to her head and prepared for the delivery, with only her own equipment to work with. Bill went foraging outside the cabin for wood. He got a fire going in the stove and then set out to find the man of the family.

Kate delivered the baby and wrapped it in an extra coat Bill had brought from the car as an emergency blanket. She received the afterbirth, praying that nothing would go wrong, and then turned her attention to the child. Something *was* wrong. The baby was a "bleeder." Kate knew that unless she could give it an immediate transfusion, it would bleed to death. But how? The mother could not afford one drop of blood. The father's blood would do, but where was he?

"I think I came the nearest I ever had to using some bad language *that* night," Kate twinkles. When she heard the sound of a car stopping outside the cabin, she held her breath. Had Bill found him? He had.

Kate controlled her anger until the emergency was over. She quickly ordered the young man to bare his arm and drew from it a syringeful of blood which she injected into the rapidly failing baby. The infant's color returned to normal, and Kate heaved a sigh of relief. Then she told the father what she thought of him for the shameful condition in which he had left his wife, without warmth or light at such a critical time. Bill was filling the lamps and adding wood to the fire. What a woman! Standing there with the lamp still blazing from her head and giving that nincompoop what-for in no uncertain terms. Kate admits that she actually enjoyed jabbing the witless father with the needle of her syringe to save his baby's life. His explanation was lame. He didn't know it would happen so soon.

Kate returned to the cabin several times to attend the

mother and to make sure the baby was safe. The couple left the area after a brief try at their job as caretakers, and Kate, of course, did not send them a bill. She never heard from them again.

Kate never sent bills, and her patients had to request an accounting of what they owed her. Like Dr. Torpy, she made up an amount she thought they could afford and thus settled the matter. Some of her patients became incensed at her vagueness about their bills and threatened to go elsewhere unless she kept better track of what they owed her. Kate would grin and ask, "Is ten dollars all right?" Ten dollars for a confinement, including prenatal and postnatal care seemed pretty ridiculous, but there was no point in trying to reform Kate's haphazard calculations, so they paid what she asked and added their affectionate gratitude to the payment.

Kate claims that while Christmas Eve has always been quiet and unbroken by calls, she has never enjoyed an uninterrupted Thanksgiving. One year the three-year-old son of Mrs. Espeseth, one of her closest friends, upset a pan of boiling water over himself while his mother was preparing the Thanksgiving turkey for the oven. Kate rushed him to the hospital at Tomahawk and remained with him until he was out of danger.

Another year, when Tommy was a senior at high school, his best friend, Dick Birkholz, was accidentally shot in the groin while out hunting deer. His companions carried him two miles through the woods to the car and then drove him fifteen miles to Kate's Rice Creek house. Kate was just about to take the Thanksgiving turkey out of the oven when the car pulled up and the injured Dick was carried into the house. The boy had lost a great deal of blood and was in a state of shock and collapse. Rather than risk mov-

241

ing him to a hospital, Kate attended to the wound in her home. The sight of the boy, who was as close to her as her own Tommy, gushing blood from the critical wound, almost unnerved the usually calm and self-possessed doctor. She shook so violently that she could scarcely bathe the wound, and Bill had to use a few volatile words to stiffen her backbone. She extracted the bullet and dressed the wound, and by the time Dick's parents arrived he was out of danger.

However, Kate had been so unnerved by the ordeal that she distractedly told Mrs. Birkholz to "put the hot water bottle on the hot water bottle." The laughter which followed brought her out of her jitters, and she ordered the hot water bottle to be put on the injured place without further chattering.

The Newcombs and the Birkholzes sat down together to a belated Thanksgiving dinner, and though the turkey was dried out, there was thankfulness at that table, for Dick was demanding his share of the feast. By evening the boy had recovered sufficiently to be moved to his own home and in a few weeks he was back at school gaily telling the story of "the hot water bottle on the hot water bottle."

Still another Thanksgiving interruption occurred on a stormy Thursday just as the family had sat down at the table. Grace had been said and Bill had raised the carving knife over the succulent golden-brown turkey when the phone rang. A groan went around the table, and Tommy came back with the bad news. Labor pains in Winchester. That meant a twenty-five-mile ride over blocked roads. Kate and Bill got up from the table and Bill readied the snowmobile.

They arrived in Winchester, after a slow and hazardous ride through snowdrifts that covered treacherous ice, just in time for Kate to deliver one of her very rare sets of twins! The grateful family wanted Kate and Bill to share their Thanksgiving feast but, hungry as they were, they headed back for home and found that the children had delayed their own dinner until their parents returned. The Newcombs are that kind of a family.

Some of Kate's stories of her northwoods practice are as mirth-provoking as they are incongruous. One day when she was making a call at some distance from her Woodruff office, she received a telephone call from a point thirty miles farther away. The woman who had tracked her down told this astonishing tale: She had been out fishing in a boat when she felt her labor pains begin. She had returned to her home and had her baby. She then got up, climbed into her pick-up truck and drove five miles to a place where there was a telephone to call up the doctor and ask her what to do next! Kate asked her if she had also delivered the afterbirth. No, the woman cheerfully replied, she had not. Kate gasped, and asked her where she was. The woman gave her the location, thirty miles away. Kate ordered her to stay right where she was, to get into bed immediately. She would get there as fast as she could.

When Kate arrived at the house from which the woman had telephoned, she learned that her patient had climbed back into the truck and returned to her own home. This, mind, without the vitally important delivery of the afterbirth! Kate hurried to the woman's home and found her sitting up in bed, bedecked in hair ribbon and bed jacket which she had put on to be tidy for the doctor's arrival. She calmly told the doctor she had prepared some tea for her and invited her to have a cup to refresh herself after her long ride. Kate, as she puts it, "nearly blew a fuse." She asked the woman if she had taken leave of her senses, and she made haste to get rid of the long-delayed afterbirth. There were no serious aftereffects, but the patient received a stern lecture on the danger of her foolhardy behavior which she was not likely to forget.

Then there was the night, in a storm, when the electric current failed. Kate delivered a baby by matchlight, and the child was known long afterward as "Dr. Kate's match baby."

Another of Kate's patients, after a difficult birth on the eve of Election, got out of bed against Kate's strict orders and went to the polls to cast her vote for the candidate of her choice. The woman took Kate's severe reprimand with good humor. Her candidate had won by that single vote!

One particularly crowded day, Kate had a call to make on a bedridden patient in a remote forest cabin. It was a sadly dilapidated hovel, the depth of poverty and squalor. Kate could scarcely find a place to put down her bag mid the chaos that littered the one-room shanty. She attended the patient and then, before returning to her car, she decided to stop at the tumble-down outhouse, as she had been too busy to attend to her own physical comfort.

When she gingerly opened the door of the grisly "Chick Sale" behind the main dwelling, she saw with astonishment that the "seat of honor" was upholstered with the furs of forest animals. The sight of such luxury, compared with the condition of the cabin, filled Kate with awe. However, the condition of the furs, from a sanitary viewpoint, was such that rather than avail herself of this dubious elegance, she decided to risk meeting the creatures in the flesh in the adjacent forest.

Kate made many of her calls over the lake ice on foot, and sometimes, when the ice thawed, she headed over the creek through the floes by boat. Norman McMahon's story, of a canoe trip through the broken ice of the creek, ending with the foundering of the craft, and with the doctor and Norman wading through the icy shallows to the shore, is only one of many more tales than could be recorded.

Kate received calls for help in treating sick horses and injured dogs, and while these unorthodox requests sometimes ruffled her feathers, she often gave directions for treatment that were of some aid to the stricken creatures. "Someday," she laughingly declared, "I'll be called on to deliver a cow of a calf!"

When Eldorah was a tiny girl, the constable's truck stopped at the Rice Creek house with a load of illegally shot deer. The constable was looking for Bill to help round up a band of illicit hunters responsible for the out-of-season kill. Eldorah, seeing the bleeding animals in the truck, rushed up to the constable and said, "Mamma isn't home now, but if you'll just leave them, she'll fix them up okay!"

In 1942, because of the rationing of gasoline, Kate opened an office in Woodruff to centralize her practice. Her quarters were in a second-floor loft over Ben Wright's general store across from the railroad station. She had scarcely moved into her new offices when she received the heartbreaking news that her father was seriously ill. Before she could make arrangements to get to him, she had word of his death. That year Kate drove many and many a mile with the tears rolling down her cheeks.

In 1942 Kate bought the house which is now her office and her Woodruff residence. One of the advantages of her move to Woodruff was her proximity to Carl's Pharmacy. Carl Krueger's drugstore, as it is today, compares favorably in size, stock and equipment—including a modern soda fountain—with any privately owned drugstore to be found in the large cities.

As for Carl himself, he is one of the leading citizens

of Woodruff. A tall, quiet-spoken man with the fair coloring of his German descent, Kate declares he has been her "right arm" in many an emergency. At any hour of the day or night, a call from her would bring Carl to her side with whatever drugs or prescriptions she happened to need. Carl claims he can judge the comparative reliability of doctors from their prescriptions. He states unequivocally that Dr. Kate's prescriptions have always been "ninety-nine per cent accurate," allowing one per cent for her conservative restraint insofar as dosing her patients with drugs is concerned. Kate has taken to heart old Dr. Torpy's conviction that "folks have a good chance of staying alive if you don't doctor them to death."

During the war years, Kate added another duty to her schedule. Tommy was attending the Arbor Vitae Woodruff High School, and Kate had entered Eldorah in the grade school there to save the Boulder Junction school bus the long trip to Rice Creek to fetch the child. On her way from Boulder to Woodruff each morning, Kate made several detours to pick up young students who needed transportation to the high school, arriving at Woodruff with a full load of young passengers, and returning them home, or sending them by her car if she was too busy to leave for Boulder herself.

Needless to say, all this meant endless mileage, but the worst trial were the long trips to Tomahawk and Rhinelander for hospital calls. She wondered how long she could keep up the gruelling grind, and her constant prayer was for a conveniently located hospital. To her own prayers, others were added.

A Quiet Wedding

THE winter of 'forty-seven and 'forty-eight found Kate going about her practice with a lighter heart. She had bought a two-story house on Second Street where she now had her office, with emergency living quarters where she could spend the night when the weather was too severe for the trip back to Boulder Junction. She had rented the upper floor to the young Dick Birkholzes who had been married the previous spring with Tommy as best man.

The hospital project was well under way. Dr. Torpy and other prominent citizens were enthusiastically promoting the venture which had now assumed official standing. The hospital committee had formed a corporation to consolidate the enterprise, calling it the Lakeland Memorial Hospital Fund. The Lions' Club added impetus to the drive by turning it into a community movement.

The people of Woodruff, Minocqua and Boulder Junction rallied behind the hospital committee with fervor. They held pie-baking contests, square dances and community suppers to swell the fund.

Plans were drawn up for a ten-room structure and while the cost estimated by the architect looked staggering compared with the slow rise of the collections, Kate felt confident that the sponsors of the fund would find means to achieve their goal, especially with so much interest being evinced by local business and summer people. Everyone seemed determined to provide "a hospital for Dr. Kate," as the venture was informally called in the community.

Another year passed and the hospital was still a maze of white lines on blue paper, with the fund still far from the necessary $110,000 which was the estimated cost of the building. With another winter of hard driving ahead, Kate drew some comfort from the knowledge that everything possible was being done to make the Woodruff hospital a reality. A site had been donated by Clarence G. Larson, a public-spirited employe of the telephone company. The lot was situated within easy distance of Kate's office, across from the Arbor Vitae Woodruff High School.

In January, 1949, an important family matter began to divert Kate's attention from the hospital fund which meant so much to her.

Tommy was attending Northland College at Ashland, where he was in his junior year. The years had flown by with the rapidity of a logging-sleigh on an "ice-road," and "Tommy Duck" had grown from lanky boyhood to the husky proportions of a football player. Six feet of flexible brawn, sinew and muscle, well tempered by his life in the forests, made him a formidable fullback on the college team. He had won his letter and was training to teach physical education as well as general subjects.

Tommy always came home late in January for the annual birthday party given for him by Mrs. Grauelle, his former grade-school teacher. This time Tommy telephoned his mother to ask whether he might bring "a girl" to spend the weekend at Boulder, as he wanted her to attend the party with him. Her name was Lola Williams and she had been a sophomore at Northland. She had cut short her college education to take a job with the Ashland Telephone Company, since she had no desire to pursue a career and thought the expense of college training a useless burden on her family. Lola sounded sensible from the very outset.

Kate assured her son she would be glad to entertain his friend. This was the only girl Tommy had ever asked her to invite to his home and Kate was naturally curious. She met the pair at the Woodruff station and found Lola a reserved, attractive and wholesome young woman, who won her immediate approval. Kate could see from the light in Tommy's eyes when he looked at Lola that this was no passing fancy. Her surmise was confirmed when Tommy confided that he had asked Lola to come with him so that she might decide whether his was a family she would like to belong to. He had not known her long, but he was sure from the first moment they met that she was the girl he would marry. Kate smiled as she remembered his father's prompt decision on the same subject. She realized with a pang that Tommy had reached the age when he was ready to build his own nest. As for Lola, she seemed to be all Kate and Bill could desire as a daughter—sensible, well-mannered, quiet-spoken, pretty in a winsome way, and obviously as much in love with Tommy as he was with her.

The approval was apparently reciprocal, for Tommy lost no time after that weekend in selecting the engagement ring, and he informed his mother that he and Lola were planning to be married in June. It seemed rather sudden, but Kate took a realistic view of the matter. Tommy was a man in body and mind, she told Bill, and it was far better to have him happily settled with this fine, wholesome girl than carousing around on the loose and perhaps getting into mischief.

Lola's parents, Mr. and Mrs. Stanley Williams, lived in Clintonville, about a hundred and twenty miles from Woodruff, and the two families lost no time in getting acquainted once Tom's and Lola's plans were definite. They were delighted to find each other highly congenial. "Boss" Williams, Lola's father, was an ardent hunter and fisherman, which suited Bill to a T. "Momo," her mother, was all that could be wished for as a real mother and homemaker and she and Kate struck up an immediate "entente" concerning everything that involved their families. Judy, Lola's younger sister, was exactly Eldorah's age and the two teenagers hit it off together from the first, while David, the only boy in the family gave Tommy his unqualified approval and listened in awe as the renowned Bill Newcomb swapped stories of hunting exploits with "Boss."

Tommy still had a year to go at Northland, and with a wife to consider, there was the problem of maintaining a household. He assured his mother they could get along very well on his allowance with Lola keeping her job to help out until he finished his studies. He would then be eligible for a teaching post, and with the extra money he earned as a guide during the summer season, he was sure they could manage.

Kate thought this over. Remembering her son's lack of a mother's care during her early years of practice, when he had expressed the wish that she were "a cookie mother instead of a doctor mother," she decided to raise his allowance so that his wife could make a proper home for him. Kate's only request was that they be married at her beloved church in Boulder Junction. Lola agreed gladly. All she wanted was a quiet wedding, and that seemed a reasonable request.

Kate looked over her list of friends with a selective eye. Which of them could she invite to Tommy's "quiet wedding" without offending the others? Her quandary became acute. There were few people in Boulder Junction and points north, east, west and south, who weren't eligible for the guest list on the basis of long friendship with the Newcomb family. By the time she got through making her list, Kate had two hundred and fifty people who simply could not be left out! Tommy was as much their boy as he was hers. They had seen him grow from a toddling baby to a strapping young college athlete, and all of Boulder Junction had "mothered" Tommy while his busy mother tended their sick. No, none of them could be left out.

She called Lola at Ashland and told her that at least two hundred and fifty invitations would have to be reserved for Tommy's Boulder Junction friends. Lola gasped. She couldn't possibly have a wedding of such proportions, she wailed in consternation.

Kate assured her that all she needed to do was to arrive at Boulder for the ceremony, and the rest would be taken care of at Kate's end of the line. She and Bill would hold the reception at the Rice Creek house. Lola wouldn't have a thing to worry about except to send out the invitations to the wedding. Lola protested against the trouble and expense to her bridegroom's family, but Kate assured her she owed her friends a party and this was a good occasion for it.

On her trip to Boulder, Tommy had taken Lola to meet his close friends, the Birkholzes. Dick's mother, Mrs. Crystal Birkholz, learning that the romance was headed toward a June wedding, suggested that the date be set for June fifteenth, the date of her own wedding anniversary. Her marriage had been a very happy one, and she believed that date would be just as auspicious for Tom and Lola. The date was set and the invitations issued.

As for the reception, Kate tacked up a notice in the Boulder Junction and Woodruff post offices announcing the reception and inviting all who could to come to the Rice Creek house and join in the celebration of Tommy's wedding, which would take place at the Boulder Junction Community Church on June fifteenth at one thirty P.M.

Attending to her practice with one hand and the wedding preparations with the other, Kate found this business of getting her son married far more than she could manage, and with the usual good neighborliness of the northwoods, her friends in Boulder and Woodruff jumped into the breach and Tommy's wedding became a community project. Kate ordered a cake only to find that the second Mrs. Larry Doolittle had also had one baked, and so there were two huge cakes for the occasion.

On the day of the wedding, the Rice Creek house, which had by this time become a large, sprawling eight-room forest villa with all modern conveniences, was crowded to capacity with the two families. Lola, her sister Judy, her brother David, and her father and mother, "Boss" and "Momo" Williams, had come from Clintonville the previous day. Lola's description of her frantic wedding morning, which was a real test of the bride's disposition, is well worth recording:

"Everybody was getting ready at once, and I flew around until the last minute in my blue jeans, T-shirt and sneakers, with my hair up in curlers, helping them all to dress. I combed Judy's and mother's hair, got mother into her girdle, zipped up everybody's dresses and pinned on their corsages. I hadn't even had a chance at the bathtub. Tommy needed a haircut and had to be shooed off with Bill to get to the barber's. They took so long that I began to get worried, but by the time I was dressed, they finally turned up and we got under way. It takes a lot to rattle me, but I will admit that morning had me pretty close to the jitters."

The simple northwoods church, its hall a golden background of waxed spruce with an arched ceiling of the same polished wood, was decorated with pine boughs, its altar glowing with tall white tapers among huge baskets of white gladioli. The pews were jammed and the road outside the building was crowded with an overflow crowd. People had come from Manitowish and Sayner, from Mercer and Ironwood and Eagle River, from Woodruff and Rhinelander and Wausau and Tomahawk, from Clintonville and even from Madison, Milwaukee and Chicago, to witness the marriage of "Tommy Duck" Newcomb and Lola Williams.

The bride wore a white suit and a small veiled hat to match. Her maid of honor was her close friend, Carol Collier, and the two bridesmaids were Eldorah Newcomb and Lola's sister Judy. The church hall radiated youth as the young Reverend Wilfred Hansen performed the ceremony and the strains of "I Love You Truly" and "Because" vibrated through the church structure. As Tom and Lola repeated their vows, the faces of that sentimental congregation streamed with tears. The years had flown so fast. Here was little "Tommy Duck," whose exuberant exploits in the woodlands had seemed the incarnation of young Pan himself, now standing solemnly beside his pretty bride, taking the vows of matrimony.

They knelt and a beautiful soprano voice sang "The

Lord's Prayer," throwing its benediction over them and the congregation.

"I think I was the only one in the church who wasn't weeping," Kate recalls, "But I will admit I had a big lump in my throat."

The ceremony was over and rice pelted the newly-weds. Tommy was so nervous that he began introducing his bride as his "girl friend." The wedding party and the entire congregation, including those who crowded the grounds outside the church, adjourned to the Newcomb home at Rice Creek where tables had been laid under the pines. The huge buffet luncheon was attended by so many people that Kate did not even attempt to count them. There was plenty of food and cake and fruit punch and coffee to go around, and enough left over for another wedding.

The bridal pair had decided to escape the usual pranks played on country newlyweds by hiding their car on a trail down the creek and heading for it in an outboard motor-boat. This had all been carefully arranged by Bill. The elated pair climbed into the waiting craft and headed down-creek toward their car, waving jubilant good-bys to their guests on the shore.

When the boat reached the middle of the creek, the motor coughed, sputtered and went dead. There they sat, in the gathering dusk, marooned on the creek. The hilarity on shore was mingled with sympathetic groans. Tommy fumed and fussed with the engine, while Lola, with the good humor that makes her a jewel among women, sat in the stern of the boat, convulsed with laughter. The madder Tommy grew, the harder Lola laughed.

Another boat took off to the rescue. Kate watched from the shore, her eyes shaded against the red of the sunset. Bill stood at her side and slipped a hand through her arm. He was shaking with laughter as he watched the rescue. Tommy's nice light wedding suit was streaked with grease and he had to come back to the house and change to second-best for his wedding trip.

Kate gave Bill a sidelong glance as Tommy and Lola dashed back into the house to the cheers and applause of the crowd.

"I suppose *you* thought that one up," Kate said to Bill severely.

Bill looked at her with indignant innocence wiping out his merriment. "*Me?*" he replied in horrified protest. "Now, Kate, you know I'd never do a thing like that!" Well, no one knows to this day whether Bill did or didn't. Of course, he is an expert mechanic, and he would know exactly how to "doodle" an engine as well as how to fix one. But he staunchly denies any complicity in the prank.

The honeymooners finally got started on their wedding trip with a cheering crowd of well-wishers throwing rice and old shoes after the car. And this, mind you, was to have been a "quiet wedding!"

Disaster at Rice Creek

TOMMY and Lola returned to spend the summer at Rice Creek and went back to Ashland in September to begin Tommy's senior year at Northland. When they came home for Thanksgiving, they told Kate and Bill that they would be grandparents the following spring.

Kate's joy over the happy news was suddenly shadowed by word of Dr. Torpy's illness. He was taken to the Sacred Heart Hospital at Tomahawk where his condition was pronounced critical. Kate went to visit him and found him shockingly wasted. She knew his time was short, but she concealed her emotion and tried to cheer him by bringing him news of the progress of the hospital fund, and reminding him that he had pledged himself to help her organize the staff. The old doctor scowled at her over his glasses and said in his frail, husky voice:

"You know blankety-blank well that you're not going to see me alive again, so cut out the——" et cetera, et cetera. Obviously his condition had not impaired his "mule-skinner" vocabulary. Then he added more gently, "I want you to do me a favor, Kate."

She assured him she would do anything he asked.

256

"Look after Pinemere for me, will you?" he implored her.

Pinemere was the girls' camp at which he was the official doctor, and it was the joy of his life. Kate promised faithfully that she would look after Pinemere and took leave of him with a heavy heart.

She received news of his death shortly afterward, and she grieved with the rest of the northwoods people over his passing.

Townsfolk, forest people, loggers, guides, Indians and summer residents all mourned the death of "Papa Zers" with a grief that has not been equalled in the woodlands. He was followed to his grave by a weeping countryside and his name is spoken with tenderness by those to whom he gave his gruff, reliable devotion during fifty-five years of selfless practice.

Dr. Torpy's death increased Kate's responsibility in the community, as many of his patients now sought her out, and she found herself busy day and night carrying the burden.

The winter lasted into April of 1950, and snow still covered the ground as May blustered into the northwoods in a series of cyclonic squalls which shook the pines and churned the waters. The wind mounted steadily until it reached a velocity of nearly eighty miles an hour. It devastated the forests, hurling down huge trees as though they were matchsticks.

On the night of Friday, May fifth, as Kate was about to start through the wind and snow for a weekend of needed relaxation under her own roof, her telephone rang, and Bill's shaking voice told her in his brusque way to stay where she was. It was useless for her to come home, he said, as there was no house for her to come home to. He was tele-

257

phoning from Boulder. Their home and everything it contained had burned to the ground.

Kate's hands turned to ice on the metal of the instrument. Her pulse throbbed like a drumbeat.

"Are *you* all right?" she managed to ask through the turmoil of her shattered senses. Yes, Bill said, he'd got out in time. Fortunately, Eldorah had gone to Woodruff to see a movie. So she was safe. But three of the dogs were gone, though he'd saved Lady, his oldest hound.

"How—how did it happen?" Kate stammered, her voice unsteady.

"The wind—it blew out the flame in the oil heater. I guess it backed the fumes down the flue and they caught fire from the red-hot feeder. The tank blew up. It all happened so fast, Kate, I barely had time to get out in my undershirt. I got the car away in time and drove over here to call you. Everything's gone, Kate, everything." She heard his voice break and she knew the grief that lay behind it.

"As long as everyone's safe, Bill," she consoled him gently.

"I'm going back and stay in the cottage. Just you stay where you are, Kate. There's nothing you can do out here."

Kate hung up the instrument with numb fingers. Her home was gone. Everything they possessed, everything they treasured, had been in that house. Their clothing, their books, their silver, their furniture—and many of Tommy and Lola's wedding presents as well! All she had left were the few things she kept at her office to make shift with during the week in case she couldn't get back to Boulder. In those days she generally managed to return home after her work was done at the office, unless an o.b. or another emergency made it necessary for her to go to the hospital at Tomahawk, or to sleep on the improvised bed in the room that adjoined the little kitchen.

She picked up the telephone and called long distance to Ashland—Tommy and Lola's apartment. Lola answered. Tommy was out for a few minutes. Kate sat there, unable to form the words to convey the terrible news. "What is it, Mother?" Lola asked anxiously. "The house at Boulder burned down——" Kate's voice broke in a sob. She could hear the gasp that signified Lola's shock. "Anyone——? Is Bill—all right?" she asked after a brief moment. "He's all right—no one hurt—tell Tommy——" Kate could not speak any more. She slid the phone back into the cradle. The tears were flowing now. Bill was safe. Eldorah was safe. Tommy and Lola were safe. She was safe. Everything else was gone, but her family was safe, and she dropped her head on her clasped hands and thanked God for His blessing.

Later she learned that Bill had been badly scorched and his leg had been injured while pulling a chest of hunting ammunition out of the path of the rapidly spreading blaze, to prevent an explosion that might set fire to the summer cottage. Other ammunition, still in the burning structure, had exploded from time to time during the night as the flames reached it.

Kate heard the story of that night piecemeal when she was finally allowed to go to Boulder. She learned that when Bill arrived at the market with the news, their friends had tried to persuade him to remain there. But he had insisted upon returning to his own place.

"Nothing is going to drive me off my place," the doughty Bill had declared. "Not even a blankety-blank-blank of a fire!" And he had limped off to his car and returned to the scene of the holocaust. By this time several cars had arrived to view the disaster. Smoke and flames still poured from the ruins, and only the snow on the floor of the surrounding forest and the wetness of the trees prevented the fire from spreading through the woods. There had been nothing to do but let it burn itself out.

When Tommy arrived late that night with two of his friends, he was dumbfounded at what he saw. Cars crowded the roadway, and the trail of smoke led to a smoldering ruin that had once been his home.

All night Bill's neighbors came, pouring into the cottage with emergency supplies. Food, bedding, shirts, shoes, soap, dishes, cooking utensils, and wood for the stove. The tragedy at Rice Creek brought all Bill's friends and neighbors for miles around to offer their help. Bill received them, steadying his shaking limbs and coughing out the smoke that had filled his lungs as he swore away his grief. Kate's home, their cherished house, their carefully planned and slowly built woodland refuge, with all the comforts they had struggled so hard and so long to install, pump, generator, modern bathroom, kitchen sink—all a smoking crackling ruin on the snowy knoll. His valuable collection of guns, carefully gathered over the years were all gone.

But the tramping boots and the rough voices that rang through the cottage around him, somehow eased his pain.

The moment the news of the fire reached Woodruff, Kate's doorstep was crowded with friends eager to be of help. Her telephone rang continuously. What did she need? What could they do for her? Hundreds of hands reached out with gifts to replace the possessions she had lost.

In the days, weeks and months that followed, the communities of Boulder Junction and Woodruff and the surrounding towns, did their best to duplicate or substitute the furnishings Kate had lost in the fire. There were no substitutes for the family albums, the heirlooms and the mementos that had gone up in smoke. But some old snapshots of Tommy and Eldorah were rounded up and reproduced to replace Kate's burned photographs of the children. Her valuable first editions of Dickens and Thackeray and Wordsworth were irreplaceable, but her friends collected what books they could to start a new library.

Bill had had a stock of lumber with which he had planned to build another addition to the house. The wood was gone, and the next morning the man he had engaged to begin work that very day appeared and said sadly that he supposed he wouldn't be needed.

"The h—— you won't!" Bill replied. "We're getting to work right now to fix up this place for an all-year residence. You can start by pulling down the back porch of this cottage so we can build a room there for my daughter. This kitchen shed comes down, too. I want a real kitchen here. Let's get to work, bub. We need a place to live and we need it quick."

Stub Nelson, Mel Kenaga's son-in-law had arrived the night before with equipment and installed a telephone so that Bill would not be isolated on the creek without communication. Bill telephoned for a new shipment of lumber and the winterizing of the cottage got under way.

His faithful friend Mel Kenaga, and another carpenter, set to work on the cottage, and Bill made an effort to help. But his leg pained and his hands shook, and at one point they found him in a heap on the ground. The shock of the fiery nightmare was taking its toll. Bill brushed off his weakness lightly and tried to fight the pain and the spells of dizziness, but he found that he was more of a hindrance than a help, and he gave up and sat in the sun, staring out at the creek. The snarling wind had subsided. An acrid spring was in the air at Rice Creek.

Kate came to the cottage and they looked into each other's eyes without needing to speak. She went with him to see the charred remains of their home, and they stood there as though beside the bier of a loved one.

The worst of the damage was to Bill himself. If only he had turned off the heater when he'd had a hunch to do so. He might have known that wind would play tricks. Unreasonably, he blamed himself for the tragedy and self-recrimination bit deeply into his conscience. Kate scolded him for his bitterness. It had been an accident. He had had no way of anticipating the vagaries of the wind. He might well have lost his life in the disaster. Bill replied grimly that it might have been better if he had. Kate comforted him as best she could and prayed that time would banish his despondency.

The cottage was soon rebuilt into a comfortable all-year home. The generator was replaced, a bathroom installed, and Kate insisted that she liked the smaller house even better than she had the big one. It was easier to take care of. Bill merely tightened his quivering lips and turned away. He did everything he could to improve their new quarters and make room for the gifts that continued to flow in from friends and well-wishers. More books, more clothing, furniture, lamps, stoves, heaters, bedding, tools, even a few guns to replace the valuable collection Bill had lost, and which he mourned almost as much as he did the beloved hounds that had perished in the fire.

There had been enough insurance on their old place to pay about half the cost of remodeling the cottage, but no payment could compensate them for their treasured keepsakes, or their pets.

Slowly, gradually, their life began to resume its old rhythm. And something more had come into it. Each article they handled spoke of the devotion of their friends. Patients, businessmen, church members, everyone was represented in the flood of new belongings that filled the rebuilt cottage.

The family silver, once rescued from the threatening fire at Stone Lake, lay in melted blobs on the charred ruins of Kate's antique cupboard. The silver they now had was ordinary kitchen ware, but it was also a message of affection. Their blankets were not only wool; they were the enveloping warmth of friendship. Their heads lay on pillows that had been placed there by hands and hearts full of concern for their comfort.

"It was a terrible thing to lose our home," says Kate, "but sometimes I think we got something much more valuable in return, something no fire can ever burn and time cannot destroy. To this day, almost five years later, we continue to receive pictures that our friends feel belong in our collection, and gifts that they think may have been overlooked."

On Memorial Day, only a few weeks after the fire, Kate and Bill received news that Lola had presented Tom with a daughter. She was named Kathleen, after her grandmother, and the Newcombs rejoiced in their new role as grandparents. The glad tidings helped them to forget the loss of their home.

In June, when Tommy graduated from Northland, Kate and Bill took a trip to Ashland to attend the exercise and to see their first grandchild. Kate admits that she has a special predilection for Kathleen, who came to them as a consolation prize for the loss of their home. She is fully satisfied that they got the best of the bargain.

Pale Horseman

THE mercurial events of May 1950, ranging from the stark tragedy of the fire to the happiness at Kathy's birth, leveled off as the spring flowed into summer and Kate watched her granddaughter bloom and grow. Tommy and Lola and the baby spent the summer in the boathouse cabin at Rice Creek, and so far as they were concerned, the world was a garden and the ruin on the knoll was an irrelevant parenthesis in their idyll of fulfillment. Tommy worked at the Birkholz filling station and garage at Minocqua to help with expenses, while Bill nursed his painful leg injury and fumed nervously at being unable to go about his usual summer engagements as a guide.

He waved wistfully as the other guides passed through the creek with their fishing parties, and confined his efforts to improving the house and renting boats to summer people. Bill's scars were deep. His sinuses and his lungs were still inflamed from the smoke he had inhaled and his nerves had been badly jarred by the shock of the fire. His hands sometimes trembled so badly that he could not hold a tool or a cup, and the frustration of his condition added fury to misery.

At Woodruff, the hospital fund had reached a total of some forty thousand dollars, which was a sizable amount considering the sparsely populated area. There had been some talk of borrowing from a bank to begin construction, but the summer passed without definitive action being taken, and with a sinking heart Kate faced another winter of snowy miles. She wondered how many more years it would take to bring the hospital out of the blueprints into solid reality.

Bill was not well enough to lend his strong arm to the wheel that winter, and Kate made her long trips around the countryside alone. One night it took her four hours to drive back from Tomahawk through a blizzard. Her car skidded into a ditch and she had to flag the passing traffic for help to get it out and rolling again. Cars were few and far between in such weather, and houses are widely spaced along the road to Tomahawk, making it out of the question to attempt to reach a telephone.

Would she live long enough to enjoy the relief of having a hospital at Woodruff, or would it be built as a memorial to her hopes only after she was gone? She knew her friends on the hospital-fund committee were doing their best, but the estimate of the total cost, including equipment, was now figured around fifty thousand dollars, and at the present rate of contributions it did not look as though an adequate amount could possibly be raised within her lifetime.

There was one consoling gleam in her overcast sky that winter. Lola was well on her way with another child. That fall Tom and Lola had moved into the apartment above the Woodruff office, when the young Birkholzes had gone to live in the new home they had built close to Dick's family home. Having Tommy and Lola and Kathy under the same roof with her at Woodruff kept Kate from being too depressed by the slow progress of the hospital project.

In May, 1951, at the Sacred Heart Hospital in Tomahawk, Kate had the thrill of delivering her second grandchild, the first to be born under her supervision. Michael Thomas Newcomb, born at eight forty-five on the beautiful spring evening of May twelfth, weighed nine pounds and eight ounces, and arrived without difficulty and without fear. Lola had been carefully instructed in the Read method in the months preceding her confinement.

The Sisters were jubilant over the event, and little Mike, a robust tow-head, was borne to the nursery by a bevy of white-clad "good fairies" who poured smiles and blessings on him as he was laid in his bassinette.

The corner room where Lola lay in smiling relaxation was a Star Chamber to the Sisters, for it was the mother of Dr. Newcomb's own grandson who was their guest, and this was an occasion for great rejoicing and the bearing of dainty gifts made by the Sisters in anticipation of the event.

Never had they seen their doctor so radiant. A stir of festivity filled the quiet halls of the old hospital as the rustling, whispering nuns, with beaming faces, gathered around Kate to embrace and congratulate her.

Young Mike thrived and was beautiful to behold. He looked like Tommy except for his pale gold hair and his blue, blue eyes. As for Kathy, she was still "Grandma's girl." Her interest in the new baby was possessive and maternal. She toddled back and forth to see if he were asleep or awake and pressed kisses on his fat cheeks and fuzzy head whenever he was within her reach.

Kathy's hair was exceptionally long for a baby, and at eighteen months she had a Page Boy bob, with straight bangs across the "japonesque" brown eyes that so resembled her grandmother's childhood photographs.

Kate's children, big and small, absorbed her every unoccupied moment, and Kathy's passionate adoration was balm to "Gramma's" weariness.

Winter meant Christmas, and this year Mike's little hand would light the Christ child candle for the Newcomb window sill.

Then it was 1952, and there was still no hospital, but the fund had reached almost fifty thousand dollars during the past year. Everything had gone according to plan for Tom and Lola. They had a girl and a boy. They wanted another girl and another boy. A family of four was their objective, and they intended to have them all while they were still young enough to enjoy them.

So far so good. Their marriage was happy and fruitful. Lola was a calm, competent mother, a gentle wife and a good cook. Tom was contented at home, and he had begun teaching the previous fall at the Sugar Camp School about twenty-five miles from Woodruff. He guided during the summers and went duck-hunting in the fall, and ice-fishing during the winter.

On Wednesday evenings he went to the Arbor Vitae Woodruff High School gymnasium where the young men of the town met for "Men's Night." Here they tossed the ball around the basketball court and relived their high-school days.

One Wednesday evening in March, Tommy returned home from the "gym" complaining of a sore throat. There had been an epidemic of virus flu in the community, and Lola surmised he had picked up a "bug." She gave him a hot drink and got him to bed early so he would have a good rest and perhaps throw off the symptoms by morning.

The next morning Tom complained of a severe headache, and the soreness in his throat persisted. His mother administered some medication and tried to persuade him to stay home from school, but he was coaching his basketball teams for a tournament and insisted upon going to Sugar Camp. Kate was concerned about the flu epidemic which was widespread and severe. She had told Lola that she was afraid this particularly virulent type of influenza might have serious complications. However, knowing Tommy's healthy resistance to any kind of illness, she did not let her mind dwell on his indisposition but went about her practice as usual through the heavy weather.

Tommy returned home Thursday evening still feeling ill. He told Lola he had had to lie down in the school infirmary most of the afternoon. He felt nauseated and ate little at supper. He was anxious to be in condition for the basketball tournament which was scheduled for the following week; he had four teams playing and he couldn't afford to miss that important event. Kate came upstairs to look him over that evening and she administered an antibiotic, hoping that it would check the symptoms of influenza which continued to distress him. He had no temperature, but his throat still felt sore and the nausea persisted.

On Friday, he felt worse and Lola kept him in bed. He complained of nightmares, and Lola remembered that he had been restless and jumpy in his sleep the past three nights. This was unusual, as he was generally a sound sleeper. On Saturday he felt worse. The congestion in his throat was so acute that he could not swallow even liquids. On Sunday he claimed he felt better and wanted to have some friends in to play cards, but Lola decided he had better rest if he wanted to be fit for the basketball tournament, which was to open the following evening with a game at Rhinelander.

By Sunday evening another symptom developed which caused Kate considerable alarm. Tommy's left arm had begun to twitch with an uncontrollable convulsive movement, and he complained that his legs ached.

On Monday morning, Tommy insisted he felt all right, if only he could get his throat cleared up. It felt sore and kept filling with mucous, and when he tried to eat a hamburger which he asked Lola to fix for him, it nearly strangled him. By afternoon, the twitching of his arm had become more pronounced and his left leg was entirely out of control. Kate had been trying to get him to agree to go to a hospital for a thorough examination, and now she put her foot down and telephoned for the local ambulance. It was not available, so she telephoned to the constable's office and asked Don Gongaware, the constable and her old friend in emergencies, if he would come by with his siren-equipped car to take Tommy to St. Mary's Hospital at Rhinelander. Don arrived with one of his aides almost before Kate could hang up the receiver. His eyes were filled with concern, for Tommy had always been one of his favorite youngsters. He had seen him grow, boy to man, and the fact that he was sick enough to need hospitalization was a deep personal anxiety to him as a family friend.

By this time the leg was twitching so badly that it was difficult for Tommy to walk without support, so the two men helped him down the stairs and into the car.

Lola had telephoned her mother in Clintonville asking her to come to Woodruff to stay with the children so she could join Tommy at the hospital. "Momo" Williams was on her way, but Lola had to stay with the children until her

269

mother covered the hundred and twenty odd miles from Clintonville.

The constable's car speeded over the snowy Highway 47 to Rhinelander with the siren wailing to clear the way. At Rhinelander, Kate asked the driver to stop at the office of Dr. Frances A. Cline, her friend and associate. She felt the need of the presence of another doctor in this hour of frightening emergency, and Dr. Cline accompanied them to the hospital. At the ambulance entrance, Tommy was lifted into a wheel chair and taken to a room where he was put to bed while Kate consulted with the resident doctors, describing her son's symptoms and registering him for observation.

Lola waited anxiously for her mother to arrive. Time dragged with agonizing slowness. With the snowy roads, it might be hours before Mrs. Williams got there. Lola's usual calm was shaken and she moved around the apartment in icy perturbation, tending the children and waiting—waiting—waiting.

At seven o'clock, Carl Kreuger, the local druggist and Kate's old friend, came to Lola and told her that Tommy was being transferred from the Rhinelander hospital to St. Mary's in Wausau. He would take her to Tomahawk to meet the Rhinelander ambulance there so she could accompany her husband to the Wausau hospital. Lola was puzzled by the transfer to Wausau, but she asked no questions. She hurriedly called a sitter to stay with the children until her mother arrived, and left for Tomahawk with Carl.

When they reached the appointed spot, they waited for about fifteen minutes with no sign of the expected ambulance. Carl went to a nearby lunchstand and telephoned only to learn that the Rhinelander ambulance had been delayed by engine trouble on the outskirts of Tomahawk, and that the Tomahawk ambulance was picking up the passengers and would meet them as soon as it could.

The Tomahawk ambulance finally arrived, and Lola got aboard. It was, grimly enough, the glass-enclosed town hearse, which was also used as an ambulance when the occasion required. This is not unusual in small communities which cannot afford both conveyances.

Kate, in the improvised ambulance with Tommy and Doctor Cline, made room for Lola at Tommy's side. She had been using a suction valve to clear his throat, as the congestion had become so acute that it was difficult for him to breathe.

As the driver helped Lola into the car, he said, "Don't worry, Mrs. Newcomb, they can't kill an Irishman on St. Patrick's Day." For the first time Kate realized that this was the fateful seventeenth of March, a day which seemed to bring strange events into her life.

Lola still did not understand the reason for the shift to the Wausau hospital. It was not until they arrived at St. Mary's that the truth was revealed to her. Tommy was taken to the isolation ward, a glass-enclosed section used for highly contagious cases. Then Kate explained that the examination at Rhinelander had produced a diagnosis which demanded immediate isolation. Tommy had symptoms of what might be an acute form of polio. Since St. Mary's at Wausau had one of the best polio wards in the state, and a laboratory for immediate analysis, he had been transferred there for further observation.

Mother and wife looked into each other's eyes, numb with the unutterable emotions that flooded over them. Dr. Cline stood by, helpless to comfort them. The case was now in the hands of Dr. Donald Greene, who was in charge of isolation cases at St. Mary's. He was examining the patient, having a spinal tap made for the laboratory, and X rays would be made of the head and spinal column.

There was nothing to be done that night except make the patient comfortable. A night nurse was available but arrangements would have to be made to engage a day nurse as there was no one at the hospital free to take that shift. Dr. Greene suggested that the women go to a hotel and return in the morning, when he would be better able to give them a diagnosis.

Dr. Cline accompanied them to the nearest hotel. They engaged a room and Dr. Cline went home, saying she would return to the hospital in the morning. Kate telephoned for a nurse to take over the day shift, but she was unable to find anyone. Nurses were scarce, and on a contagious case —well—they became scarcer. Lola telephoned the apartment. Her mother had arrived and all was well there. What about Tommy? No change, said Lola. They would know tomorrow.

There was no sleep for either Kate or Lola that night. They lay in the darkness, staring into the black fear of tomorrow. Kate got up and called the hospital. There was no change. No, he was not asleep. He was being made as comfortable as possible. The telephone rang. It was Bill. He was at Woodruff. He had come down from Boulder. What was it? Evasively, Kate told him they would know in the morning. Everything was being done; he wasn't to worry. People were telephoning, he said. They wanted to know. She would call him tomorrow, Kate said.

Early the next morning, mother and wife left for the hospital. Since they had been unable to engage a day nurse, they would take care of Tommy themselves during the daytime hours. They put on the sterile gowns and caps and entered the isolation ward. Tommy had been moved to a room where an iron lung stood in readiness outside the door. Kate's heart sank as her eyes fell on the significant equipment. Lola looked at her; both their faces blanched.

Dr. Greene stepped out of the room and said he would like to question Lola in order to complete his diagnosis. Kate said she would take over from the night nurse and entered the room. Lola followed Dr. Greene to his office, where he questioned her at some length. Had her husband shown any previous symptoms of nervousness or erratic behavior? No, he had not. The doctor asked her innumerable questions which puzzled her. What was he trying to get at? He explained that he wanted to eliminate all contingent possibilities.

At last Kate and Lola heard the diagnosis. Tommy was suffering from a virulent type of polio known as "bulbar," complicated by meningitis and encephalitis. Encephalitis was an infection of the brain tissue. Kate heard the verdict with anguished realization. She knew that "bulbar poliomyelitis" was most virulent when it attacked a vigorous organism. She knew that it paralyzed the throat and respiratory system and that its mortality rate was very high.

Dr. Greene had only two fragments of encouragement to offer. He told them that if Tommy lived through the attack, he would have no serious aftereffects. The malady either killed, or it subsided without inflicting the paralysis produced by other types of polio. He also told them that, so far as he could determine, the patient's lungs had not been affected. Only his throat was involved, but there was a positive reading of meningitis in the laboratory test of the spinal fluid, and there was inflammation of the brain tissue.

Kate felt as though she were split in two parts. One wrung its hands and prayed for the life of her son. The other, calm and clinical, consulted with the physician and observed the condition of the patient. When Dr. Greene gave her the encouraging news about the normal condition of Tommy's lungs, she measured the information in terms of percentage for or against recovery, and told the mother in herself that while the chances were favorable, she must not hope too much.

All day Tuesday, Kate and Lola, in the sterilized white gowns and masks required by the isolation ward, took turns in caring for Tommy. His throat had to be siphoned continually, his elimination had to be attended to, and intravenous feedings and hydration had to be watched and regulated. Both Dr. Kate and Mother Kate realized the sturdy fiber of Tommy's wife in those hours of ordeal. The women worked in four-hour shifts until the night nurse again took over. Hardly a word was spoken as they cared for the boy who was dearer to them than anything on earth.

Tommy babbled in a strangled voice. Lola listened. His inflamed brain was conjuring horrors—pursuit—torture —conspiracy to kill him.

Dr. Greene administered heavy doses of penicillin. He told Kate later how heavy they had been, and that he had injected them directly into the spinal cord. Had she known it at the time she might have been alarmed, as this maximum dosage of the antibiotic into the spinal cord was still in an experimental stage. Yet Dr. Greene administered it, for he knew that only the most extreme treatment would be of any avail against the killer that had Tommy Newcomb by the throat.

Bill came to the hospital and stood at the bedside in the masquerade of sterile white, staring blindly at his beloved son. Kate's eyes met his bleakly over their gauze masks. These two had never needed words to express what they felt, nor did they need them now. She led him to the door and told him to go to the hotel and wait there for her.

Bill went to the dressing room and removed the investiture, washed his hands four times according to strict regulations, and went to the hotel to wait there for Kate. "Boss" Williams was there. To his questioning look Bill replied only by shaking his head. He went to the window and looked out at the still whiteness of the night. It was too still. Even the stormy temper of March had subsided, waiting. Kate arrived and both men looked at her face; white and worn it told them nothing. "Boss" asked her if she would eat something. She shook her head. She had had some tea and toast at the hospital. Then she told them how bad it was. Bill sat down beside her and took her hands and they clung to each other with silent sobs. "Boss" dropped his head in his hands. Others came. The telephone rang. The word had already reached Woodruff.

That day and the next many people came to Wausau from Woodruff and from Boulder, a distance of over sixty miles. Dick Birkholz came every day, though he was not permitted to enter the sickroom. Only Tom's mother, his wife, and Crystal Birkholz, the most intimate family friend, were admitted to his bedside. Other visitors stood at the glass wall of the isolation wall, with faces of helpless despair, some streaming with tears, some too frozen with horror to weep. Only two springs ago they had seen Tommy, straight and radiant at the chancel of the Boulder Junction church, a glowing bridegroom. Less than a year ago they had rejoiced with him at the birth of his son. And now he lay stricken and rigid in a hospital bed, with tubes and needles and jars suspended around him and white-clad figures hovering over him like ghosts.

In Woodruff, in Boulder Junction, and in all the communities where Dr. Kate and her family were known and loved, a pall hung over the roads, the streets and the forests. People walked through the streets or met at the shopping centers, their faces drawn with anxiety. Meeting, they searched each other's eyes for a sign of relief from the suspense and fear that haunted them. What could they do for her who had done so much for them? Nothing. They could only wait and pray. Yes, they could pray, and they did pray.

Services were held in the little church at Boulder, and in every church in that area. People who had never gone to church before, went now to pray for Tommy Newcomb and for his anguished mother, their beloved Dr. Kate, who had been assailed by an enemy far more cruel than any they had encountered. Masses were held at the Catholic altars, and in the chapel of the Catholic hospitals where Kate had worked, the white coifed sisters prayed in a continuous chain. The citadel of heaven was besieged on all sides for Tommy Newcomb's life.

The first Sugar Camp team played the opening game of the basketball tournament at Rhinelander the Monday night that Tommy was taken to the hospital, but after that the games were cancelled and Tommy's pupils were placed under a precautionary quarantine once the seriousness of their teacher's illness was known. They went to class, then straight to their homes. They were forbidden to go to any public places, or to visit other families until symptoms of possible infection had been given a chance to appear. None did, fortunately.

One of Tommy's pupils, lying awake in sleepless anxiety, woke his father and asked him to help him pray for his teacher. The father, deeply touched, knelt with the boy, and they prayed together. On Wednesday, he asked his father to take him to see Mr. Newcomb. He was sure that if he could just see him, his teacher would surely get well. The snow had begun again, with violent north winds, and that trip to Wausau was made through blinding storm. But young David Sowinski's father would not deny his boy the comfort of seeing his teacher and bringing his prayers in person.

On Wednesday afternoon, Tommy began fighting the intravenous equipment. He had some fantastic hallucination that the doctor was a secret agent of a sinister power, who was extracting his blood and carrying it away to harm others. Lola was the only one who could understand his strangled and incoherent ravings. Kate was so unnerved by her boy's violence that the doctor ordered her to return to the hotel and wait. Tommy, in a burst of insensate fury, had stripped off the intravenous feeding equipment and flung himself at the doctor. He had to be forcibly restrained, and Kate feared the worst. His brain condition must have reached a critical and perhaps fatal stage, she wept, as she told of the terrifying development to her friend, Crystal Birkholz, who was waiting at the hotel for her. Mrs. Birkholz went to the hospital, leaving Kate with her son and daughter-in-law who had come down from Woodruff with her. She put on the sterile gown and mask and entered the isolation ward. Lola met her and led her to Tommy's bedside, hoping the presence of this dear friend who had been as close as a mother to him during his high-school years, would reassure and calm him. He mumbled something undistinguishable and tossed his head from side to side, his face twisted with a torment he could neither escape nor assuage.

Lola sat on one side of his bed and Mrs. Birkholz on

the other, and each of them took hold of one of Tommy's hands. They sat there, perfectly still, for a long time, holding the sick boy's hands, and their two loving hearts poured their longing for his relief into him as surely as though it were a healing current. In about a half hour, the rolling eyes closed and Tommy was asleep for the first time since he'd entered the hospital. The two women did not move.

The night nurse came on duty and sent for Dr. Greene. He noticed that the patient was really asleep, but he did not remark about it.

Lola and Mrs. Birkholz removed their sterile attire, washed their hands carefully the required four times, and went through the snowy night to the nearby hotel. Lola entered the hotel room with a look of hope in her eyes.

"Mother," she said as Kate's agonized eyes met hers, "I think he's better. He fell asleep holding our hands. It's the first time he's slept since last Friday, and I really think he's going to be better."

Kate looked at her, fearing yet longing to believe what Lola believed. The others exchanged questioning looks.

"But I really mean it," said Lola quietly. "I *know* he's going to get well now."

Kate dropped her face into her hands. This sudden hope was too much for her. She sat there trying to recover her control. Lola's sweet, earnest affirmation had unsettled her completely. Kate's friends tried to persuade her to take a sedative and try to sleep. No. She was afraid she might be called in the night and did not want to be befuddled by a drug. She would lie down, but she had to remain alert for a call. The dreaded summons did not come.

Early the following morning, when Kate and Lola went to the hospital, the nurse met them with a faint smile on her lips. She told them Tommy had had a good night. Kate swayed and Lola slipped an arm around her.

Dr. Greene appeared looking haggard and white. He had spent many weary hours, by day and by night, at Tommy's bedside, coming to examine him at all hours to observe the effects of his medication, the condition of his throat, his pulse and his temperature, his respiration and his muscular reflexes. Obviously, Dr. Greene had left nothing to chance which was within his power to control.

"Doc," he said, taking Kate's hand, "I think the boy is over the hump." Kate went to Tommy's bedside. He was still more than half asleep, so he did not see his mother's tears. " 'Over the hump.' " What beautiful words they were!

There was still a long way to go before Tommy could be called well, but he had passed the crisis. Dr. Greene told Kate he was convinced the maximum doses of penicillin in the spinal cord had done the trick.

Kate turned to Lola. "You'd better call Dad," she said.

But Dad was already there. He trailed in with heavy feet, set for the blow he expected. Lola looked at him and smiled. He looked at Kate. She smiled. Bill turned away, reaching for his handkerchief in his back pocket. Kate followed him to the hall where he blew and blew his nose, a stream of meaningless profanity rolling out under his breath from the sheer necessity of letting off steam.

"Well, don't get your hopes up too much, Mother," he said stubbornly. "Just stick right with him and see they don't mess around." It took a long time to convince Bill that it wasn't Kate, and Kate alone, who had pulled Tommy through.

At Woodruff and Minocqua, at Boulder and Tomahawk, in the snow-swept forests and on the shores of the frozen lakes, they all heard the news about Tommy being "over the hump," and the pall lifted. Of course, there were still weeks of convalescence ahead, but their prayers had been answered. Tommy was "over the hump." The tense faces relaxed. The subdued voices were raised in cheerful greeting.

"Hi, Carl, isn't it great?"

"Yep, but it was sure a close shave."

"Boy, *was* it close!"

"It was the kind that kills. It doesn't cripple you, it just knocks you off."

"Well, if it was me, I'd rather be killed than crippled."

"They're giving him some kind of thing—therapy—whatever that is."

Woodruff, Minocqua, Boulder, Tomahawk, Rhinelander, Winegar, Lac du Flambeau. Now they could talk about it with their heads up and their faces cheerful. Now they could meet on the streets, in the shopping centers, at their churches and schools without fearing to look into each other's eyes, lest the news they found there might be unbearable. Now they could talk about Tommy's rugged constitution, and—— "You can't kill an Irishman on St. Patrick's Day." Now they could discuss the disease, theorizing inaccurately about whether polio was meningitis, or something entirely different, and get into arguments, knowing less when they finished than when they began. Kate's boy was "over the hump"—that's all that mattered. He was going to get well. Her cheerful, reassuring face would still be among them, for they had feared that if the worst happened to Tommy, Dr. Newcomb would not remain in the northwoods, but go away somewhere to forget—or worse, she might not survive the tragedy. She was getting on in years. A blow like that could kill a woman. Those who had gone to Wausau had seen her age right before their eyes. She looked like a different person—old and broken. But now, everything would be right again. It would take time, but it would be all right with Tommy and Dr. Kate.

Ministers in their pulpits, nuns and priests at their altars gave thanks for the mercy of God, who had spared the son of Dr. Kate, His faithful servant.

At the hospital, Tommy was put through the exercises and baths that would bring back the strength to his muscles, and Dick Birkholz took time off from his job to be with him. When he was brought home, a crowd gathered at the Woodruff office and his appearance, leaning on Lola and Dick, brought cheers, and a few happy tears as well, as his infectious grin greeted his well-wishers. Dick came every day to help his friend with the rigorous pulling and stretching exercises which required the aid of a strong arm to perform.

Lola, with the buoyancy of the young, quickly recovered from the nightmare. The clouds melted behind her, and she took up her daily routine with smiling composure. Her mother stayed with her to help with the children while Lola pampered and waited on Tommy, who enjoyed it all immensely.

On May fourth, Tommy returned to his classroom, and as he entered and took his place at the desk, the class burst into a wild cheer of welcome. Pandemonium broke loose as his elated pupils pounded each other for sheer joy at having "old Newcomb" back.

Tommy had some trouble with the lump in his throat, so he let them howl awhile before he rapped for order.

He told them he was glad to be back, and thanked them for all their good wishes, and he warned them that he was in good shape to wallop them if they misbehaved. They roared with glee. "Old Newcomb" was a real "cool" guy, and it had been a pretty bad deal to almost lose him.

Not that it improved their behavior especially, after the novelty of having him back wore off, says Tommy. They soon went back to being demons again, which made things normal.

The only effect Tommy has felt from his illness is that his legs get stiff and ache when he sits in a boat too long on a fishing excursion, which he does regularly during the season.

As for Kate, her hair was grayer, her step was slower, and there was a weariness in her eyes that had not been there before, not even when her home burned down at Rice Creek.

The Million Penny Parade

THAT spring, with fifty thousand dollars in cash and pledges in the hospital fund, and an incalculable surplus of good will and determination in their hearts, the people of Woodruff clamored for the long delayed hospital for Dr. Kate.

The Board acknowledged that the hospital was long overdue, and, encouraged by the many offers of building materials and volunteer labor, they decided to carry the construction as far as it would go with the funds on hand. It was hoped that once the building was begun, public enthusiasm might well boost contributions over the top so that the building could be completed.

The Boulder Junction Community Church had been a good example of what could be done when a community made up its mind to accomplish a project which seemed all but impossible at the outset.

Early in the summer the site was cleared by a crew of high-spirited and energetic volunteers and building materials began to accumulate around the grounds, some donated and the rest bought at cost from the hospital fund.

On July third the ground-breaking ceremony was

held, and as the first spadeful of earth was turned, three four-leaf clovers were found in the sod. A cheer arose from the watching crowd as this happy augury was announced. Kate stood there, blinking and smiling as the lucky clover leaves were presented to her as a memento of the occasion.

Enthusiasm fired the hospital board members when they saw the people of Woodruff, Minocqua and the surrounding townships vie with each other to help with the work. Additional funds were obtained from one of the local banks on notes signed jointly by the hospital board and several individual businessmen, and the work on the hospital got under way.

The basement area was dug and the foundations were poured. As the cement hardened, the hospital site seethed with activity. Up went beams and joists under the argus-eyed supervision of the construction foreman who inspected every detail to see that the work was carried out according to specifications. All summer the busy builders toiled and the building grew.

On September fourth an article appeared in Minocqua's *Lakeland Times* which gives a succinct report of the work's progress:

LAKELAND HOSPITAL CORNERSTONE TO BE LAID IN SUNDAY PROGRAM

The cornerstone of the Lakeland Memorial Hospital will be laid at ceremonies scheduled for Sunday afternoon (Sept. 7th) at 2 o'clock. The hospital board has invited all interested persons to attend the event and observe the progress being made in the construction of the hospital. Part of the cornerstone laying program will be a joint concert to be provided by the Minocqua and the Arbor Vitae Woodruff high school bands.

It is understood that the main floor of the structure will be completed this week and that the roof will be in place before the snow flies. Both main floor and roof will be of prefabricated concrete, the first of its kind to be used in this part of the state and representing the latest and most modern planning in fireproof construction.

Then followed a list of new contributors too numerous to be recorded here. The article further stated that "Casey" Lambert of Minocqua was pledging one thousand dollars and placing his photographic laboratory and his electrical and machine shop at the disposal of the hospital during the time of construction and maintenance. The report concluded:

The hospital board stated it was pleased to report the interest reflected in the many favorable comments and in the financial support given by camps, summer home owners, tourists, and Lakeland area citizens.

The cornerstone was laid and the work continued until all the funds on hand were exhausted. When the first flurry of snow fell late in October, Woodruff had the shell of a hospital building, but there were no more materials for the willing and eager hands of the volunteer workers.

The hospital for Dr. Kate, so auspiciously begun, would be useless to her until the structure was completed and equipped, and the community resumed its drive to replenish the treasury of the hospital fund. Contributions trickled in slowly. Prospects of finishing the hospital were discouragingly dim. Providence seemed to have drawn the line at interceding further for the Lakeland Memorial Hospital, as it had done for the Community Church of Boulder Junction. Discouragement dampened the high hopes of the townspeople.

If this lifeless shell was all they could accomplish, they had failed in their attempt to bring a working hospital to Woodruff. The bare, unfinished structure stood on the snowy site, a monument of failure.

That winter, Dr. Kate had to continue her slow, skidding rides over the miles to other hospitals, but she was philosophical about another hard-riding winter. She was so grateful to Almighty God for having spared her son's life that nothing could down her spirit. As she drove through the thickening snow flurries, she thought of the uncompleted hospital building, and the fact that it had reached even that stage of completion made her feel better. It would be nice, of course, to have her hospital ready, but it would take several tens of thousands of dollars to finish it, and as for the equipment, that would require at least—— Suddenly the words of Pastor Radford flashed into her mind:

"If you would stop thinking about the money and begin to have a little more faith, you would find that much more would be accomplished."

Kate smiled. It was as though the good pastor's spirit had whispered in her ear. Firmly she fixed in her mind the vision of a completed hospital, ready to receive her patients. Somehow, the work would be finished, in the Lord's good time, and in plenty of time for her to enjoy it. She did not know that the completion of the hospital was already on its way, in a classroom of the Arbor Vitae Woodruff High School.

Mr. Otto Burich, the mathematics teacher at Arbor Vitae Woodruff High, was attempting to illustrate to his class of sixteen pupils how much a million actually was. They measured the ceiling and counted the holes in the squares of acoustical tile, multiplying the result until they had extended the ceiling into one which would contain a million holes. Someone observed that the holes were about as big as pennies, and one pupil wondered how big a pile a million pennies would make. They figured the pennies in dollars.

"What would we do with a million pennies?" was the next question.

"We could give them to Dr. Kate to finish her hospital!" piped up another student.

"Say! That's not a bad idea!" declared their teacher thoughtfully. The class jumped at the suggestion. So the drive for a million pennies for the Lakeland Memorial Hospital Fund was conceived. People wouldn't mind giving pennies, where they might not be able to afford dollars.

And so the project was begun, and it was promptly called "The Million Penny Parade." The idea spread from Mr. Burich's class to the entire school, and the pupils of Arbor Vitae Woodruff High began to devise ways and means of earning the pennies and also of extracting them from the inhabitants of Woodruff and the surrounding communities. "Why not the entire country?" it was proposed. "Why not the entire world?" someone added. The drive was on.

The English classes held a competition to see who could write the best letter which would explain the purpose of the campaign and bring in the pennies. A thousand mimeographed copies were made of the best letter, and mailing lists were collected wherever they were obtainable. Resort owners, summer-camp managers, drugstores, markets, a list of Dr. Kate's patients, names of friends and relatives in far places, every available address book was combed for names and addresses. When the community learned of the school project, contributions were offered to defray mailing costs.

Other thousands of copies of the letter had to be turned out. More stamps were donated by enthusiastic teachers and businessmen, and "The Million Penny Parade" began to roll in earnest. So did the pennies. Hundreds, thousands, hundreds of thousands of pennies poured in by mail and were handed to the young solicitors by enthusiastic townsfolk. The Indians at Lac du Flambeau added their efforts to the drive, for Dr. Kate was their faithful friend in sickness, and they were happy to do their part.

The youngsters worked hard all winter, opening mail and counting the rapidly increasing pile of pennies that swelled on the floor of the high-school gymnasium. The students of the Arbor Vitae Woodruff High School were getting a practical demonstration of what a million pennies looked like. Pennies continued to pour in—from the church congregations in various towns, from business houses throughout the country, from soldiers in the armed forces. Pennies came from all the forty-eight states and from twenty-three foreign countries. They represented contributions from almost sixty thousand people.

"The Million Penny Parade" became the subject of nationwide publicity. Newspapers and magazine articles were written about the drive for pennies for a hospital being so successfully conducted by the pupils of a small-town high school. Dr. Kate's smiling face appeared in the articles as the inspiration of the project. There had been enough talk of "juvenile delinquency." Here was proof of juvenile enterprise and competence. There had been little studying done at the Arbor Vitae Woodruff High School that winter and spring, but the sense of accomplishment these youngsters had acquired was far more valuable than anything they could have learned from their books. They had begun a project and seen it through to victory, and the effect it had on their morale and self-confidence was something no child psychologist could have achieved with all the scientific theories contained in a boatload of textbooks.

This little northwoods doctor had done more than achieve a hospital. She had redeemed the good repute of the young people she loved.

By April the penny campaign had reached its quota of a million and continued to climb, and a parade was planned to celebrate the achievement. The "Penny Paraders" selected Miss Donna Behn, a sparkling brunette as their queen, and four high-school beauties as her court of princesses.

Dr. Kate looked on in happy amazement. All this had been done for her sake. Most of the children were her own "babies" and they had undertaken this tremendous project to bring her a finished hospital. It was all too wonderful. The bank rallied to the spirit of the "Penny Paraders" and offered to advance thirty-two thousand dollars to assure the building's completion. The plans were expanded from ten to sixteen rooms, with a surgery, kitchen, nurses' quarters, nursery and laboratory, and a private office for Dr. Kate.

Thirty-one years had passed since Kate had first arrived in the northwoods, twenty-two years since she had resumed her practice here. Her mouse-brown hair was grizzly white, and the lines in her face attested to the many years and the many hardships she had lived through, but her brown eyes were bright behind the glasses as she beamed on the lifted faces of her zealous "babies." She stood before them in the auditorium at a high-school rally one afternoon and tried to tell them her gratitude for what they had done for her. The cheers and applause that rang in the hall after her halting speech brought the laughing tears to her eyes, and she scurried off the platform, whispering to the beaming Otto Burich that she had to rush to Tomahawk.

Bill was waiting impatiently in the car. Lola was at the Sacred Heart in Tomahawk, expecting the third of their scheduled brood of four, and Kate was to be on hand to deliver her third grandchild.

Barbara Ann Newcomb was born at eight fifty-six on the evening of April fourth. She was a ten-pound beauty with long dark hair and as lively from her first chirp as a bright-eyed chickadee. Again the sisters rejoiced with their happy Doctor Newcomb, and it was a double rejoicing, for she would soon have the hospital they had prayed for. It meant that she would no longer be with them, but their loss would be her gain, and they were accustomed to renunciation for the good of others.

Lola's confinement safely over, Kate returned to Woodruff. Late one night, when all her calls were made, she went to the hospital site and walked around the ghostly building that would soon become a living hospital. A qualm of anxiety began to trouble her. Upkeep? Equipment? Some of the more practical businessmen in the community had questioned the ability of a small hospital in a sparsely settled area to support itself and keep up the mortgage payments, but Kate brushed their doubts aside. "Stop thinking about the money and begin to have a little more faith."

One step at a time, the dream was coming true. Somehow, the hospital would be provided for.

By the middle of May, one million, two hundred thousand pennies had been received, and on Memorial Day, 1953, the town of Woodruff held its first "Million Penny Parade," sponsored by the Arbor Vitae Lions Club. From all the surrounding areas, twenty thousand visitors streamed in to watch the monster demonstration held to celebrate the success of the penny campaign.

Visitors who came to view the huge heap of pennies in the gymnasium threw more pennies on the pile, and the total reached one million, seven hundred thousand pennies, seventeen thousand dollars to continue the work on the Lakeland Memorial Hospital.

That summer Kate watched the hospital building transformed rapidly from a hollow shell to a finished reality. The architect kept in close touch with her to make sure everything would be exactly as she wanted it. Within the next six months, the Lakeland Memorial Hospital was completed. A medical staff was selected and a corps of nurses was chosen from the many applicants who had expressed their eagerness to join the hospital staff. Everything was ready except for the necessary equipment.

Early in 1954 the Lions Club started a drive of stamp selling to raise funds to equip the hospital. The stamps bore a picture of Dr. Kate with one of her babies and sold at a dollar for a sheet of one hundred. But the proceeds were slow in arriving. Medical equipment had increased enormously in price. It would take many thousands of dollars to furnish the hospital so that it would be a complete unit for the care of all kinds of cases.

"We decided to open and do the best we could with what we had," says Dr. Kate, "but many facilities were lacking, and it looked as though I would have to continue to send my patients to the better-equipped hospitals for a while. I kept remembering what Pastor Radford had said to me, and I knew it would all be taken care of in time. But the way it was taken care of never entered my mind. That's another story, and it was the surprise of my life!"

The Doctors' Convention

EARLY in March, 1954, Dr. Kate received an invitation to attend a doctors' convention the week of March fifteenth in Los Angeles, California, with all expenses paid. Kate felt flattered at the invitation, but she decided she could not spare the time from her busy schedule to make the trip. Her family urged her to go, but Kate shook her head. Her patients needed her right there. Her hospital was about to open its doors and there was too much to be done. She was surprised when a representative of the Wisconsin Medical Association arrived from Madison to see her about the convention in Los Angeles. She had been selected, he said, to represent her state, and the convention was expecting her to attend. It was being held in honor of Sir Alexander Fleming of London, the doctor who had given penicillin to the world in a form that could be used for clinical purposes.

Kate realized that she could not decline the invitation. It would be a disservice to her state not to attend the meeting and she agreed to go. Her family was delighted at her decision. They felt that she needed a vacation, and they helped her to get ready for the trip. It would be her first to California since 1924, and she hoped for better luck with the weather this time.

She made the necessary arrangements to leave her patients in the able hands of Dr. Frances Cline and Dr. Gale Huber, and as tickets had been sent her in advance, there was no need to make reservations. Kate had attended other medical conventions, but never with all her expenses paid. She reflected that the Los Angeles Medical Association must be very prosperous to stand the expense of such a costly trip.

She boarded the train at Woodruff the evening of March thirteenth with her family waving good-by from the platform. She was scheduled to arrive in Los Angeles on the evening of the fifteenth, although the date of the testimonial dinner for Sir Alexander was March seventeenth. Kate noted the date. Important things always happened to her on St. Patrick's Day. This time it was to be an official dinner. She hoped all would go well. The suggestion had been made that she arrive a little earlier, so she could visit the city and meet some of the doctors before the appointed evening.

Kate was surprised that the Medical Association had not only supplied her transportation but had even secured a stateroom for her all the way through. She spent most of the time between Chicago and Los Angeles catching up on much-needed sleep. The past few months had been crowded with so many extracurricular activities connected with The Penny Parade and the hospital.

The Santa Fe "Chief" was a luxurious train and she felt like a queen, being waited on hand and foot instead of waiting on others as she had for so many years.

The train arrived at Los Angeles late in the evening and she was met at the station by a nice-looking young man who introduced himself as Donald Boehme, a hospital superintendent, who had been assigned to look after her comfort and to show her the hospitals and the sights of the big city. He took her to the Town House where a suite had been reserved for her. "A suite, no less!" Kate said to herself. They were really doing things up brown for the representative from Wisconsin.

She slept comfortably in her luxurious hotel suite, and after breakfast, which she had in her room, Mr. Boehme appeared and they started out to visit the various hospitals which he knew would be of interest to her. He seemed to know all about her work in the northwoods and her long dream of having a hospital at Woodruff which had finally been realized. He had read the article in the January issue of *Woman's Day*, and the doctors she met at the hospitals also knew about her and her hospital. Kate began to feel her old shyness overtake her and she hoped people wouldn't make a fuss over her; she dreaded being made conspicuous, especially among strangers.

In the afternoon Mr. Boehme took her to see the renowned Forest Lawn Memorial Park where she saw the beautiful stained-glass reproduction of Da Vinci's "Last Supper," and the enormous painting of the Crucifixion, by a Polish artist whose name she could not pronounce. They also visited the Observatory at Griffith Park where Kate peered through the big telescope and marveled at the models of the earth and the moon, and the charts of the familiar constellations she had seen over the northwoods forests.

Mr. Boehme was an animated conversationalist and asked her about the radio and television programs she had seen and heard, inquiring about those she preferred. Kate told him she had not had much time to listen to radio in recent years, and as for television, she had seen very little of it. In fact, she knew almost nothing about this new medium, although her family had talked of getting a television set. Mr. Boehme frequently excused himself to make telephone calls, and Kate assumed he was checking with his hospital to see that all was well during his absence. She told him she would like to take a trip to Long Beach where her friends Mr. and Mrs. Sam Williams were spending the winter. She also wanted to get in touch with her old friend Mrs. Donna Hall, who lived in Beverly Hills. Donna was a member of Kate's old Buffalo crowd and she had not seen her in over thirty years. She had tried to reach Donna by phone several times, but had not been successful, nor had Donna returned her calls. Kate was somewhat concerned over her old friend's failure to communicate with her. She had left not one but several messages. It was very strange.

Mr. Boehme, who seemed far more interested in his own plans, assured Dr. Newcomb that she could visit with her friends to her heart's content after the dinner. For the present, they would follow the program which had been laid out for her by the medical people.

They were joined at dinner by Mr. Boehme's very attractive wife, Jan, and the trio went to a musical revue starring Bea Lillie. Kate had never seen the famous comedienne before and was fascinated by her quips and antics. But she felt rather tired by the time the performance ended and was glad to return to her hotel for a night's rest.

The next day was March seventeenth, the day of the dinner. Again, in the morning, Kate tried to reach Donna Hall by telephone without success. It seemed downright peculiar that there had been no return calls from Donna.

Kate hoped she would not have to leave California without seeing her old friend.

Mr. Boehme had another full day planned. She asked him again if they couldn't drive to Long Beach as she was anxious to see the Williamses, but he put her off, explaining that they were going to visit the Will Rogers Ranch and go to the Will Rogers State Beach. It was a long drive, during which Mr. Boehme pointed out the homes of various motion-picture stars. They meant little to Kate, whose movie attendance had been very limited for years.

The weather was not particularly favorable for a visit to the beach. She was having no luck with the California weather. She wondered when the much talked-about "sunny" season began. But she enjoyed seeing the Will Rogers Ranch and the exhibit of the great actor's possessions, as she had always admired him.

When they returned to her hotel in the late afternoon, Mr. Boehme suggested that Kate be ready early that evening, as he still had a couple of places to take her before dinner, which was scheduled for eight o'clock.

Kate dressed in a simple tailored suit and small hat, her usual costume for all occasions, and Mr. Boehme drove her to see the Hollywood Bowl. He then headed the car into Hollywood and Kate saw its famous Boulevard. She was amazed at the enormous growth of the city. When she had last seen it, it had been a straggling area of vacant fields and orange groves, with a business center at the lower end and a mushroom sprinkling of barnlike studio buildings and bungalows dotting its vast western expanse.

Mr. Boehme stopped across from a theater which bore the sign "El Capitan" and suggested that Kate might like to see how a television program was produced. Kate was not overanxious to go in. She was afraid they would be late for the dinner. But Mr. Boehme assured her he would get her there in plenty of time. The television production might be an interesting experience to tell her friends and family about when she returned to Wisconsin. Kate agreed that it might.

Mr. Boehme drove the car into a huge parking lot behind the theater and escorted Kate to the entrance. They were told that the theater was filled, and Mr. Boehme seemed very much disturbed at the door manager's refusal to admit them.

Kate started back toward the parking lot, somewhat relieved that she would not have to spend time in the theater. It was nearly quarter to seven, and she was very punctilious about keeping appointments. It would be a long ride back to Los Angeles, and she thought they should be getting started.

Mr. Boehme caught up with her as she was almost halfway back to the car, and he told her that two empty seats had been found in the theater. Kate knew it would be useless to protest, as Mr. Boehme was a man of determination. She allowed him to lead her back to the theater and they went in.

All the seats in the spacious hall seemed to be occupied, but they were ushered to two empty places at the front and Kate slipped past the people in the two aisle seats and took her place. Mr. Boehme seated himself beside her. She saw a big screen over the curtained stage with a large sign projected on it reading: "THIS IS YOUR LIFE." A stream of lights ran around the edge and a voice was announcing that this was Ralph Edwards' "This Is Your Life" program. Kate wondered what the show would be about. Mr. Boehme told her they sometimes called on people in the audience, and they might call on a doctor in honor of the Doctors' Convention. Kate wondered if the doctor would be Sir Alexander Fleming, and she turned her head to see if she could catch a glimpse of the distinguished visitor in the audience. Mr. Boehme was saying it was a great honor to be called upon and that he would feel highly flattered to be selected. Kate replied, "*I* wouldn't."

Now a very good-looking, genial-faced man came down the aisle carrying a microphone. The audience applauded and he greeted them in a warm, friendly voice. He was stopping to speak to people, asking their names and where they came from and then moving on to the next stop. Kate hoped he wouldn't come to her, but he stopped at their row and singled her out, asking her name. She murmured, "Newcomb," so softly that he asked her to repeat it. She did, this time a little louder. He asked her what she did and she told him. He asked her where she came from and she replied "Wisconsin," and wished he'd go on to someone else. But he asked her what city she came from, and she replied, "Woodruff." He drew a book from under his arm and asked her if she would please read what was printed on it. Kate stared at the leather-bound book and Mr. Edwards spoke aloud the words she saw:

"This Is Your Life, Dr. Kate Newcomb!"

Kate looked up at him sharply. What did this mean? How had *her* name got on that book? She was baffled and bewildered. Now this Mr. Edwards was asking her to step up to the stage. Kate's heart sank. She turned to Mr. Boehme and asked, "Do I have to?" Mr. Boehme was smiling and getting up from his seat, helping her up. Panic was flooding over her. What was happening? Mr. Edwards took her arm as she slipped through to the aisle. He was leading her toward the stage and up the steps where a divan stood before a backdrop of draperies. Mr. Edwards led her to the divan and invited her to take the "seat of honor." She slid into the cushions, glad to be sitting down, for her knees had begun to shake. What was going to happen? How long would it take? She was worried about being late for the dinner.

Mr. Edwards was talking about her. He was telling about her practice in the northwoods and said her entire life was right there in the book he was holding. There were cameras moving in all around her and she felt silly and nervous. Mr. Edwards was telling the audience she was born in Wellington, Kansas, and he gave the year as 1866. Kate protested and Mr. Edwards corrected himself and apologized, laughing. He'd meant 1886. That was better. Kate relaxed a little. The audience seemed to enjoy the joke, and Kate chuckled with them. Then Mr. Edwards told about her mother's death when she was three, and about her happy years with her grandmother in Leoti, Kansas, until her father married again and they moved to Buffalo. He mentioned her five brothers and sisters. How did he know all this? She couldn't remember that any of these intimate details had been in the magazine article.

Now a voice came from somewhere off stage, a woman's voice, and it said, "Kate always mothered all of us, and we called her 'nuther mother." Kate was startled. Who was that? Mr. Edwards asked her if she recognized the voice, but she was too stunned to identify it. Mr. Edwards gave her a hint and she said uncertainly, "My sister Marge?" The curtains parted at one side of the stage and a familiar-looking figure stepped out. Kate looked at her. Was it really Marge, or just an actress made up to look like her? Marge lived in Cleveland. It *couldn't* be she. This "Marge" hugged Kate and kissed her, but Kate still couldn't believe this wasn't a trick. Marge told how Kate persuaded her father that she was not cut out to be his hostess. She told of the mishap with the squab, and then Kate knew it must be Marge.

A picture of Kate in her middy-blouse was flashed on a television set on the stage. Where had they got *that?* Probably from Marge.

Mr. Edwards was telling about the years when Kate taught school in Buffalo. He mentioned the Parkside Baptist Church and the happy times she'd had with the old Buffalo crowd. A picture of three smiling young ladies appeared on the screen, and now another voice spoke from off stage, a woman's voice, talking about Gull Lake and Muskoka and some of the other vacation spots around Buffalo. Kate's head went up as she listened. "Donna!" she exclaimed. "Donna Hall." And her old friend Donna stepped through the curtains. "Donna!" "Kate!" They had not seen each other in over thirty years. They were both gray-haired grandmothers now, and their embrace was tremulous with emotion.

"Where have you been keeping yourself?" Kate asked severely. "I've been trying to reach you by phone ever since I arrived." Donna laughed and so did Mr. Edwards, and so did everyone in the audience. Donna did not explain, and the strange and bewildering comedy went on, with Kate feeling like Alice-in-Wonderland and not at all sure she wouldn't be waking up in her bed.

Another voice came over the sound mechanism, and Kate said, "That sounds like one of the Schlenker girls." She did not know which, for all three of the Schlenker sisters sounded exactly alike. This one was Anna May, and she came through the curtains with her arms outstretched and such hugging and squeals of joy and surprise you never did hear. Anna May lived in Buffalo, and Kate wanted to know how she happened to get here. But there was more to the show.

What was this? A picture of Bill had flashed on the screen of the monitor set on the stage. Was Bill here? Kate wondered. But Mr. Edwards was saying that since her husband couldn't be there, he had sent her a hug and kiss by her son Tommy. Tommy?

Tommy's voice came from off stage and Kate was sure these people had made a recording. Why, Tommy was in Woodruff. He had put her on the train. Tommy's voice told how Kate had gone to the wilderness when his father became ill, and had "made a new man of him." Tommy stepped through the curtains and Kate gasped. She touched him as he kissed her to make sure he was real. Tommy told how Dr. Torpy had used mule-skinner language to make his mother resume her practice. Kate clung to her son's hand. Yes, it was really Tommy, all right. How had they done it? Surely, this was the crowning surprise of the evening, she thought.

But another voice came over the sound equipment, telling of Tommy's childhood, and there was no mistaking the voice of Norman McMahon who had played such an important part in Tommy's up-bringing. Norman stepped out and Kate embraced him heartily. He reminded her of the time they had gone over the creek in a canoe through the ice floes, and how they had to wade to shore when the canoe foundered. How had these people found Norman? Kate decided to stop wondering. It was all too much for her.

Here was the picture of the old snowplow, and the voice on the track was that of Larry Doolittle, telling of the time he sent the plow for her, and how the plow skidded into a ditch, and she trudged the two miles to his house on snowshoes, and saved his daughter-in-law's life. Larry—and here he came, grinning like a jackanapes. Kate felt she couldn't take much more. But there was more. There was Sam Williams who had rescued her from the snow the time her car stalled—and now, here was Otto Burich! And with him was Eva May Clausen, the student who had suggested the penny drive. There they all stood, and Kate peered at them through her misty glasses and wondered if she was going to wake up and find herself in her office cot in Woodruff.

Her entire life story had been told, and here were the people who had been a part of it. Who had done all this?

Mr. Edwards gathered Kate's friends around her and began handing her gifts—a movie camera, a projector with which she could show the film of the program which would be presented to her; a beautiful gold charm bracelet, each charm representing an event in her life. He also gave her the book with her name stamped on it, and now he was handing her a key and telling her it was the key to a beautiful new car which she was to pick up in Chicago at the Cole Finder Agency, a 1954 Mercury sedan to carry her on her calls. Kate was overcome. Why? Why had they done all this for her? She was just a plain country doctor. There were hundreds, yes, thousands of country doctors who took care of people in the small communities, with no one ever giving them a second thought. Why her? She felt humble and grateful for the honors and gifts that had been poured upon her. Mr. Edwards was saying there would be a party for her at the Hollywood Roosevelt Hotel that evening.

It was too much for her to take in all at once. Gradually she'd find out how it was done.

Mr. Edwards was telling about the new hospital, and saying he hoped some of the people who were watching the program would gather up their pennies and send them to Dr. Kate Newcomb at Woodruff, Wisconsin. Her name and address were flashed on the screen of the monitor set. Now, that was nice of him, thought Kate. Every penny counts when there is a sixteen-room hospital to equip, and Kate hoped the audience in the theater would be kind enough to help. Mr. Edwards said he would let them know next week how many pennies had been collected through the program.

It was over now, and everyone gathered around to hug and kiss Kate again, and they started out through the wings where Tommy and all her friends had been hiding. And there she found—Lola! And Mrs. Larry Doolittle—and Hulda Barden, Mrs. Doolittle's sister and a particularly dear friend of Kate's. The three women were wiping their faces and blowing their noses. "What's the matter?" Kate asked. "You were just wonderful!" Lola explained, and they all laughed because they'd been crying. "Where are the kids?" Kate asked, looking around. By that time she fully expected to find the entire Newcomb clan in the theater. Why not? Everything else that was impossible had happened! But Lola said they had left the children with her parents in Clintonville. She and Hulda and Mrs. Doolittle had been sitting up in the balcony crying their eyes out and telling each other there was nothing to cry about.

Kate began to piece the puzzle together. She knew now why Lola's parents had come all the way from Clintonville to see Doc off on the train. They had come to get the children, so Tom and Lola could leave. But when she asked questions they only grinned and said, "You'll hear all about it later."

As they were leaving the theater, Kate noticed a man standing near the entrance wiping his eyes and blowing his nose. He was wearing glasses and had to take them off to wipe them. Kate's heart went out to him. She pointed him out to Tommy and said she wondered what might be the trouble. Tommy laughed and the weeping man came toward them. He took Kate's hands, and Tommy introduced Axel Gruenberg, the producer and co-writer of the show, to his mother. Mr. Gruenberg's tears were a tribute to what he said was "a great story."

"Well," replied Kate, "if it was great, it's because you made it great."

Mr. Gruenberg shook his head and answered, "No, doctor, it was you who made it great."

He said other kind and flattering things to her which made her blush, and he thanked her for appearing on his program. She assured him that it was none of her doing, and that if she'd known about it beforehand, she'd probably still be running. The producer laughed and asked her how much she thought the hospital fund would get from Mr. Edwards's appeal.

"Oh, maybe a hundred dollars, if we're lucky," replied Kate cheerfully. Mr. Boehme appeared, grinning sheepishly over the trick he had played on her. She asked him about the dinner, and he replied that it would be the next night, and they'd discuss it with her later.

The entire party adjourned to the Hollywood Roosevelt Hotel, where they had a gala dinner. Kate found Mr. Edwards just as charming off stage as he was on, and she admits she still has a "real crush" on him. At ten o'clock a rebroadcast of the "This Is Your Life" program appeared on the television set in the hotel dining room, but Kate was so dazed by everything that was happening to her that she does not remember seeing herself on the screen.

She spent the night at the Roosevelt with her sister Marge and her old friend Anna May Schlenker. There was not much sleeping, but there was a great deal of chatter as they caught up with the news of the intervening years.

The following morning at breakfast in the hotel dining room, Kate caused a lot of laughter by saying, with a look of blank and tardy comprehension, "Well, I guess there isn't going to be any dinner for Sir Alexander Fleming after all. . . ."

Kate had to hear all about the conspiracy, how it had been planned weeks ahead, and what a time they'd had keeping it from her, for she is shrewdly observant. But she admitted they had her completely fooled. She learned that Mr. Boehme, who really was the superintendent of the Encino Hospital, was also the husband of Mr. Edwards' "contact woman," Jan, who had done the research and planning for the program. He had been assigned to keep Kate under surveillance and see to it that she was brought to the theater at the appointed time. And they had almost been turned away!

The next two days were a continuation of the dreamlike events of Wednesday evening. Every facility and courtesy of the big modern hotel were placed at the disposal of the Newcomb party. Kate's things had been moved from the Town House to the Roosevelt the day after the program, so she could be with her friends. Kate marveled at the warmth and hospitality she found in the city. These people were as kindly and hospitable as her own Wisconsinites. The waitresses in the dining room came to her with their tips to add to her penny fund for the hospital.

People she'd never seen before spoke to her in the lobby and on the street. They wanted to shake her hand and tell her how wonderful they thought she was. They handed her pennies and even bills and wished her luck with her hospital. Kate beamed and thanked them and handed Otto or Tommy the contributions until their pockets were worn through by the weight of the coins they collected.

Kate received wires from Woodruff and Boulder Junction and from all the towns where she practiced. They had all seen the broadcast and they were very proud of her. But how did they know about it? Lola and Tom told her they had notified everybody they could after she had left town and told them to spread the word. The children of the Arbor Vitae High School sent her a wire that brought happy tears to her eyes. Her kids! They were mighty wonderful.

Kate felt like a celebrity, and she thoroughly enjoyed the experience, although she didn't think she deserved it.

They spent Thursday seeing some of the city, although the March weather was drizzly and damp. Tommy and some of the others went to see a television show called "Truth and Consequences," and Tommy was amazed at being singled out and given a round of applause by the audience because he was "Dr. Kate's" son.

On Friday, Otto Burich's wife telephoned from Woodruff and told him that seven sacks of mail had arrived for Dr. Kate. What was to be done with them? Kate was astounded. Seven sacks of mail? What was in them? Pennies, of course, said Otto. They were heavy. "Well, for heaven's sake," said Kate, "tell her to open them and start counting them." Seven sacks! So soon? It was really amazing.

More Pennies for Dr. Kate

THE Newcomb party was scheduled to leave Los
Angeles on Friday, March nineteenth, by plane.
Dr. Kate had her choice of flying with the others or re-
turning to Woodruff by train. She gave the problem serious
consideration. Bill had strictly forbidden her ever to set
foot in an airplane. However, she came to this conclusion:
"As long as you're all going by plane, I'm going with you.
If it goes down, we'll all go down together."

The entire party went to the airport, although some of
them were remaining behind.

Kate went up the ramp to the big aircraft which was
mighty handsome. Kate felt a little apprehensive as the
trim uniformed hostess settled them in their seats, but the
others were so gay and confident that she decided it was
foolish to be frightened. Mr. Arthur Rubloff had telephoned from Chicago to congratulate her and said he was
having a dinner for them when they arrived in the Windy
City. That meant he was sure they would arrive safely, and
somehow, it reassured her.

Of course, Bill would be furious, but she'd always
been curious about this flying business, and now she was
going to find out what it was really like.

More Pennies for Dr. Kate

At last the doors were closed, the belts were fastened and the big engines roared. That made Kate's heart beat a little faster but everyone else seemed calm, so she relaxed in her seat. Tommy sat beside her, the Doolittles behind her, Otto and Eva May in front and Lola and Hulda across the aisle.

The plane started smoothly and Kate watched the swiftly passing airport. Before she realized it, the scenery was swimming below her and the plane was off the ground. She wondered if she would get "air-sick." She felt fine so far.

As Los Angeles sank lower and lower, Kate had the impression that the plane was hovering in mid-air, gradually going higher, but not moving ahead. From the window, she saw a bird's-eye view of roads, fields and toy houses.

Everybody began asking her how she felt and how she liked it.

"Fine! Fine!" she replied. "But are we getting anywhere?"

Tommy laughed. "We're going about two hundred and fifty an hour right now. They're just beginning to pick up speed."

Kate gasped. Two hundred and fifty! She asked him if he meant miles. That's what he meant, all right. "How fast do they intend to go?" asked Kate.

"Oh, about four hundred miles an hour," replied Tommy. Kate shook her head. That was impossible. Why, it meant, she calculated, almost seven miles a minute. Woodruff to Tomahawk in less than five minutes. And yet they seemed to be standing still! Well, there was nothing she could do about it. She might just as well relax.

The pretty hostesses went around seeing to it that

everyone was comfortable. Kate watched the horizon for a while and then began to feel drowsy. Tommy tipped her seat back and adjusted the pillow under her head. Whenever there was anything of interest to see she roused herself and peered down. The Rockies looked like toy mountains. The Grand Canyon was an impressive sight, even from this enormous height. But otherwise, the trip was not the least bit exciting. In fact, it was smooth and monotonous. So this was flying! Well, there was nothing alarming about it, and she'd tell Bill so. Their luncheon, served on trays, was delicious, although Kate had little appetite. She'd had so many regular meals in Los Angeles that she was beginning to worry about her girdle feeling so tight.

As they neared Chicago, the sun was setting—a magnificent sight. But over the city they found a heavy layer of clouds. The plane circled over the airport, waiting for a break in the thick bank of clouds below. This went on for such a long time that Kate wondered what was happening. Tommy explained that the weather was impeding their landing.

"But why do they keep going around like that? Why don't they just stop and wait until it clears?" said Kate. A shout of laughter went up from the seats around her. Tommy explained that if the plane stopped it wouldn't remain in the air. "Oh!" said Kate. She had a lot to learn about planes, she admitted.

The co-pilot came from the cockpit at the front of the plane and announced that because of weather conditions over the Midway Airport, the plane would go on to St. Louis. Now, that was just too bad, wailed Kate. They wouldn't get back to Chicago in time for Mr. Rubloff's dinner. That would make two dinner dates she'd miss in a week. Not that it was unusual for her to miss dinner engagements while she was practicing. But she had hoped to make this one. She was very anxious to tell Mr. Rubloff about the seven bags of mail and the pennies that were being counted. Besides, she hated disappointing him when he had been so nice as to plan a dinner party for her. But it couldn't be helped.

They landed at the airport in St. Louis where they had dinner, and Tommy decided to remain in St. Louis overnight to visit friends. The rest of the party got back on the plane and returned to Chicago. This time they were able to land at the Midway Airport without difficulty. By now Kate felt like a veteran air traveler. Take-offs and landings were just routine matters, and she hadn't felt even slightly air-sick.

It was one A.M. when they reached the Palmer House in Chicago. They found a message from Mr. Rubloff, saying he would come by in the morning. He had waited until ten o'clock, and then given up his plans for the dinner. Kate was sorry to have missed seeing her old friend but there was also a new friend who had come to meet her. A representative of the American Medical Association had waited faithfully to bring her the greetings of the Association. Its officials, he said, felt that she had done the profession of medicine a great service by appearing on the television program. Again Kate protested that she had had nothing to do with her appearance, but she accepted his kind words with thanks. She hoped her story would bring the work of country doctors into prominence and thus make them better appreciated. She bade her distinguished visitor good night and started for the elevators to go to her room. But the day's surprises were not yet over.

Otto Burich came running to tell her another piece of news. He had telephoned his wife in Woodruff and he was shaking with excitement as he told her that *sixty* bags of mail had been received at the Woodruff post office for Dr. Kate!

Kate stared at him. Did he say *sixty*—or sixteen?

"Sixty!" cried Otto. "I made her repeat it several times. I couldn't believe I was hearing straight."

"You mean—letters with pennies in them?" asked Kate.

"Pennies—dollar bills—checks—money orders." Otto stumbled over his words. "They're opening all the mail and counting the money so they'll have a total ready for the next Edwards program." Kate looked at him in a daze. Sixty bags of mail since Wednesday night. She wondered how many people had seen the program. Otto said he thought it had between thirty and forty million viewers. Kate steadied herself on Otto's arm. The figures were beginning to make her dizzy. She'd better get to bed before her legs gave out.

That night clouds of pennies whirled through her dreams. The next morning early she came down to have breakfast with her "gang." Tommy had phoned to say he would fly in and meet them at the Cole Finder Agency where they were to pick up the new car. And Mr. Rubloff was coming in his limousine to take them there. She'd almost forgotten about the car in her excitement about the mail bags. *Sixty* of them! Everyone looked awed. Otto, Eva May and the Doolittles had to hurry off to catch the early train for Woodruff.

Mr. Rubloff arrived and Kate greeted him with the exciting news about the sixty mail bags. He beamed and said he knew the TV program would do the trick for the hospital. And on the way to the agency, he confessed his complicity in arranging the Edwards broadcast. He showed them copies of the correspondence in which he suggested Dr. Newcomb as a subject for the "This Is Your Life" program and Kate could only shake her head and marvel at the way she had been completely bamboozled into going to Los Angeles, fooled "hook, line and sinker" into thinking she was going to a doctors' convention!

Tommy arrived while they were inspecting the car. It was all Mr. Edwards had said it would be. A beautiful, bright red, streamlined Mercury sedan, and the men at the agency were so nice that one would think Kate was doing them a favor by accepting the magnificent gift! It took a little time to arrange all the business about ownership and insurance, and then the Newcomb luggage was transferred from Mr. Rubloff's car into the Mercury. This important Chicago businessman was as excited and enthusiastic as a boy over the whole procedure. He helped his chauffeur with the bags, laughing and joking with Kate about her new "fire engine," and warning her not to get too reckless with the high-powered motor, or she'd be a sitting duck for a ticket from the constable. Kate reminded him that she had doctors' privileges and invited him to come to Woodruff and try out the roads with her.

When the time came to bid their friend good-by, Kate thanked him warmly for his part in the dramatic event which now looked as though it would pyramid the hospital collections into ample funds for the needed equipment. With Tommy at the wheel the red Mercury took off.

Their first stop was for a snack. Eldorah met her family at the restaurant, and after lunch they headed northward toward Clintonville to pick up the children at the Williams home.

Kathy, Mike and Barbara had been allowed to stay up to see Grandma, and there was pure bedlam when she arrived with Mommy and Daddy and Aunt Dory. Kathy and Mike both talked at once, while Barbara, who at eleven months was beginning to have her say in volume if not in clarity, completed the confusion. Out of it one could gather, with some difficulty, that they had seen Grandma and Daddy on television, and why hadn't they answered when they called to them? Mike's voice boomed in deep indignation, "Daddy wouldn't talk to me." It was only after they'd been quieted down and put to bed that Kate could tell "Momo" and "Boss" and Judy and David all about everything that had happened in Los Angeles.

The Newcombs stayed at the Williams home overnight, and early the next morning, which was Sunday, they started for Woodruff. Mike and Katy were beside themselves over Grandma's fine bright red car, and Barbara repeated everything they said in pidginese, adding screams and squeals for emphasis. "Momo" went along to help keep the "thundering herd" under control, and the story of the television program was told in detail, with Lola supplying the accurate particulars, and Eldorah complaining at having been left out. "Well, *I* was left out," commiserated Lola, as indeed she had been. After all, Eldorah had a job to keep in Chicago, and besides, she was the youngest and they couldn't put in *everybody*. Kate was inclined to agree that Eldorah *should* have been on the program, and that made her feel better.

From Tomahawk, Tommy telephoned to Woodruff to announce their imminent arrival. Eldorah, who is a superlative driver, took over the wheel, and as the red car left Hazelhurst, it was met by a police escort on motorcycles. They entered Woodruff behind this impressive convoy, with all sirens blasting to clear the way for Dr. Kate who was even more amazed than the motorists who pulled aside to let the red Mercury pass.

As they drove through Woodruff, the town looked strangely deserted, but then, it *was* Sunday. They stopped at Kate's office and found Bill there along with a crowd of friends waiting to welcome her. "Momo" and Lola got out with the children, who had to be given their lunch, and Dory drove Dr. Kate and Tom to the high-school gymnasium.

Here the deserted appearance of the town was explained. Everyone in Woodruff was at the gymnasium. The big hall was jammed with people, and a welcoming committee was at the door to meet Dr. Kate. As she stepped in, a cheer went up from the crowd. She saw that rows of tables had been placed around the vast area, and it seemed the entire population of Woodruff and Minocqua were seated at them, counting pennies, opening mail from the mountainous pile of letters, cartons, boxes, jars and containers of every description. As the pennies rattled into the kettles, buckets, pans and basins that had been accumulated to hold them, they made a roar like metal hail.

Kate stood there, her eyes wide and her mouth agape, while her friends crowded around, shaking her hand and congratulating her on the success of her television program. Kate's eyes filled and she felt her control giving way. The news about the mail bags had been overwhelming; the reality was too much for her. Her friend Reverend Leisman came forward to greet her, and his reassuring smile and handclasp bolstered her crumbling composure. She learned that the bank had remained open to handle the flood of donations which had poured in by the sackful since Thursday morning, swamping the post office and turning the town into a volunteer counting house. The count had reached sixty-thousand dollars so far, with many more pieces of mail still to be opened.

From every state in the union, from the big cities and the small towns, from the army and from the navy, from doctors and from lawyers, from clergymen and their congregations, from the entire personnel of business houses and industrial establishments, from schoolchildren and from their mothers and fathers—in letters, in boxes, in jars and in cartons—on strips of tape in rolls, in bean pots and even in beer cans, sealed in by a brewery—pennies and checks and currency poured in.

A separate count was being kept of these gifts resulting from the television program. By Wednesday the count (calculated in pennies), had entered its eleventh million, and Ralph Edwards was given the news by phone. The actual contribution figure was one hundred and six thousand dollars, or ten million, six hundred thousand pennies, (though most of the funds were sent in checks, money orders and paper currency to avoid the cost of mailing the heavy pennies).

The money was only part of the staggering mail. Medical supply houses sent cartons of supplies for Dr. Kate's new hospital. Baby powders, baby oil, gauze, antiseptics, cotton, safety pins, tissues, nursing bottles, diapers —their variety and quantity are too numerous to itemize.

Kate's brain reeled from the stunning outcome of her television appearance. How could she thank all these generous people? she asked herself. The job of writing each donor individually would require a staff of office workers, writing letters for weeks, even for months, as there were almost four hundred thousand pieces of mail which would have to be answered—a colossal undertaking. So she is thanking them here, each and every one, with all her heart, for the blessing they poured on the people of Woodruff and its surrounding towns, who will be the beneficiaries, with her, of their kindness.

"The miracle of The Penny Parade and the broadcast it inspired cannot be measured in the number of pennies and dollars and cases of supplies," says Kate. "It can only be written in the Big Book kept by the Recording Angel, on the credit side of our great American nation, whose generosity to those in need is the brightest jewel in its crown of achievement."

As Kate stood in the gymnasium, marveling at the phenomenon that had swept into Woodruff since her departure, she was summoned to the telephone. One of her o.b. cases required her presence at Sacred Heart in Tomahawk. The crowd cheered as Larry Doolittle whisked her into his car and they headed over the snowy road for Tomahawk. This would be the last year of her wintry rides, she rejoiced, as the car sped over the miles to the hospital.

The little girl who was born that night was called "Penny" in honor of Dr. Kate's triumph. Her mother was Mrs. Emma Fralix, a niece of Kate's old friend, Sam Williams.

His Excellency, The Governor

THE summer season of 1954 moved into Woodruff with the fanfare, as Kate puts it "of a three-ring circus." Summer visitors, news-reel cameramen demanding "shots," press interviews, invitations to address hospital-fund committees in other areas, wires and letters from old friends who had seen the program, or who had missed the program but read about her in the papers or in the *Reader's Digest*. Kate's head swam with the realization of what it meant to be a national celebrity.

Luckily, the tedious hours of driving to Tomahawk for her hospital cases were no longer a part of her schedule, and she managed to sandwich everything in between her calls and her hospital work with a fair degree of equanimity. But the strain of keeping everybody content, and this writer fed with material, made it a trying summer. Kate was glad when the summer began to wane and the crush abated.

The question has been often asked, "How did the banks handle those millions of pennies?"

A million pennies weigh three and one half tons. Between The Penny Parade and the television broadcast, some three million, three hundred thousand pennies had to be counted and part of them transported to the Federal Reserve Bank in Minneapolis. The first load was moved by the First Wisconsin State Bank as a voluntary donation to The Penny Parade. The second flood was gratuitously transported to Minneapolis by the Miller Brewing Company through the good offices of Fred Miller, whose tragic death just before the holidays brought sorrow to the northwoods communities. His private plane crashed as it was about to make a landing at the Milwaukee airport, killing him, his eldest son and two young pilots. Fred Miller's generosity, his warm, neighborly interest in the community where he spent his vacations, made him a loved leader in the business and social life of the lakeland country. His death threw a cloud of mourning over that holiday season in the northwoods.

After the first flood, pennies and checks continued to trickle in, and William D. Goodsmith, a retired naval engineer and a long-time friend of Dr. Kate's, was appointed a deputy warden by the constable. Together with Carl Kreuger, Woodruff's pharmacist, he was given control of the collections and the deposit of these donations. "Dr. Kate" cans were placed in the various shops and markets to receive further contributions for the hospital. The shopkeepers expedited the penny problem by writing their checks for the amounts collected each week and turning them in to the custodians of the fund.

Mr. Goodsmith, familiarly known as "Bill," has the collection figures on the tip of his tongue. He tells of the five hundred dollars collected by the post office in excess postage, adding cheerfully, "Nobody minded paying *that* charge."

With upward of one hundred and six thousand dollars in its new fund, the Lakeland Memorial Hospital began to come to life in earnest. Its notes, amounting to some forty-eight thousand dollars, were paid off at the bank. Equipment was purchased and rooms were furnished, many as gifts or as memorials to departed members of families. On their doors gleam brass plates engraved with the donors' names and the dedication.

With mortgages paid off and furnishings and equipment complete, the hospital fund showed a balance of some thirty thousand dollars in reserve to carry Lakeland Memorial through its initial stage of operations.

Contributions continued to arrive from well-wishers who knew the problems involved in maintaining a small new hospital in a sparsely populated community. The hospital was an accomplished fact, but it still remained to be seen whether it could support itself and upon this would depend the certification of the state examiners who would arrive for an inspection late in December.

As for the Sisters at Sacred Heart Hospital in Tomahawk, their joy was complete.

"It took a few years to accomplish this blessing," said Sister Hedwig, "but at last Dr. Newcomb has her hospital. We are so grateful to all the good people who helped the Lord in His design to relieve Dr. Newcomb of her long trips to attend her hospitalized patients. We are so happy for her, but oh, how we miss her! It was a sad day when we removed her name from the locker, and when the callboard no longer signaled her presence. She is one of us in her devotion to the sick, and although she is of a different faith and has her own family, we feel that she is our sister in God and in her unswerving faithfulness to those who need her help. Some of her things are still in the closet in her old room, and there are two new gowns hanging there for her use if she ever has a case here at Sacred Heart."

Lakeland Memorial Hospital is an important "character" in the story of Dr. Kate Newcomb. While photographs of the hospital building have been published, they do not convey the living breathing spirit of its personality, and it should be described for the benefit of the many thousands who have contributed to its creation.

The building is a long, low structure of modern design, consisting of one floor and a basement, and it stands with its back to the waters of Larson Lake which divides Woodruff from the island town of Minocqua. It is pleasantly uninstitutional in appearance, and its red brick and fieldstone façade might well house a golf club.

The driveway leads to a portico with low steps and upon entering the wide glass doors one finds an atmosphere that is the modern antithesis of the subdued aura of Sacred Heart. The entry walls are painted a soft green. There is a bright red soft-drink dispenser and, at this writing, a glittering Christmas tree, giving the eye a cheerful boost of color. There is a glass-enclosed switch board at the left and as one enters the hospital proper, the desk of the reception nurse faces the stairway across the hall that leads to the lower floor. On the right wall beside the inner door, hangs a large framed photograph of Dr. Kate, wearing her office coat over a gingham dress, and a smile that reveals her small, sound, even white teeth and the elusive dimples that belie her years.

The interior walls are painted a soft, pleasing green and on the light wood doors along the corridor gleam the brass dedication plates. Through the partially opened doors one catches glimpses of the rooms, painted in various pastel colors, and soft-footed nurses in crisp white uniforms and caps busy with their patients.

At the end of the hall, to the left, are two surgeries, one dedicated, with a polished copper plate, to "THE MILLION PENNY PARADE," and the other with a brass plate to "RALPH EDWARDS AND HIS TELEVISION PROGRAM 'THIS IS YOUR LIFE.'"

To the right are the administration offices.

On the lower floor is the furnace room, the kitchen, the staff dining room, doctors' and nurses' lounges, lavatories and utility rooms, and last, but by no means least, one half of the floor is given over to obstetrics.

Beside the doorway is a brass plate which reads:

OBSTETRICS
DEDICATED TO OUR PIONEER DOCTORS
Dr. T. G. Torpy
Dr. Gale W. Huber
Dr. Kate Pelham Newcomb

Here there are rooms for the mothers, private and semi-private, also in pastel colors. There is also a labor room, a delivery room, and the sparkling, glass-enclosed nursery furnished with plastic bassinettes and incubators. The newborn babies, plainly visible, look like "mama dolls" in a toy shop.

On the nursery door is a plate which acknowledges the donation of bassinettes by the St. Patrick Altar Society and the Lake Tomahawk Women's Club.

The entire atmosphere of the hospital is one of friendliness and reassurance. Its head nurse, Mrs. Otto Burich, a striking brunette, lends adornment as well as competence to her staff of carefully selected nurses. Mr.

H. H. Helminiak, the hospital administrator, keeps the administrative machinery in good working order.

There you have the Lakeland Memorial Hospital as it emerged from Dr. Kate's long and patient dream, a perfect reality, thanks to her many thousands of friends.

Small wonder, then, that the second Memorial Day Penny Parade was a march of victory, and its triumphant surge along Woodruff's Main Street was a traffic-halting event.

Wednesday, July 21, 1954, was set as the day for the dedication of the new hospital. The hospital board considered the occasion sufficiently important to warrant inviting Governor Walter J. Kohler, Jr., to be present at the ceremony. He replied that he would consider it an honor to attend.

The Governor arrived at Rhinelander by plane, and was met by a committee, headed by "Casey" Lambert, president of the hospital's Board of Trustees. Crowds lined the streets and cheered as the official car drove through Woodruff.

A grandstand had been erected on the hospital grounds, and the staff stood at the entrance to receive their distinguished guest of honor. Dr. Kate, as Chief of Staff, did the honors for the reception committee, and the Governor was escorted to the grandstand where flags and bunting flashed in the bright July sunlight, and eager hundreds cheered as the officials ascended the platform.

This was the supreme moment, when the toil and the faith of these northwoods people was being recognized and honored. The children of the Arbor Vitae Woodruff High School Band gave everything they had to the strains of "K-K-K-Katy, beautiful Katy."

The Governor beamed at Dr. Kate and she grinned

and shook her head at the familiar tribute. The members of the dedication committee took their places beside the two honored guests. Doctors Huber, Burnett, Pfeiffer and Cline represented the medical staff. The clergy was represented by Reverend Milton Leisman, Reverend Johnson and Father Griffin. "Casey" Lambert, Palmer Hansen, Clarence White, Clarence Sturm represented the hospital board and the Lions' Club.

The playing of the Star Spangled Banner opened the program, and the entire assemblage stood reverently at attention.

Otto Burich then introduced John Wadd, radio announcer of Rhinelander, who was to be the master of ceremonies.

John Wadd, in turn, introduced Pastor Leisman, who delivered the invocation, asking God's blessing upon the enterprise which had been accomplished by His grace, reflected in the hearts of the people of Woodruff and neighboring communities, as well as many, many thousands throughout the nation and the entire world.

The master of ceremonies then introduced the Governor of Wisconsin and cheers and applause rang loud and long as he stepped to the microphone.

As he began to speak, with simplicity and earnestness of Dr. Kate's accomplishments, Kate heard the town ambulance siren wailing along the street leading to the highway. She turned and looked at Dr. Huber who sat beside her. He looked blank and shrugged slightly. Kate heard the Governor refer to her as a "genius," and she wondered just how she could qualify for such an exalted appellation. That ambulance—where was it going? What was wrong? The encomiums of the Governor's address were very beautiful to hear, but doctor's blood is restless when there is trouble in the offing. Kate looked over the crowd. Where was Bill? She had wanted him to be on the platform with her, but it was the old story of leading a horse to water. She had got him as far as Woodruff, but he was nowhere in sight in the crowd.

". . . for it was her very selflessness and devotion, her very courage," the Governor was saying, "which appealed to the imagination of her fellow citizens. . . . On the one hand she had the dedication of a Florence Nightingale. Yet on the other hand, she was still one of you, a friend and neighbor. . . ."

While the crowd was applauding the Governor's words, the ambulance could be heard coming back from its mission. Who was in it? Was one of her patients or one of her friends in trouble? Kate wished the ceremony were over and done with so she could go about her work.

The Governor was appealing to the community to stand back of the new hospital and help it become an inspiration to other communities. "Like a star in the sky, it will beckon wise men onward to discovering ever-new ways of serving mankind."

The crowd applauded. Someone came to the steps of the platform and the word was passed on to Dr. Kate. There had been an accident at Crystal Lake. A father and son from one of the resorts had fallen into a treacherous hole while wading in the lake. They had been rescued and promptly taken to the Lakeland Memorial Hospital where they were being treated. Well, at least, she knew.

The program continued. Clarence Sturm, director of the Lions' Club, told of the proud part his organization had played in the hospital project.

The dedication was read by the Reverend Eldred P. Johnson of Woodruff. The hospital was solemnly dedicated to the people of Woodruff and its surrounding districts, and a benediction was invoked by Father James Griffin of Minocqua.

The ceremony was over. Again the band played "K-K-K-Katy, beautiful Katy," and the crowd picked up the song. They surged around the platform, seeking autographs and snapshots, trying to shake hands with Dr. Kate and the Governor.

The next stop was the high-school gymnasium where the Governor viewed the horde of two million pennies piled on the floor and the hundreds of thousands of pieces of mail that had arrived after the television show. He was photographed lifting a shovelful of the pennies, and he pitched some of his own pennies into the big iron kettle at the center of the pile.

The hospital was holding "open house," and the Governor's party attended the festivities. There was to be a dinner later at the Country Club in Minocqua, although Governor Kohler regretted that state duties would prevent him from being present. Kate, of course, would be there—she thought.

She slipped away from the gathering to have a look at the emergency cases and found Dr. Cline in charge. Though the boy was out of danger, the father was in serious condition.

Kate returned to the party where everyone crowded around to shake her hand and congratulate her on the formal opening of her hospital. But her anxious thoughts remained with the emergency case.

Members of the Dedication Committee were glancing at their watches. They were taking the Governor to the airport, and then going to the Club for the dinner. Dr. Kate would be picked up at six o'clock sharp.

But at six o'clock Dr. Kate was at Dr. Cline's side, fighting for the life of the immersion victim. She remained there the entire night. A man's life meant infinitely more to her than a dinner party.

The Winter Forest

IT is the Christmas season. The northern woodlands present a picture of a sparkling white landscape with a sharp fringe of dark pine-tops outlined against the clear blue of the sky. On the surrounding slopes, the towering balsam and tall Norway pines look down their snow-laden branches on the curving ribbon of river waters that ripple under the highway bridges, linking the frozen lakes in an endless pattern, like white medallions on a silver chain. Soon the rivers will freeze over, but it will take much colder weather to silence the wash of running waters.

On a frosty morning, the bare trees and the pine needles are coated with ice, and the early sun sparkles on a crystal forest.

Driving along the winding highways at night, with flurries of snow dancing in the glow of the headlights, one sees lamplight through the trees from the far-spaced forest dwellings, and there are wreaths outlined against their windows.

In the towns, the shop windows are framed with ever-green boughs and holly, and the municipal Christmas trees shine with colored lights. Snow-booted shoppers hurry in and out of the busy shops, carrying packages, and the snow clings to the cars that wait at the curb, covering their tops like frosting on varicolored cakes.

It is a time to plan for the holiday, and rehearsals are held in the lighted churches for the entertainments that will celebrate the holy season.

In the Fellowship Hall of the Boulder Junction Community Church of a Saturday evening, the congregation has gathered to honor Dr. Kate. There is to be a screening of her appearance on the Ralph Edwards's program, projected with the apparatus presented to her on that happy occasion. But, as usual, the stork interferes. Dr. Kate is detained at the hospital and her filmed facsimile must take the place of her hoped-for presence.

There is a chorus of children carolers, and a choir singing Dr. Kate's favorite hymns, "The Old Rugged Cross" and "I Would Be True." After the film, Tommy, who is there to represent his mother, accepts the gifts that the church people have for Dr. Kate—a portable blood-testing instrument of considerable value, and a box of Christmas cookies. Tom thanks the donors in his mother's name. A piece of the big Christmas cake, a delicious confection baked by Mrs. Syd Doolittle, is wrapped and sent to the busy doctor, and Syd Doolittle tells of her years of work toward the building of the church that was his late mother's dream so many years ago.

There are babies in arms and small children in the gathering, for the forest people bring their families to the house of worship. The young Reverend Nelson and his pretty wife, Myrtle, with her tiny baby in her arms, circulate among the guests and speak sadly of the recent death of Mrs. Leona Kenaga, who played an important part in the church project. There is peace and friendliness in the big warm hall with its waxed wood halls and ceiling hung with evergreens and bright with modern lighting. The spirit of Christmas fills the air and in their midst everyone speaks of Dr. Kate and her tireless service to the community. They are happy to know a book is being written about their doctor, and they are eager to tell of the many hours she has given to them and to their families, by day and by night, with no thought for her own rest or comfort. Their love for her is indeed "a temple without hands," and it will tower above these forests long after she and the tellers are gone.

The church party is over. The young minister stands at the door, speaking to each departing guest, and the cars roll back over the night roads to the backwoods homes. These are no longer the rude cabins that Kate found there when she first arrived. They are cheerful, modern homes, well warmed by oil furnaces and lighted by electricity. They have modern plumbing, and the antennas of television sets rise from many of the roofs.

The people of the northwoods have kept up with the times, and they are interested in everything that goes on in the world around them. They read the newspapers and magazines and listen to radio broadcasts; and discuss their local and state issues with the enthusiasm of alert and informed Americans.

Compared with what it was thirty-three years ago, when the Newcombs first came to the Jackson resort at Eagle River, the area now seems almost a metropolis. The roads are well paved. There is the sound of planes over the quiet forests. Cars wind over the highways that are cleared by state and county snowplows. There are churches and shopping centers in the growing towns, and there is a busy hospital in Woodruff.

But the natives still pursue the sports that have always provided their winter entertainment. On the wide expanse of snow-covered ice that marks the lakes, one sees dark figures, well padded against the cold wind, watching beside the fishing holes where the small scarlet floaters wait for the tug of perch or wall-eyed pike. As the floater bobs and disappears, the fishermen jerk the thread-like line and pull the short rod quickly away from the ice hole. The yellow and silver perch flaps for an instant and then turns to a curved icicle in the freezing cold air. Ice-fishing is a favorite sport in the northland. The winter catch is a relished delicacy. Its meat is light and sweet, and a "deep fry" of the small fillets is a golden feast for the fisherman and his family.

On the pine-topped slopes that are said to be the path of ancient glaciers, young skiers and tobogganers, in plaid coats and bright wool pants and scarves, fill the air with color and gaiety as they glide down the snowy inclines, their cheeks rosy and their breath congealing in the frosty air.

The gay parody of "baseball on snowshoes" brings teams onto the snow-covered lake ice to try their luck at "stealing bases," though the cumbersome northwoods footwear more often than not sends the players headlong, with the ball sinking in the snow to be dug for, and hilarity making a higher score than the game itself.

December is a lively month. The temperature hovers between thirty and zero, and the cold of thirty, forty and fifty below has not yet set in. The deer hunt is over and the danger from amateur hunters is past. The lust of the chase has given way to the genial spirit of "good will toward men."

After office hours, Dr. Kate buzzes around her Woodruff headquarters, alternating between phone calls to the hospital for a report on her patients, accumulating packages and addressing Christmas cards to be mailed to reach the four corners of the nation where she has friends. Christmas is another day nearer.

Upstairs, the sound of running feet signals the romping hour before bedtime. Kathy, Mike and small Barbara are finding pretexts for postponing the "lights out" signal from their mother. Sometimes a howl goes up as the maneuvers become a trifle rough, and rotund Barbara is tumbled in the fracas.

At Rice Creek, in the fastness of the forest, Bill holds the fort with the hounds, Benny and Betsy, and the beagles, Shorty and Duke. The cats lick their chops as they watch the birds feeding at the rack hanging high on a pine branch, out of their reach. Bill's old hunting cronies, Orlando Chada and Judd Blaisdell, drop in to smoke a pipe with him. They talk of old times, when the forest was a rich hunting ground for the predators that were their favorite game. Now that the tracks of wood creatures are few and far between, even the beasts of prey are scarce in this area. They have gone to seek their quarry in more remote cover, for civilization is creeping into their habitat and driving them still farther north to unsettled timberlands.

Some of the old-timers remember the days of the early loggers, when the mule skinners drove teams of steaming oxen and mules over the dangerous curves and slopes of the old "ice roads," risking men and animals as the sled of heavy logs groaned down the steep inclines, braked only by the adroit flinging of a steel chain under its runners. Many a driver and many a team were crushed to death in those days when a brake chain failed to check the descent of the log-filled lumber sleigh, and the great load of logs came hurtling down a glassy slope like a giant juggernaut, leaving death in its wake.

Through the "snow fences" of young trees planted along the highways by the Foresty Department, acres of black stumps, topped with snow, stand like solemn gravestones, marking the ravaging of the forests.

Law and order has replaced the lawless reign of the lumberjacks. The grandchildren of the men who, enamored of the forest, remained to settle the towns, now go to modern local schools and then to faraway colleges to become men and women of note in other parts of the country. But the northwoods has put its seal on them and they return to their forest haunts during the hunting and fishing seasons and sometimes at holiday time.

It is Christmas Eve. The Newcomb family and their friends gather at the house on Rice Creek for the annual celebration. The old "summer cottage," which became their refuge from the fire, is now a comfortable home, snug against the cold. Its long living room looks out upon the snow-banked creek where the idyllic island shines in the sun, its pine-fringed outline breaking the expanse of frosty creek waters.

The Christmas tree stands proudly against the glass panels of a door that leads to the shore. Its branches are covered with such glory as it never dreamed of when it stood in the forest just a few days ago.

On the waxed wood of one wall, among pine boughs and holly, hangs a bandeau of white beads designed in a pattern of rising steps and woven with symbolic Indian figures. A proud eagle feather juts from the knotted doeskin thongs at the back. It is the headdress of a Chippewa princess, and is the symbol of Dr. Kate's adoption into the tribe of the Chippewas. The ceremony took place in early September at a colorful "pow-wow"—or ceremonial dance —held at the Indian Bowl in the Lac du Flambeau Reservation. There Indians and townspeople gathered to honor the white "lady doc" for her faithful work among the sick and needy on the reservation. Flaming torches and campfires lighted the scene as the Indians, resplendent in full regalia, complete with war bonnets of eagle feathers and skunk fur, crowned Dr. Kate with the symbolic bandeau and conferred upon her the Chippewa name of "Gi-Way-Duc-Nu-Quay," which means "Lady of the North," welcoming her as their beloved sister, a distinction bestowed upon few white men and only one other white woman. The bandeau adds a note of barbaric beauty to the traditional Christmas decorations that festoon the living room.

The guests arrive in the late afternoon—"Boss" and "Momo" Williams with David and Judy, Mr. and Mrs. Chada, the Myron Gravelles with their daughter Guida, and Mel Kenaga, significantly and sadly alone.

At five o'clock the Christmas Eve feast is served, and it is the same every year—baked ham with pineapple, scalloped potatoes, fruit salad, vegetable salad, relishes, hot rolls and always plenty of good coffee, made in an enormous two-gallon coffee pot which Bill hauls out of hiding each year for the occasion. Dessert will come later.

At ten minutes to seven, Tommy reads the Christmas poem. Its authorship is unknown, and its words are simple:

The Winter Forest

"They said that every Christmas night
    The Christ child came to walk below,
And so we set a candlelight
    To guide his footsteps through the snow,
And there behind the window glass
We sat and watched to see Him pass.

Our candle shone so clear and red
    We thought the Christ would see it thus
And maybe He might turn His head
    And smile a tender smile at us.
But drifted snow piled high and white
And almost hid our little light.

And then, within the candle's arc,
    There came a vision clear of things
That shine beyond the deepest dark.
    We saw it's sharing life that brings
Christ close within our candle's glow.
He smiles at us through friends we know."

Then Kate lights the Christmas candle, a large taper made from the remnants of candles of many previous years. Other candles glow around the living room, but this is the votive light.

The youngest member of each family goes into the adjoining bedroom where they are given their candles and candlesticks to be lighted and placed in the window. The youngest member of Kate's immediate family is Eldorah. The youngest of Tom's family is a new arrival, William David, born in October, on the twenty-first, at the Lakeland Memorial Hospital, the first of Kate's grandchildren to be born in the new Maternity Ward. Now Tom's and Lola's family is complete, according to their own plans for two girls and two boys.

Lola holds the ceremonial candlestick in her infant son's hand. The other "youngest" carry theirs, Mrs. Chada, Eldorah, Judy, Guida Gravelle, and finally, Mel Kenaga performing the ritual in memory of her who was a participant for many years—Leona, the absent one. They march solemnly into the living room as the radio supplies appropriate Christmas music. Each walks up to the votive candle and lights his own from it. Then the lights are placed on the window sills of the several windows, where the flames are mirrored in the glass and their golden light falls upon the dancing snowflakes outside.

By now it is seven o'clock Boulder Junction time—the hour for Christmas carols—and everyone joins in "Silent Night." Throughout the country, at this exact moment, others are performing the same ritual and singing the same carol. Gilbert Gravelle, who is serving in the army, received his Christmas candlestick by mail, and he too is joining in the ceremony many miles away.

More carols follow, until "Bless This House" ends the ritual, and the gay lilt of "Jingle Bells" and "Rudolph the Red-nosed Reindeer" breaks the solemnity as the children shout the familiar words with joyful enthusiasm.

The Christ child's birthday cake is carried in, a single candle glowing on the white frosting, on which is inscribed "Happy Birthday, Baby Jesus" in bright red letters. Mike blows out the candle, assisted by Kathy and Barbara Ann. The cake is cut and served, with ice cream and coffee, and cocoa for the children, to complete the Christmas feast.

The guests depart, and it is time for the children to hang up their stockings. These are special stockings, of generous capacity, knitted in bright-colored wool, with each child's name at the top.

Mike comes running with a book in his hands and the excited children quiet down while Grandmother Kate reads them "The Night Before Christmas," a significant hint that it is bedtime. They must be especially good tonight, and go right to sleep. Quiet reigns as small Bill finishes his last bottle and closes his eyes.

Then there is a mysterious bustle as the stockings are filled and boxes and packages pile up around the tree. Then silence. . . .

Christmas morning dawns over the snowy creek and there is a stir in the wide bed as three chirping Christmas-eyed Newcombs scamper into the living room. The packages are there, under the tree, but the rule is that they must not be touched until after breakfast. The stockings are fat with goodies and little toys—oranges, apples, nuts, candy, whistles, balloons to be blown up.

The children tear into the kitchen and slide into their places at the breakfast table. Dutifully, they eat their breakfast, their eyes shining with anticipation. Grandmother is preparing the Christmas turkey for the oven so that she will be free to join the fun of opening the packages while the festive bird roasts.

Now the great moment has come. The children race back to the living room in a frenzy of excitement. There are gifts for everyone, so many that it takes hours to open all the packages.

Barbara trots from one to the other, stumbling in her excitement and Mike gallantly comes to her rescue, subduing her humiliated howls by offering her one of his toys. The tears dry on her fat cheeks.

Kate exclaims over the gifts her grandchildren have selected for her. Bill watches, grinning. He hordes his packages, refusing to open them for all to see, and carrying them off to his room. His children protest, until he finally returns, wearing a new lumberjack shirt, dark woodsman's trousers, new socks and carrying a can of his favorite pipe tobacco under his arm. The family exclaims with approval, admiring the fit of the new finery. Bill maintains a solemn countenance, but with one eyebrow cocked and a twinkle in his eye that brings Barbara running to clutch at his legs and demand "up." Grandpa picks her up and she pries at the cover of the tobacco can, demanding cookies. But when Grandpa opens the can, she wrinkles her nose in distaste.

Small Bill howls from his basket for attention and Lola goes to quiet him. It is an exciting day, and when it comes to an end and Tommy and Lola and the children have started back for Woodruff, their car loaded with toys and boxes, Kate and Bill relax for a quiet chat before bedtime.

It has been a wonderful year, sighs Kate. It has brought her the best gift of all, a hospital at Woodruff. Just before Christmas the news came that the state authorities had given Lakeland Memorial their seal of approval as an accredited hospital. Kate pours a grateful blessing on all who helped her achieve her dream. She has one more wish. If she could find a young doctor, man or woman, who would be willing to undergo the rigors of country practice and to whom she could pass on the methods and tradition she has established in her beloved northwoods, her happiness would be complete.

"The income from rural practice cannot be compared with what doctors earn in the large centers," she admits, "but the range of experience and the sense of accomplishment and dedication more than make up the economic difference."

The saga of Dr. Kate has brought renown to the obscure communities of Northern Wisconsin whose small towns may someday become centers of industry. But the forests are wide, and though the towns may grow, there will always be room for a man to breathe and stretch his legs in these invigorating woodlands which restored a dying man to health and brought fame to an obscure country doctor.

S. Clara Co. W